Time of Arrival Based Infrastructureless Human Posture Capturing System

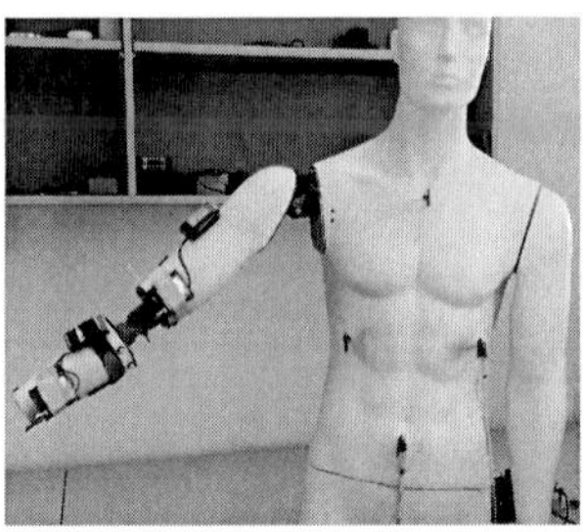

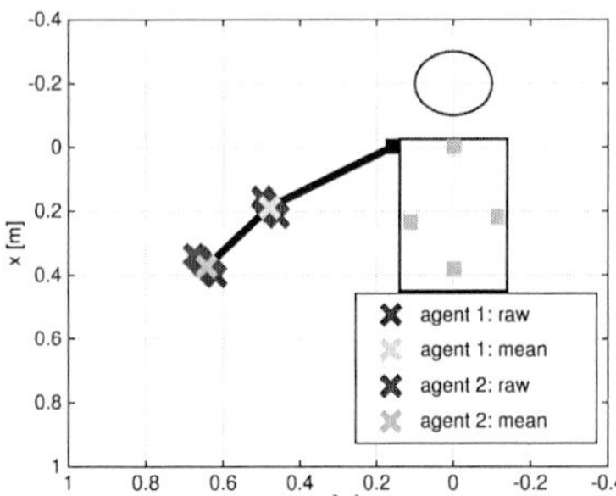

Zemene Walle Mekonnen

λογος

Series in Wireless Communications
edited by:
Prof. Dr. Armin Wittneben
Eidgenössische Technische Hochschule
Institut für Kommunikationstechnik
Sternwartstr. 7
CH-8092 Zürich

E-Mail: wittneben@nari.ee.ethz.ch
Url: http://www.nari.ee.ethz.ch/

Bibliographic information published by the Deutsche Nationalbibliothek

The Deutsche Nationalbibliothek lists this publication in the Deutsche Nationalbibliografie; detailed bibliographic data are available in the Internet at http://dnb.d-nb.de .

ISBN 978-3-8325-4429-4
ISSN 1611-2970

Logos Verlag Berlin GmbH
Comeniushof, Gubener Str. 47,
10243 Berlin
Tel.: +49 030 42 85 10 90
Fax: +49 030 42 85 10 92
INTERNET: http://www.logos-verlag.de

Diss. ETH No. 23262

Time of Arrival Based Infrastructureless Human Posture Capturing System

A dissertation submitted to the
ETH ZURICH

for the degree of
Doctor of Sciences

presented by
ZEMENE WALLE MEKONNEN
Master of Science, University of Kassel
born January 19, 1986
citizen of Ethiopia

accepted on the recommendation of
Prof. Dr. Armin Wittneben, examiner
Prof. Dr. sc. techn. Dirk Dahlhaus, co-examiner

2016

Date of Doctoral Examination: February 24, 2016

Abstract

Human posture capturing systems have a wide range of applications in the fields ranging from clinical medicine to sports and entertainment. In this thesis, a time-of-arrival (TOA) based human posture capturing system is proposed and studied. The key advantages of the proposed system compared to existing commercially available human posture capturing systems are simplicity, low-cost and independence from external infrastructure.

In the first part of the thesis, the proposed human posture capturing system setup, which is based on ultra-wideband (UWB) communication technology, is presented. To exploit the potential of UWB communication technology, a highly asymmetric system that consists of three types of radio nodes is considered: ultra-low complexity and ultra-low power transmit-only agent nodes, low-complexity relay nodes called anchors and a cluster head. Such a highly asymmetric system, among others, implies that it is practically infeasible to synchronize the clocks of all the radio nodes in the system. We present a TOA measurement model that takes into account the offsets of the clocks between the radio nodes. Furthermore, a possible non-line-of-sight (NLOS) situation between the agents and the anchors, due to occlusion of different body parts, leads to a TOA measurement with unknown positive bias. To cope with this problem, we propose a method to identify NLOS and discard the corresponding TOA measurements, which is based on the likelihood ratio test of the received signal features (e.g. signal to noise ratio).

In the second part of the thesis, the problem of TOA based human posture capturing is abstracted to the general problem of wireless sensor network localization problem. The maximum likelihood (ML) solution of the localization problem that takes into account the clock asynchronicity of the agents and their position constraints (e.g. due to the kinematic constraint of the body) is shown to be a non-convex optimization problem. To deal with this problem, we propose a two-step localization method. In the first step, the ML estimator is relaxed to a semi-definite programming (SDP) problem by applying convex relaxation techniques. The SDP problem can be efficiently solved by readily available optimization toolboxes. Then in the second step, the solution of the SDP problem is refined by the ML estimator. The proposed localization method is also extended to take into account the position uncertainty of the anchors, e.g. due to the movement of the body and calibration errors. To enable system operation without relying on external infrastructure, and hence unleash ubiquitous use, we propose a simple and cost effective calibration method that reuses the localization system itself.

In the third part of the thesis, the proposed localization and calibration methods are applied and analyzed for the specific setup of human posture capturing. The performance evaluations provide key insights about the tradeoffs that are involved when choosing system parameters, such as system complexity, accuracy, and computational complexity. Furthermore, the localization and calibration methods are evaluated using measurement hardware that practically demonstrates the proposed human posture capturing system.

The thesis concludes with the summary of the main findings of the project and an outlook on future research topics in the area of TOA based human posture capturing.

Kurzfassung

Systeme zur Erfassung der Körperhaltung, im Folgenden Human Posture Capturing genannt, haben breite Anwendungsmöglichkeiten in der klinischen Medizin, im Sport und in der Unterhaltung. In dieser Arbeit entwickeln und analysieren wir ein solches Human-Posture-Capturing-System, das auf Time-of-Arrival (TOA) Schätzungen basiert. Einfachheit, niedrige Kosten und Unabhängigkeit von externer Infrastruktur bilden dabei die wichtigsten Vorteile des vorgeschlagenen Systems gegenüber herkömmlichen und kommerziell erhältlichen Alternativen.

Im ersten Teil dieser Arbeit wird der Aufbau des Human-Posture-Capturing-Systems präsentiert. Dieses basiert auf der Ultra-Wideband (UWB) Kommunikationstechnologie. Um die Möglichkeiten von UWB voll auszuschöpfen, betrachten wir drei verschiedene Typen von Übertragungsknoten: Sendeknoten von sehr geringer Komplexität sowie sehr niedriger Sendeleistung, Relayknoten (auch Ankerknoten genannt) von geringer Komplexität, sowie einem Clusterhead, der höhere Komplexität aufweisen kann. Ein solch hoch asymmetrisches System impliziert unter anderem, dass es praktisch unmöglich ist, die verschiedenen Knoten im System zu synchronisieren. Zu diesem Zweck entwickeln wir ein TOA-Mess-Modell, das Taktverschiebungen zwischen den einzelnen Knoten berücksichtigt. Zusätzlich können die TOA-Messwerte einen unbekannten positiven Bias aufweisen, z.B. bei Übertragungen ohne Sichtverbindung (non-line-of-sight (NLOS)), wenn einzelne Körperteile verdeckt sind. Um auch diesem Problem gerecht zu werden, schlagen wir eine Methode vor, welche NLOS Situationen identifiziert, womit die zugehörigen TOA-Messungen verworfen werden können. Die Identifizierung erfolgt dabei mittels eines Likelihood-Ratio-Tests von Signalmerkmalen wie z.B. dem Störabstand.

Im zweiten Teil dieser Dissertation abstrahieren wir das TOA basierte Human-Posture-Capturing-System und formulieren ein allgemeingültiges Lokalisierungsproblem in drahtlosen Sensornetzwerken, das die Taktasynchronität sowie Bedingungen die aus der Körperhaltung folgen (z.B. kinematische Bedingungen) berücksichtigt. Dieses Lokalisierungsproblem kann mit einer Maximum-Likelihood-Schätzung (ML) gelöst werden. Wir zeigen jedoch, dass das mathematische Optimierungsproblem nicht konvex ist, was eine effiziente Lösung erschwert. Um dieses Problem zu lösen, schlagen wir eine Lokalisierungsmethode in zwei Schritten vor. Im ersten Schritt wird die ML-Schätzung mit einer konvexen Relaxation in ein semidefinites Programmierungsproblem (SDP) umgewandelt. Das SDP-Problem kann dann mit herkömmlichen Optimierungsverfahren effizient gelöst werden. In einem zweiten Schritt wird die Lösung des SDP-Problems mit dem ML-Schätzer verfeinert. Die vorgeschlagene Lokalisierungsmethode erweitern wir danach so, dass auch Positionsunsicherheiten an den Ankerknoten (beispielsweise durch Bewegungen des Körpers oder durch Kalibrierungsfehler hervorgerufen) mitberücksichtigt werden können. Damit das System ohne Hilfe externer Infrastruktur betrieben und somit jederzeit und überall eingesetzt werden kann, entwickeln wir eine einfache und kosteneffektive Kalibrierungsmethode, welche durch das Lokalisierungssystem selbst vorgenommen wird.

Die vorgeschlagenen Lokalisierungs- und Kalibrierungsmethoden werden dann im dritten Teil der Arbeit anhand spezifischer Human-Posture-Capturing-Situationen eingesetzt und analysiert. Durch die Auswertungen erhalten wir wichtige Einblicke in die Leistungsfähigkeit des Systems, sowie in die Wechselwirkungen verschiedener Aspekte wie Komplexität, Genauigkeit oder Rechenaufwand und diskutieren den Einfluss verschiedener Systemparameter auf diese Grössen. Anhand Hardware-Messungen demonstrieren und evaluieren wir schliesslich die Lokalisierungs- und Kalibrierungsverfahren an einem praktischen Human-Posture-Capturing-System.

Die Arbeit schliessen wir mit einer Diskussion der wichtigsten Resultate des Projektes ab und geben einen Ausblick über zukünftige Forschungsschwerpunkte im Gebiet der TOA basierten Human-Posture-Capturing-Systeme.

Contents

1. Introduction

1.1. Motivation

Human posture capturing refers to the process of estimating the position and/or orientation of the human body parts. Continuously capturing the posture of the different body parts enables the tracking of the person's movement. Hence, the name human motion capturing or human motion tracking is also used to refer to such systems.

Capturing and assessing the posture of a person is of great interest in various disciplines. In clinical medicine, for instance, human posture capturing system can assist the rehabilitation process of patients with gait disorders, e.g. stroke patients and people with Parkinson's disease. By recording and analyzing stroke patients' posture, human posture capturing systems can guide them to adjust their gaits [1]. The progression of Parkinson's disease can be studied by analyzing the posture of the patient, which is critical in deciding the type of treatment the patient has to undergo [2]. In sports, human posture capturing systems can help athletes to improve their performance by recoding and analyzing movements during training [3]. For example, in gymnastics, diving and synchronized swimming, where the movement accuracy, rhythm, coordination and balance are key components of the total score [4], posture capturing systems can help athletes to optimize their performance. The entertainment industry also employs posture capturing systems to record the movement of actors [5]. The recorded data can later be used to create realistically animated computer generated imagery.

Ideally, such a system fulfills the key requirements of human posture capturing which can be summarized as follows:

- *Accuracy*: the posture capturing system should be able to estimate the position of the body parts precisely. The requirements may range from "sub-mm accuracy" (for capturing fine movements such as eye blinking) to "cm accuracy" (for capturing large scale body movements such as walking).

- *Update rate*: to enable a meaningful analysis of the person's movement, the system should be able to capture and update the posture at a sufficient speed.
- *Robustness*: the performance of the posture capturing system should be robust against the potential influence of the body and the surrounding environment. The system should be robust against external interferences such as magnetic field, light, sound and heat [6]. Moreover, if the system relies on the line-of-sight link between the different sensors in the system, it needs to be robust against occlusion of different body parts.
- *Simplicity*: the system should be simple to use. Ideally, a user wears the posture capturing system, the system calibrates itself and starts recoding postures without requiring skilled operators and external infrastructure. Furthermore, to allow a non-restricted movement of the person, the posture capturing system should be convenient to wear, i.e. the nodes in the system have small form-factors and are preferably inter-connected wirelessly.
- *Cost*: meeting the aforementioned requirements, the system should be affordable. The cost considerations include installation (or startup) costs and operation costs (e.g. skilled operator and power consumption).

Clearly, these requirements are not independent. For example, to achieve a high update rate, the posture capturing algorithm needs to be computationally simple and efficient. However, this might lead to a degradation in accuracy. Similarly, the system can be made robust by adding some redundancy in the system, which comes at the expense of increased system complexity and cost. Hence, it is practically difficult to find a system that can outperform all others in all requirements [6]. In light of this difficulty, the design goal of human posture capturing systems is oriented according to the targeted application.

In this thesis, we focus on capturing the posture of large body parts, i.e. we are interested in large scale movements such as arm movements and walking. One of the main requirements of the considered human posture capturing system is that it needs to be simple and self-contained, which does not rely on external infrastructure. Moreover, to enable ubiquitous use, the system is required to be of ultra-low cost, ultra-low power and ultra-small form factor (with a potential to be installed subcutaneously). On the other hand, the accuracy and the update rate requirements of the considered system are less stringent compared to the systems which are targeted for capturing fine movements.

Although this thesis is focused on capturing large scale movements, to get a complete picture, we start with a brief summary of the state-of-the-art human posturing systems in Section 1.2, including those targeted for fine movements. Then, in Section 1.3, an overview of radio based localization techniques is provided and the motivation behind the choice of time of arrival (TOA) based localization for the application of human posture capturing is described. Previous related works that apply TOA based localization for the purpose of human posture capturing are discussed in Section 1.4. The challenges of such systems and the main contributions of this thesis are then presented in Section 1.5.

1.2. Human Posture Capturing Systems

According to the sensor technology they use, human posture capturing systems can be categorized into two main classes – namely vision based systems and non-vision based system [7]. Vision based systems (also referred to as optical systems) use optical sensors, e.g. a camera, to capturing the posture of a person. Non-vision based systems on the other hand use non-optical sensors, such as inertial, magnetic and radio sensors, to perform human posture capturing.

This section provides a brief overview of the human posture capturing systems from both categories. The main goal of this discussion is to provide insights about the trade-offs that are involved when designing such systems. For a detailed survey of human posture capturing technologies however, the reader is referred to [6–8].

1.2.1. Vision based systems

Depending on the technique they use, vision based systems can further be divided into two groups: those which use reflective markers and those which do not.

Vision based systems with markers

For this systems, reflective markers are placed on the parts of the body whose postures are of interest. The cameras, which are placed outside body, emit lights. The lights are reflected by the markers and then detected back by the cameras. The posture of the person is then estimated by combining the images that are captured by multiple cameras.

To enable accurate posture capturing, the cameras and the reflective markers have to be carefully installed [7]. This is because the images that are captured by the cameras are 2-dimensional (2D) images. Hence, to capture the 3-dimensional (3D) posture of the person from 2D images, the cameras need to be placed such that they provide multiple view points. Moreover, the cameras can only see the markers which are in their line-of-sight (LOS), which further emphasizes the need for careful installation.

Currently, there exist several commercial vision based human posture capturing systems that use reflective markers, e.g. Vicon [9], Raptor [10], Motus [11], Qualisys [12] and OptiTrack [13]. Despite the description of the products in their respective company's website states that accurate motion capturing is achievable, independent tests which provide the exact specification of the achievable accuracy of the systems are difficult to find [14]. To get an insight about the performance of these systems, we briefly revise the result in [15] which compares the Vicon-MX and OptiTrack motion capture systems. The Vicon-MX is a more expensive system, which costs $250,000$ £GBP at the time of purchase in 2010 [15]. The OptiTrack is a relatively cheaper system, which costs $4,750$ £GBP at the time of purchase in 2011 [15]. The specifications of the two systems and the achievable accuracy is given in Table 1.1. For the test, 4 reflective markers are placed on the lower-left leg and the inter-marker distances are measured using the two systems. The accuracy figure shown in Table 1.1 is the largest standard deviation of the distance measurement error.

We see that an accuracy in the range of millimeters (OptiTrack) and sub-millimeters (Vicon-MX) can be achieved by vision based systems that use reflective markers. Despite such high accuracy, the main bottleneck of these systems is that they require complex settings and highly skilled operators, which makes them expensive. The motion capturing system also requires a dedicated infrastructure and the subject person is required to be confined inside the space which has infrastructure support [16]. Furthermore, the use of cameras raises privacy concerns which further limits the application areas of the systems.

Table 1.1.: Comparision of Vicon-MX and OptiTrack motion capture systems [15].

System	Number of Cameras	Update rate	Accuracy (largest std. of error)
Vicon-MX	12	100 Hz	0.3 mm
OptiTrack	10	100 Hz	3.67 mm

Vision based systems without markers

These systems do not require reflective markers to be attached on the body. The system estimates the posture of a person by directly processing the 2D images captured by multiple cameras. The main advantage of these systems is that the person does not need to wear a special suite.

One of the approaches these systems use is to combine the *a priori* information of the human body and the information from the 2D images captured by the cameras [17]. To capture the *a priori* information about the human body, a likelihood function which models the different human body parts positions and the constraints between them is constructed. Then given the 2D images from the cameras, the most likelihood posture of the person is estimated.

Although these systems may alleviate the complex setting problem of marker based systems, they are computationally intensive [7]. Hence, substantial research is required to prove their feasibility [17]. Moreover, as these systems also use cameras, their applications are limited because of privacy concerns.

1.2.2. Non-vision based systems

In non-vision based systems, sensors are attached on the different parts of the body to collect movement information [7]. The posture of the person is estimated by combing the movement information from the sensors and the *a priori* knowledge of the kinematics of the body. The sensor technologies that are employed by such systems include inertial, magnetic and radio sensors.

The human posture capturing system considered in this thesis, which estimates the posture of a person based on the signals that are communicated by radio sensor nodes attached on the body, falls in this category. Hence, in this sub-section we briefly summarize non-vision based systems which are based on inertial and magnetic sensors. Then, in Section 1.4, radio based human posture capturing system is discussed in detail.

Human posture capturing based on inertial sensors

These systems use the measurements from inertial sensor units, which comprise accelerometers and gyroscopes, to capture the posture of a person. The accelerometers measure acceleration and the gyroscopes measure the rate of turn (or angular velocity) of the body parts they are attached to.

Figure 1.1 shows a conceptual flow diagram that describes procedure of estimating a position and orientation from inertial sensor measurements. The procedure, which is described in [6], can be summarized as follows.

Estimating the orientation is relatively straight forward. It results from integrating the gyroscope measurement. Estimating the position of the sensor, on the other hand, involves some steps. The accelerometer measures the sum of a linear acceleration (due to the displacement of the sensor unit) and gravitational acceleration. Since only the linear acceleration is of interest (which carries information about the location of the sensor unit), the gravitational acceleration needs to be subtracted from the accelerometer measurement. To do so, the acceleration measurements are transformed to a known reference coordinate system using the orientation estimates calculated from the gyroscope measurements. The gravitational acceleration, which is known in the reference coordinate system, is then subtracted from the acceleration measurements. Double integrating the linear acceleration results in the displacement, which is then used to estimate the position of the sensor unit.

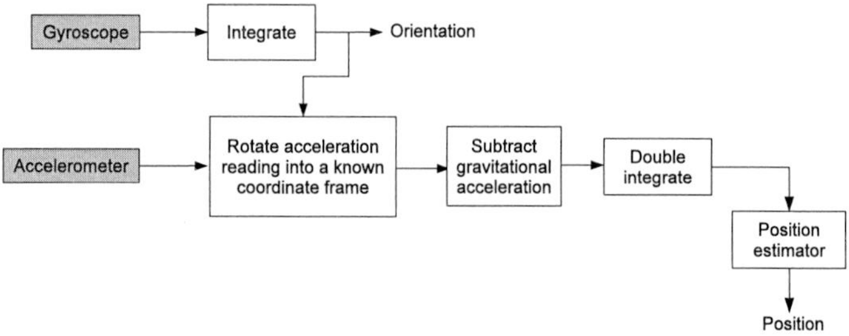

Figure 1.1.: Position and orientation estimation from inertial sensor measurements [6].

Commercial human posture capturing systems, which use inertial sensors, are currently available on the market, for instance Xsens-MTV [18], InertiaCube3 [19] and Inertia-Link [20]. The comparison of the systems is given in Table 1.2. Here, we need to make a remark that these systems first measure the orientation of the limbs. Then the locations of the limbs is calculated by fusing the kinematic model of the body and the measured orientations. Hence, the accuracy values given in Table 1.2 are the root mean square (RMS) of the orientation estimation accuracy in degrees.

We see that inertial based systems has a high update rate. Another advantage of these systems is that they are self-contained, i.e. no external infrastructure is required.

Table 1.2.: Comparison of inertial based motion capture systems [21].

System	Sensor dimension	Update rate	RMS accuracy	Connectivity
Xsens MTV	$3.8 \times 5.3 \times 2.1\,\text{cm}^3$	120 Hz	$2°$	wired
InertiaCube3	$3.13 \times 4.32 \times 1.48\,\text{cm}^3$	120 Hz	$< 1°$	wireless
Inertia-Link	$4.1 \times 6.3 \times 2.4\,\text{cm}^3$	100 Hz	$2°$	wireless

They also don't have a LOS restriction problem. And most importantly, they are non-invasive systems which do not invade the privacy of the person. The main weakness of these systems however is that they are prone to drift errors, which accumulates due to the integration process [6]. Hence, the accuracy of the position and orientation estimates deteriorates through time. Furthermore, as can be seen from Table 1.2, the form factor of the sensor nodes is not small (a dimension in the range of centimeters).

Human posture capturing based on magnetic sensors

Posture capturing systems that are based on magnetic sensors rely on the measurement of magnetic field induced at the sensor units. There are two types of magnetic positioning systems, which are realized by magnets and by quasi-static magnetic coils [22]. For the systems in the first category, a magnetic dipole, which serves as the excitation source, is realized by a magnet [23, 24]. For the second approach, on the other hand, magnetic coils are exited by a low-frequency alternating currents (ACs) to generate magnetic signals [22, 25, 26]. For both approaches, the magnetic signal which is coupled at the sensor unit is measured and the positions of the sensors relative to the locations of the excitation sources are estimated by applying appropriate algorithms.

The main advantages of the systems which are based on magnets are that the magnetic source does not need power and it is easily realizable [22]. However, the main bottleneck of these systems is that they are prone to interference from nearby ferromagnetic materials. The presence of such materials distorts the magnetic field induced at the sensor units as they act as unintended field sources [6]. Since, the field source of the magnet is constant, the system cannot cope with perturbation from the unintended field sources [22]. The systems which are based on magnetic coils, on the other hand, can be designed to be robust against such interference with appropriate excitation pattern and by applying the right signal processing at the outputs of the sensor units [22]. Nevertheless, the mutual coupling (more specifically the mutual inductance) between the source and the sensor decays proportional to the distance between them to the third power [26]. Hence, such systems are suitable for applications where the ranges between the sources and the sensors are short [6], e.g. hand gesture tracking.

Examples of commercial human posture capturing systems that use magnetic sensors are Patriot-Wireless, G4 and Liberty, which are all from Polhemus [27]. The performance of the Liberty hand motion capture system is tested in [28]. The hand motion capturing system setup is shown in Figure 1.2. For both hands, the transmitter (the source) is placed on the wrist and 16 sensors are placed on the hand. The source has a dimension of $2.3 \times 2.8 \times 1.6\,\mathrm{cm}^3$. The sensors, on the other hand, have a dimension of $9.6 \times 9.6 \times 9.6\,\mathrm{mm}^3$. The measurement results in [28] show that a positioning accuracy of 0.1 mm is achieved by this system.

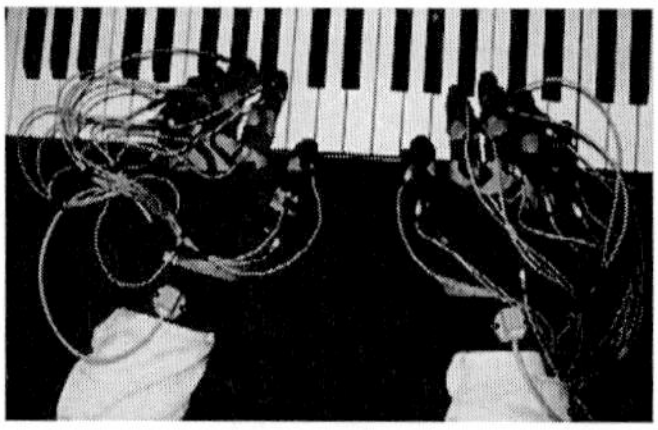

(a) Liberty hand motion capture system.

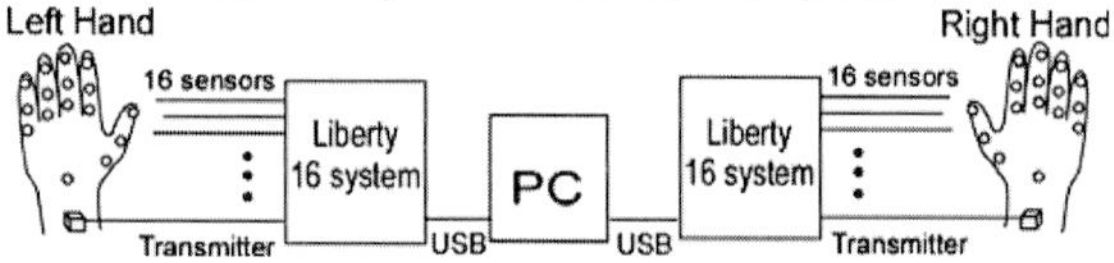

(b) System setup.

Figure 1.2.: Liberty hand motion capture system [28].

On top of the high position accuracy of these systems, we note that magnetic systems have a small form-factor [29], which makes them convenient to use. We also note that, as magnetic fields can pass through the human body, these systems also do not have LOS restriction problem. Furthermore, they are non-invasive systems. Despite the aforementioned advantages, the main bottleneck of these systems is that the supported range between the sources and the sensors is short [6], which limits their application.

The different classes of human posture capturing systems, which are discussed above, can be summarized as shown in Figure 1.3. Vision based systems, which use reflective markers, provide reliable posture capturing. However, they require expensive laboratories, complex settings and skilled operators. Vision based systems, which do not use markers, require a relatively less complex setting. But they are computationally intensive and achieving accurate posture capturing is still a challenge. Moreover, the use of camera raises privacy concerns, which limit the application areas of vision based system.

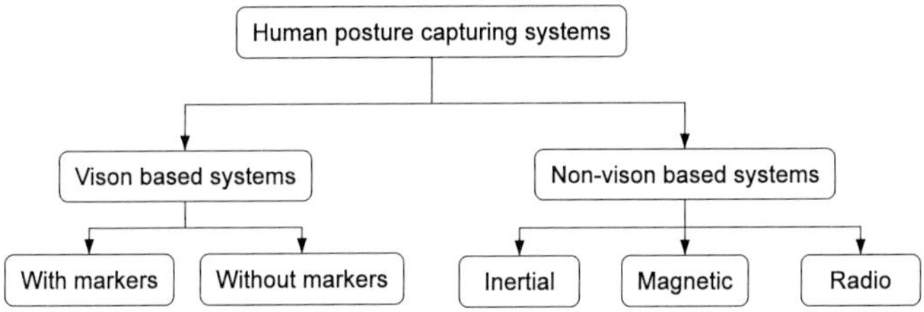

Figure 1.3.: Summary of the different classes of human posture capturing systems.

Non-vision based systems, which use inertial and magnetic sensors, do not have a privacy concern (as they are non-invasive) and their performance are not affected by NLOS situations. However, inertial systems are prone to drift errors and magnetic systems suffer from the interference from nearby ferromagnetic and conductive materials, which deteriorates posture capturing accuracy. To alleviate this problem, in [30–32], hybrid systems that fuse the measurements from inertial and magnetic sensors are proposed. Although hybrid systems might solve the reliability problem of the individual systems, they come at the expense of increased system cost.

Table 1.3.: Comparison of the different classes of human posture capturing systems.

	System			
Characteristics	Vision (with marker)	Inertial	Magnetic	Radio (potential)
Accuracy	high	medium	high	low
Update rate	high	high	high	high
Robustness	high	low	low	low
Simplicity	complex	medium	medium	simple
Cost	expensive	medium	medium	cheap

The comparison of the different classes of human posture capturing systems can be summarized as in Table 1.3. In this thesis, we consider a human posture capturing system which is based on the TOA measurement of the signals that are communicated between radio nodes attached on the body. As shown in the table, the potential distinct advantage of the considered radio based system over the state of the art systems is that it is low complexity (simple) and cheap.

The system we are considering is based on ultra-wideband (UWB) radio communication technology, which has distinct advantages compared to conventional communication systems that makes it attractive for the considered application. Section 1.3 provides a brief summary of UWB radio technology and localization based on radio signals. It is shown that, among the different radio based localization techniques, TOA based localization is the one most suited for the considered application. That is why, in Section 1.4, TOA based human posture capturing is discussed in detail.

1.3. Localization based on UWB Radio

UWB radio communication is thoroughly discussed in [33–35]. A comprehensive overview of UWB radio based localization can further be found in [36–38]. The goal of this section is to summarize the key features of UWB radio which makes it an attractive choice for human posture capturing.

According to the definition by the U. S. Federal Communications Commission (FCC), UWB signals have an absolute bandwidth larger than 500 MHz or a fractional bandwidth larger than 20 % [37]. Although the history of UWB radio dates back to the early days of radio communication [39], it received much of the attention after the FCC allowed unlicensed UWB operation in the spectrum ranging from 3.1 GHz to 10.6 GHz [36]. This very large bandwidth, which is free to use with a regulated transmit power [40], enables a wide range of applications.

By exploiting the very large signal bandwidth, UWB nodes can determine their relative distance with a very high spatio-temporal resolution and perform precise localization using the measured distances. Furthermore, UWB has the potential for low-cost, small form-factor and low-power implementation [34]. These key features of UWB makes it attractive for low-cost human posture capturing. In order to understand the reasoning behind the choice of time-of-arrival (TOA) based localization for human posture capturing, next we briefly summarize different localization techniques that are applied in wireless radio communication systems.

Localization techniques for wireless radio communication systems, in general, differentiate between two types of nodes: *anchors* (whose locations are known) and *agents* (whose locations are unknown). Localization in these systems then refers to the process of estimating the locations of the agents based on the signals that are communicated between the anchors and the agents. Radio based localization methods can be classified into two main categories: geometric localization methods and fingerprinting localization methods [41].

Geometric localization methods

Geometric localization methods typically involve two steps. In the first step, signal parameters that contain information about the geometry formed by the anchors and the agents are extracted from the signals that are communicated between them. The signal parameters include angle-of-arrival (AOA), received signal strength (RSS) or TOA. Then in the second step, the location of the agents is estimated using the extracted signal parameters and the known locations of the anchors.

AOA based methods estimate the angles between the agents and the anchors, which is done by a means of antenna arrays [36]. Given the AOA measurements, the locations of the agents is estimated by applying triangulation [38]. Let us consider anchors with uniform linear antenna-arrays (ULAs) with N antenna elements and inter-element spacing l. Assuming an additive white Gaussian noise (AWGN) channel, the root mean squared error (RMSE) of any unbiased estimate of the angle ϕ between the agents and the anchors is lower bounded by [37]

$$\mathrm{RMSE}(\hat{\phi}_{\mathrm{AOA}}) \geq \frac{\sqrt{3}c_0}{\beta l \cos\phi \sqrt{2\pi\gamma\, N(N^2-1)}},$$

where c_0 denotes the speed of light, β represents the effective[1] bandwidth of the transmit signal and γ is the received signal-to-noise ratio (SNR). We observe that AOA estimation accuracy is improved with increasing signal bandwidth β, SNR γ, number of antennas N and antenna spacing l.

One of the main bottlenecks of AOA methods that make them unsuitable for UWB based localization is that they require antenna arrays. This translates to increased system complexity and cost, which makes them unattractive for the considered application of human posture capturing. Moreover, due to the very large bandwidth, the number of observed multipath components might be very large, which makes the AOA estimation a computationally intensive multi-dimensional search [42].

[1] The effective bandwidth corresponds to the root mean squared (RMS) bandwidth of the signal and is formally defined in Section 2.3.

RSS based methods assume that the pathloss model of the communication channel between the agents and the anchors is known. Hence, the relative distance between the anchors and the agents can be calculated from the measured received signal strength. Given the relative distances, the locations of the agents can then be estimated by applying trilateration [38]. In [43], it shown that the RMSE of any unbiased estimate of the distance based on the RSS is lower bounded by

$$\mathrm{RMSE}(\hat{d}_{\mathrm{RSS}}) \geq \frac{\ln 10}{10} \frac{\sigma_{\mathrm{sh}}}{n_{\mathrm{PL}}} d,$$

where d is the distance between the agent and the anchor, σ^2_{sh} is the variance of the Gaussian random variable which models the log-normal shadowing effect and n_{PL} is the pathloss exponent.

We see that the accuracy of the RSS based distance estimates depends on the channel parameters, which suggests that the method is very sensitive to the accuracy of the channel model [42]. Most importantly the key feature of UWB (its huge bandwidth) is not exploited by RSS based methods.

TOA based approaches typically assume that the clocks of the anchors and the agents are synchronized[2] and estimate the distance between them from the flight time of the communicated signals. Considering an AWGN channel, the lower bound on the RMSE of any unbiased estimate of the distance based on the TOA is given by [44]

$$\mathrm{RMSE}(\hat{d}_{\mathrm{TOA}}) \geq \frac{c_0}{2\pi\beta\sqrt{\gamma}}.$$

We note that the accuracy of the TOA based distance estimate is improved for increasing effective bandwidth β and SNR γ. Hence, the huge bandwidth of the UWB signals can enable a precise distance estimation, which in turn leads to accurate localization performance. This is intuitive because the very large signal bandwidth (which corresponds to extremely short duration transmit pulses) makes it possible to distinctively resolve multipath components and hence accurately estimates the TOA.

[2]There exist TOA based localization methods, including the methods presented in this thesis, which only require the clocks of the anchors to be synchronized. But the clocks of the agents can be asynchronous. This is discussed in detail in Chapter 3.

Fingerprinting localization methods

Fingerprinting methods use the location specific features of the propagation channel to perform localization [41]. Localization using fingerprinting also involves two phases: training phase and localization phase. In the training phase, the signal features (fingerprints) corresponding to the known training locations of the agents is gathered and stored to a database. In [45,46], parameters of the received signal, such as mean excess delay, RMS delay spread, maximum excess delay, received signal power and the number of multipath components, are used as a fingerprint. In [47,48], on the other hand, the multipath structure of the channel impulse response (CIR) is used as a fingerprint. In the localization phase, the unknown location of the agent is estimated by comparing its fingerprint with the database entries and selecting the best match [41].

The key advantage of fingerprinting methods is that they can enable localization in harsh propagation environments with dense multipath and non-line-of-sight (NLOS) situation. However, in order achieve a good localization accuracy, fingerprinting methods require a large amount of training data [49], which makes the training phase complex and limit a practical implementation of such methods [41]. Furthermore, even with large amount of training data, the localization accuracy achieved by fingerprinting methods in [41] is in the order of deci-meters. Clearly, such localization accuracy is not sufficient enough for the application of human posture capturing.

In summary, among the different radio based localization techniques, TOA based methods are the most suited for UWB systems, as they can enable precise localization by exploiting the very large signal bandwidth. UWB communications systems, in turn, have the potential for low-cost and low-power implementation, which makes them very attractive for the application of human posture capturing.

1.4. TOA based Human Posture Capturing Systems

TOA estimation of UWB signals is a well investigated topic. Several TOA estimation methods, which trade-off computational complexity and accuracy, have been studied. Considering coherent receivers, maximum likelihood (ML) based TOA estimators are presented in [50–52] and different sub-optimal estimators are proposed in [53–55]. Similarly for non-coherent receivers, ML based TOA estimators are studied in [56–58] and sub-optimal TOA estimators are presented in [54, 59]. For a detailed comparative survey of the different TOA estimation methods, the reader is referred to [60, 61].

Also there exist several previous works that consider the general problem of localization based on TOA measurements. The ML solution of the localization problem, which is a non-convex optimization problem, is presented in [37, 38, 62, 63]. The relaxation of the ML solution to convex optimization problem is studied in [64–66] (relaxation to semi-definite programming (SDP) problem) and [67, 68] (relaxation to second order cone programming (SOCP) problem). Other sub-optimal solution which consider the approximation of ML estimator with a linear least squares problem are investigated in [69–72].

However, the above previous works on TOA based localization methods consider the general problem of wireless sensor network localization. It is typically assumed that locations of the anchors are fixed and known. The clocks of the anchors and the agents are also assumed to be perfectly synchronized and hence, there is no clock offset between them. As discussed in Section 1.5 however, for the considered low-complexity and infrastructureless TOA based human posture capturing system, such assumptions on the anchors and the agents are not realistic. It should also be noted that the specific setup of the TOA based human posture capturing system can be exploited to provide location information about the agents. For example, the agents which are located on the same arm have a distance constraint between them due to the kinematic constraints of the body. A detailed discussion on the challenges of the considered human capturing system and the main contributions of this thesis is given in Section 1.5. Before that however, next we discuss previous works that considered the application of TOA based localization for human posture capturing.

Previous related works that studied the specific application of TOA based localization for human posture capturing are relatively few. In [73], the impact of the on-body channel propagation on TOA estimation is studied. It is shown that, for the case of LOS or slight diffraction[3], even sub-optimal estimators (such as maximum energy search [53] and a threshold based scheme [54]) can achieve accurate range estimates (with a RMSE accuracy in the order of sub-centimeters). However, when the diffraction effect is severe (i.e. NLOS situation), it is shown that even ML based TOA estimators cannot achieve accurate range estimates.

UWB based systems that can measure movement parameters, which are relevant for analyzing a person's gait, are proposed in [16, 74]. The system in [74] consists of two UWB transceiver nodes (which can both transmit and receive) that are attached on the foot. One is placed at the heel and another at the toe. Using these two nodes,

[3]A slight diffraction is, for example, when the LOS link is blocked by the arm.

the system measures the foot clearance[4] of a person by estimating the TOA of the signal reflected from the ground. The work in [16], on the other hand, considers a system where UWB nodes are attached on both heels and knees. The heel-to-heel and heel-to-knee distances are then measured by estimating the TOA of the signals that are communicated between the nodes.

A TOA based human posture capturing system, which estimates the locations of the different parts of the body, has been considered recently in [75]. For the considered system, the agents are attached on the body and the anchors are placed outside the body. Given the TOA measurements between the agents and the anchors, the locations of the agents are estimated by applying a localization method which is based on the linear least squares approximation of the ML estimator. However, the main pitfalls of this system are the following. The anchors are located outside the body which means that the posture capturing system is not fully wearable and hence, the person is required to be confined in the area where the anchors are installed. Also the considered linear least squares solution of the localization problem is sub-optimal which is suitable only when the agents are located inside the convex-hull of the anchors and the TOA measurement errors are small [70]. Furthermore, the clocks of the anchors and the agents are assumed to perfectly synchronized, which is difficult to achieve in practice when low-complexity agents are considered.

Although the application of TOA based localization for human posture capturing is appealing and is receiving attention, substantial research is required to realize such systems. In this thesis, we propose and analyze a low-cost, low-power and low-complexity TOA based human posture capturing system, which does not rely on external infrastructure. The localization accuracy requirements of the considered application coupled with the need to make the system low-cost and self-contained pose several challenges that need to be tackled to enable the feasibility of the proposed system. The next section discusses the main challenges and the contributions of this thesis.

1.5. Main Challenges and Contributions

The proposed human posture capturing system comprises three types of nodes: agents, anchors and a cluster head. The agents, which are located on the limbs, are considered to be extremely low-power and low-cost transmit-only beacons with a very small

[4]Foot clearance is defined as the vertical distance between the foot and the ground during walking [74].

form-factor that can easily be integrated into different pieces of a cloth or implanted subcutaneously. These specifications imply that it is impractical to assume the clocks of the agents to be synchronized with the clocks of other nodes in the system. Hence, the posture capturing system needs to cope with the clock asynchronicity of the agents.

The anchors are low-complexity nodes which are located on the relatively static parts of the body, e.g. the torso. As discussed in Section 1.3, TOA based localization techniques assume the anchors' locations to be known and their clocks to be synchronized. Since the system is required to be self-contained, it should be able to calibrate the locations and clocks of the anchors without relying on external infrastructure.

Although the anchors are located on the relatively static parts of the body, their locations cannot be assumed to be fixed as the person is mobile. Furthermore, the anchors' locations are determined from a calibration phase, which is prone to errors. Hence, the human posture capturing system should be able to cope with uncertainties in the locations of the anchors.

Since the agents and the anchors are located on the body, the LOS between them might be obstructed. The TOA measurements under NLOS situations contain unknown positive biases which, if unaccounted, lead to a considerable degradation in localization performance.

The cluster head, which can for example be a smartphone, captures the posture of the body by estimating the locations of the agents based on the information that is relayed by the anchors. Noting that the computational capability of the cluster head is limited, the posture capturing algorithm needs to be computationally efficient while meeting the accuracy requirements of the application.

The work in this thesis has addressed the aforementioned challenges and the main contributions can be summarized as follows:

In Chapter 2, the proposed TOA based human posture capturing system setup, the signal model and the communication protocol is described. The TOA based range measurement model, which accounts for different possible clock synchronization cases between the nodes in the system, is presented. A NLOS identification method, which enables the system to detect NLOS situations and to discard the corresponding range measurements from the posture capturing process, is discussed. It is shown that a simple likelihood ratio test using the SNR of the received signal can achieve a reasonably accurate NLOS identification.

For the discussions in Chapters 3, 4 and 5, the TOA based human posture capturing system is abstracted to the general problem of wireless sensor network localization. The motivation for this approach is twofold. On one hand, known methods from wireless sensor network localization can be applied to the considered problem. On the other hand, the algorithms that are proposed in this thesis can be easily applied to other systems which have similar type of problems.

In Chapter 3, assuming phase synchronous[5] anchors with known locations, the problem of localizing clock asynchronous agents which have position constraints is considered. The position constraints of the agents, which are located on the limbs for the considered human posture capturing setup, is inspired by the kinematic constraints of the body. The ML solution of the localization problem is presented and shown to be non-convex optimization problem. The relaxation of the ML solution to a SDP problem, which is convex and can be efficiently solved with standard convex optimization toolboxes, is presented. The proposed two-step localization algorithm, where the SDP solution is refined with the ML estimator, is compared with the corresponding Cramér-Rao lower bound (CRLB) and shown to be efficient.

The problem of localizing asynchronous agents while considering anchors with location uncertainties is discussed in Chapter 4. The ML solution of the localization problem, which jointly estimates the locations of the agents and the anchors, is formulated and shown to be non-convex. A previous related work in [76] assumes that the anchor location errors are small and simplify the ML estimator by performing prior approximation of its objective function. We instead propose to relax the ML estimator to a SDP problem without performing prior approximation. It is shown that our proposed method outperforms the existing scheme, notably when the anchor location errors are dominant compared to the range measurement errors.

In Chapter 5, a self-calibration method that estimates the locations and clock offsets of the anchors based on the TOA measurements gathered between the anchors and the agents. The agents' locations are not surveyed and hence, the multiple agents' locations can be realized by a single moving agent. This makes the calibration procedure simple and cost effective. Instead of considering a specific clock synchronization scenario, we systematically classify the different clock synchronization cases that may arise in practice and provide a generalized formulation of the self-calibration problem that covers all the synchronization classes. The ML solution of the calibration problem and its relaxation to SDP problem is presented. It is shown that the proposed method is

[5]Phase synchronous nodes implies that the clocks' of the two nodes are synchronized both in phase and frequency. The different clock synchronization classes are discussed in Section 2.3.

capable of accurately calibrating TOA based localization systems.

The proposed localization and calibration methods, presented in Chapters 3, 4 and 5, are analyzed in the general framework of wireless sensor network localization. In Chapter 6, the performance of the localization and calibration methods are evaluated for the specific setup of human posture capturing. The performance evaluations provide insights about the tradeoffs that are involved when choosing system parameters, such as accuracy, system complexity and computational complexity.

In Chapter 7, the proposed human posture capturing system is implemented and demonstrated with a real-time demonstrator system. The agent nodes are prototype transmit-only nodes that continuously transmit pseudo-random noise (PN) sequences. The anchors are realized by a low-complexity digital receiver board, which uses 1-bit analog-to-digital convertors (1-bit ADCs).

2. TOA based Human Posture Capturing System

In this chapter, the proposed TOA based human posture capturing system is described in detail. We start with the description of the system setup. This is then followed by the discussion of the signal model and the communication protocol employed by the system in Section 2.2. The model of TOA based range measurement, which takes into account clock asynchronism of the agents and the anchors, is discussed in Section 2.3. A simple (but accurate) NLOS identification method, which is implemented as a likelihood ratio test on the channel parameters, is presented in Section 2.4.

2.1. System Setup

The human posture capturing system that we are considering can be depicted as shown in Figure 2.1. The system comprises three type of nodes, namely agents, anchor relays and a cluster head.

- *Agents*: are extremely low-power and low-cost transmit-only beacons, which can be implemented with a small form factor. Such nodes can easily be integrated into different pieces of a cloth, attached on the body or implanted subcutaneously, and hence enable ubiquitous use.
- *Anchor relays*: receive the beacon signals (which are transmitted by the agents) and forward them to the cluster head. For short, the anchor relays are also referred to as anchors. In principle, the anchors can be realized as low-complexity nodes that implement a variant of amplify and forward (AF) relaying [77]. In the scope of this thesis however, the wireless second hop channel from the anchors to the cluster head is not treated. Instead, we consider the setup where the anchors are wire connected to the cluster head. An outlook on a possible extension of

this work to a wireless channel between the anchors and the cluster head is given in the outlook chapter.

- *Cluster head*: receives the signals from all the anchors and s the signals that are communicated between each agent-anchor pair. The TOAs for each agent-anchor pairs are then estimated from the resolved signals. The locations of the agents is then jointly estimated using the TOA measurements. By fusing the knowledge of the kinematics of the body and the agent location estimates, it then captures the posture of the body.

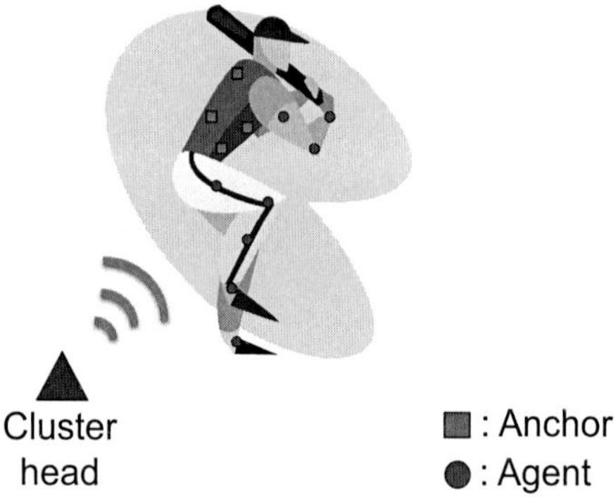

Figure 2.1.: TOA based human posture capturing system setup.

The posture capturing system that we are considering is aimed at capturing the change in the human posture due to limb movements. In other words, fine movements, such as eye blinking and finger movements, are not considered. To enable posture capturing based on TOA measurement of the signals that are communicated between the agents and the anchors, the nodes in the system are placed as follows. The agents are placed on the limbs, i.e. on the arms and the legs. The anchors are placed on the torso, which is considered as the relatively static part of the body. The location of the cluster head, on the other hand, is not relevant.

With this system setup, the posture capturing process that we are considering involves two phases: a calibration phase and a localization phase. During the calibration phase, system parameters, which are required to be known for TOA based localization, are estimated. Such system parameters include the anchors' locations, the clock offsets of the anchors and the constant signal propagation delays between the anchors and the cluster head. Then during the localization phase, the location of the agents (and hence the posture of the limbs) is estimated based on the TOA measurements of the signals received by the cluster head.

2.2. Signal Model

To minimize (and if possible avoid) the interference between the agents and the anchors, the posture capturing system employs a multiple accessing scheme. The two most commonly used multiple accessing schemes for UWB transmission are based on direct sequence (DS) and time hoping (TH) [35]. Both multiple accessing schemes use a node specific pseudo-random noise (PN) chip sequence to separate the simultaneous transmission from different nodes. The main difference between the two schemes however is that in the DS based scheme, the PN chip sequence is used to randomly flip the polarity of the transmitted pulse. On the other hand, in the TH based scheme, the PN sequence randomizes the transmit time of the pulse.

To ease the discussion and keep it short, we consider a transmission system that uses DS multiple accessing scheme. It should however be noted that the posture capturing methods that are proposed in this thesis can readily be applied to systems with TH based multiple accessing.

Let T_{ch} be the chip period and N_{ch} be the number of chips of the PN sequence. Then the unmodulated[1] DS signal transmitted by the agents is a periodic signal with period $T_s = N_{\mathrm{ch}} T_{\mathrm{ch}}$. To this end, the periodic DS signal that is transmitted by agent m, within the time window $(s-1)T_s \leq t \leq sT_s$, $s \in \mathbb{Z}$, can be expressed as

$$s_m(t) = \sum_{i=0}^{N_{\mathrm{ch}}-1} c_{m,i} p(t - sT_s - iT_{\mathrm{ch}}), \tag{2.1}$$

where $c_{m,i} \in \{+1, -1\}$, $\boldsymbol{c}_m = [c_{m,0}, \ldots, c_{m,N_{\mathrm{ch}}-1}]$ represents the PN chip sequence of the mth agent and $p(t)$ denotes the pulse that is transmitted within one chip period.

Here, we make a distinction about the transmit pulse $p(t)$ depending on the signaling scheme that is used. Namely, direct sequence spread spectrum (DS-SS) and direct sequence impulse radio (DS-IR) signaling.

For the case of DS-SS signaling, the pulse $p(t)$ is a rectangular pulse with a duration

[1]As the TOA estimates of the received signals at the cluster head are not affected by the transmitted symbols, we can consider the unmodulated signal without loss of generality.

T_{ch}, i.e.

$$p(t) = \begin{cases} 1/\sqrt{T_{\text{ch}}}, & 0 \leq t \leq T_{\text{ch}}, \\ 0, & \text{otherwise.} \end{cases}$$

For this case, the PN chip sequence is important both for separating the transmit signal between different agents and for spreading the spectrum. As discussed later in this chapter, the accuracy of the TOA estimates is inversely proportional to the bandwidth of the transmit signal. Hence, the parameters T_{ch} and N_{ch} need to be chosen such that the transmit signal in (2.1) has a spectrum that is wide enough to achieve the target TOA estimation accuracy.

On the other hand for DS-IR signaling, the transmit pulse $p(t)$ is an ultra-wideband pulse with pulse duration $T_p \ll T_{\text{ch}}$. Examples of such pulses are Gaussian monocycle pulse, Gaussian doublet pulse and Hermite pulse [78]. The main difference of this scheme to that of DS-SS is that the transmit pulse $p(t)$ in this case already has a wide spectrum and hence, the PN sequence doesn't further spread the spectrum [35]. However, the PN chip sequences enable the separation of the transmit signals from different agents. We further note that without the PN chip sequence, the transmit signal is periodic with period T_{ch}, which leads to a spectrum with strong spectral peaks. The presence of such spectral peaks leads to undesirable limitation of the total transmit power such that it meets regulatory requirements, e.g. the spectral limit by FCC [40]. The PN chip sequence effectively solve this problem by randomly flipping the polarity of the transmit pulse, which smoothens out the spectrum of the transmit signal.

The signals transmitted by the N_{t} agents are jointly received at a given anchor n as

$$r_n(t) = \sum_{m=1}^{N_{\text{t}}} \sum_{l=1}^{L_{mn}} a_{mn}^{(l)} s_m(t - \tau_{mn}^{(l)}) + w(t), \tag{2.2}$$

where $h_{mn}(t) = \sum_{l=1}^{L_{mn}} a_{mn}^{(l)} \delta(t - \tau_{mn}^{(l)})$ represents the propagation channel between anchor n and agent m with path amplitudes $\{a_{mn}^{(l)}\}$, path delays $\{\tau_{mn}^{(l)}\}$ and number of paths L_{mn}, and $w(t)$ is an additive noise.

Figure 2.2 depicts the model of the received signal at anchor n, which is then forwarded to the cluster head for further processing. The wired second hop channel between the anchor and the cluster head is modeled as a channel which introduces a constant propagation delay and signal attenuation. To this end, the signal received at

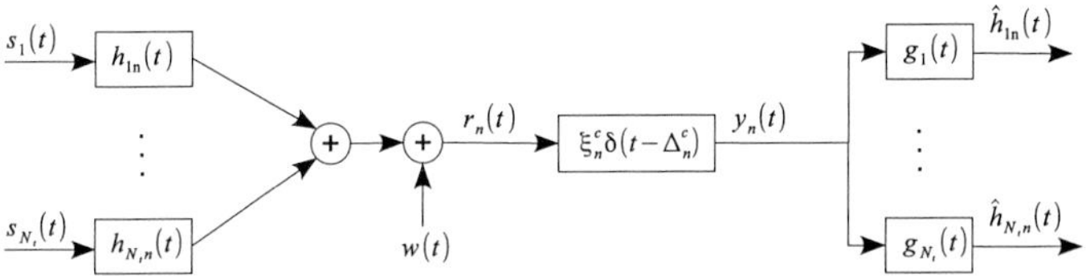

Figure 2.2.: Signal model: estimates of the channel impulse responses between all agents and anchor n.

the cluster head from anchor n can be expressed as

$$
\begin{aligned}
y_n(t) &= \xi_n^{\mathrm{c}} r_n(t-\Delta_n^{\mathrm{c}}) \\
&= \sum_{m=1}^{N_{\mathrm{t}}} \sum_{l=1}^{L_{mn}} \xi_n^{\mathrm{c}} a_{mn}^{(l)} s_m(t-\tau_{mn}^{(l)}-\Delta_n^{\mathrm{c}}) + \xi_n^{\mathrm{c}} w(t),
\end{aligned} \tag{2.3}
$$

where ξ_n^{c} and Δ_n^{c} are the signal attenuation and delay introduced by the cable connecting anchor n with the cluster head. Both ξ_n^{c} and Δ_n^{c} are assumed to be constant, but they are not required to be known.

At the cluster head, the signal transmitted by agent m and received through anchor n is detected by passing $y_n(t)$ through a filter $g_m(t)$, which is matched to the transmitted signal. The output of the matched filter $\hat{h}_{mn}(t)$ can hence be expressed as

$$
\begin{aligned}
\hat{h}_{mn}(t) &= y_n(t) * s_m(-t) \\
&= \sum_{l=1}^{L_{mn}} \xi_n^{\mathrm{c}} a_{mn}^{(l)} R_{s_m s_m}(t-\tau_{mn}^{(l)}-\Delta_n^{\mathrm{c}}) \\
&\quad + \sum_{m'=1, m'\neq m}^{N_{\mathrm{t}}} \sum_{l=1}^{L_{m'n}} \xi_n^{\mathrm{c}} a_{m'n}^{(l)} R_{s_{m'} s_m}(t-\tau_{m'n}^{(l)}-\Delta_n^{\mathrm{c}}) + \xi_n^{\mathrm{c}} w(t) * s_m(-t),
\end{aligned} \tag{2.4}
$$

where $R_{s_m s_m}(t)$ is the autocorrelation of the transmit signal $s_m(t)$ and $R_{s_{m'} s_m}(t)$ is the cross-correlation between $s_{m'}(t)$ and $s_m(t)$, for $m \neq m'$. From (2.4), we note that the first term in $\hat{h}_{mn}(t)$ represents the relevant signal part. The second term, on the other hand, represents the interference caused by other agents. The transmit signal $s_m(t)$ is chosen such that its autocorrelation approximates a dirac-delta signal while its cross-correlations is close to zero. These two requirements, however, are not independent and in practice a tradeoff is required. Some of the commonly used PN sequences, which provide such tradeoffs, are M-sequences, Gold sequences and Kasami sequences [79].

Representing the superposition of the interference and the noise terms in (2.4) as an additive noise $n(t)$, the estimate of the channel between agent m and anchor n can be rewritten as

$$\hat{h}_{mn}(t) = \sum_{l=1}^{L_{mn}} \tilde{a}_{mn}^{(l)} R_{s_m s_m}(t - \tau_{mn}^{(l)} - \Delta_n^{\mathrm{c}}) + n(t), \tag{2.5}$$

with $\tilde{a}_{mn}^{(l)} = \xi_n^{\mathrm{c}} a_{mn}^{(l)}$. The noise $n(t)$ is modeled as a white Gaussian random process with a two-sided power spectral density (PSD) of $N_0/2$.

Given the channel impulse response estimate $\hat{h}_{mn}(t)$, the TOA estimator then estimates the delay of the first multipath component $\tau_{mn}^{(1)}$. Note however that, due to the propagation delay between the anchor and the cluster head, the TOA estimator actually estimates $\tau_{mn}^{(1)} + \Delta_n^{\mathrm{c}}$. Hence, the unknown but constant delay Δ_n^{c} needs to be accounted by the posture capturing method.

2.3. TOA based Range Measurement Model

The signal model presented in Section 2.2, and hence the channel impulse response estimate in (2.5), tacitly assume that all the nodes in the system share the same reference clock, with time t. This in other words means that the clocks of the agents, the anchors and the cluster head are synchronized both in phase and frequency. However, for the considered highly asymmetric system, where the agents are extremely low-power transmit-only beacons and the anchors are low-complexity relays, such an assumption is impractical. To account clock asynchronocity in the TOA based range measurement model, next we briefly revise the different clock synchronization classes in wireless sensor networks.

Clock Synchronization Classes

Let t be the time at the reference clock. The time at the clock of node i can be related with that of the reference clock as [80]

$$t_i = \alpha_i t + \beta_i, \tag{2.6}$$

where α_i and β_i are the skew and shift of the clock of node i with respect to the reference clock, respectively. The clock model assumes that the clock parameters α_i and

β_i are constant. However, in practice, they may change overtime due to temperature, atmospheric pressure or hardware aging [81]. For the model to be valid, the clock synchronization has to be performed periodically, where the period is chosen such that the clock parameters do not experience a recognizable change.

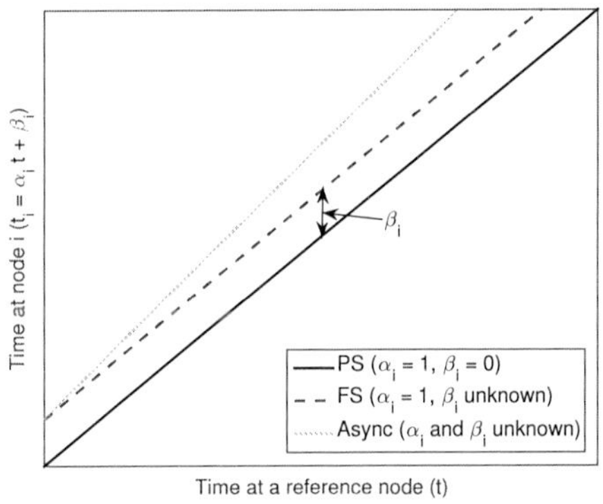

Figure 2.3.: Relation between the time at node i and the time at a reference node for the three different synchronization cases.

Given the clock model in (2.6), the *offset* of the clock of node i with respect to the reference clock at a reference time t then takes the form

$$\Delta_i = t_i - t = (\alpha_i - 1)t + \beta_i.$$

To this end, we make three distinction for clock synchronization between node i and the reference node. Namely,

1. *Phase synchronous (PS)*: The two clocks are completely synchronized, i.e. $\alpha_i = 1$ and $\beta_i = 0$. Hence, the clock offset $\Delta_i = 0$.
2. *Frequency synchronous (FS)*: the two clocks are frequency synchronized, i.e. $\alpha_i = 1$. However, the clock shift β_i is unknown. Hence, the clock offset $\Delta_i = \beta_i$ is unknown but it is constant overtime.
3. *Asynchronous (Async)*: the two clocks are neither phase nor frequency synchronized, and hence, both α_i and β_i are unknown. For this case, the clock offset $\Delta_i = (\alpha_i - 1)t + \beta_i$ is unknown and dependent on time.

A graphical depiction of the three synchronization cases is shown in Figure 2.3.

Range Measurement Model

To capture the effect of clock asynchronicity on the TOA based range measurements, we consider the most relaxed synchronization case where all the anchors and the agents are asynchronous with each other. Assuming that a node starts transmission and recording at a rising edge of a trigger, the timing diagram of the communication between agent m and anchor n can be depicted as shown in Figure 2.4.

The rising edge of agent m occurs at the time instant t_m^{transmit} and hence the node starts its transmission at this point in time. The signal propagates through the channel and is received at anchor n at the time instant $t_n^{\text{received}} = t_m^{\text{transmit}} + \tau_{mn}^{(1)} + \tau_m^{\text{tx}} + \tau_n^{\text{rx}}$, where $\tau_{mn}^{(1)}$, τ_m^{tx} and τ_n^{rx} are the propagation delay of the signal over the air, the transmitter and receiver circuitry (e.g. the cable connecting the RF front end with the antennas), respectively. We further note that since the clock of agent m is asynchronous with the reference clock, it has a clock offset of $\Delta_{\text{t},m}$. Similarly, the clock of anchor n has an offset of $\Delta_{\text{r},n}$ with respect to the reference clock.

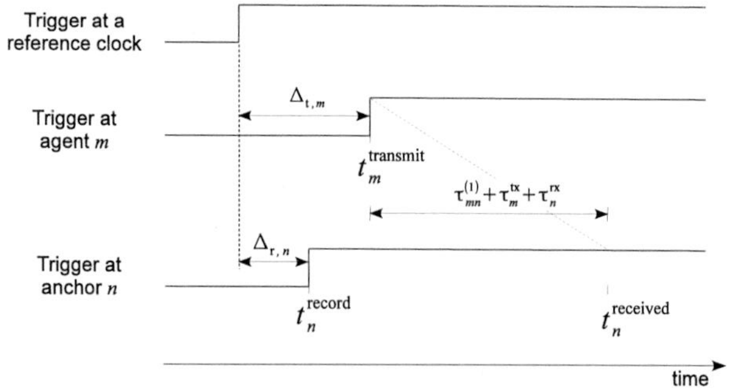

Figure 2.4.: Timing diagram: communication between agent m and anchor n.

Hence, the error free TOA[2] measured at anchor n for the signal transmitted from agent m is given by

$$\begin{aligned}\text{TOA}_{mn} &= t_n^{\text{received}} - t_n^{\text{record}} \\ &= \tau_{mn}^{(1)} + \underbrace{\tau_m^{\text{tx}} + \Delta_{\text{t},m}}_{\equiv\bar{\Delta}_{\text{t},m}} + \underbrace{\tau_n^{\text{rx}} - \Delta_{\text{r},n}}_{\equiv\bar{\Delta}_{\text{r},n}} \\ &= \tau_{mn}^{(1)} + \bar{\Delta}_{\text{t},m} + \bar{\Delta}_{\text{r},n},\end{aligned} \tag{2.7}$$

[2]Here we slightly abuse the definition of Time of Arrival (TOA) to refer to Time of Flight (TOF).

where $\bar{\Delta}_{t,m}$ and $\bar{\Delta}_{r,n}$ are the timing offsets of agent m and anchor n, respectively, which account the clock offset and the propagation delay through the circuits.

Let $\boldsymbol{t}_m$ be the location of agent m and $\boldsymbol{r}_n$ be the location of anchor n. The error free range measurement between agent m and anchor n then takes the form

$$\begin{aligned} d_{mn} &= c_0 \, \mathrm{TOA}_{mn} \\ &= \|\boldsymbol{t}_m - \boldsymbol{r}_n\| + b_{t,m} + b_{r,n}, \end{aligned} \tag{2.8}$$

where $c_0 \approx 3 \times 10^8 \, m/s$ is the speed of light, $b_{t,m} = c_0 \bar{\Delta}_{t,m}$ is the ranging offset of agent m and $b_{r,n} = c_0 \bar{\Delta}_{r,n}$ is the ranging offset of anchor n.

We see that for the case when the anchors are asynchronous with each other and with respect to the agents, the clock offsets $\Delta_{r,n}$ and $\Delta_{t,m}$ in (2.7) are unknown and change over time. Hence, the ranging offsets $b_{r,n}$ and $b_{t,m}$ in (2.8) are also unknown and time dependent. We further note that the agent locations $\{\boldsymbol{t}_m\}$ are also unknown.

Assuming that the signals from all anchors are measured simultaneously, the range measurements between all agents and anchor n have the same anchor ranging offset $b_{r,n}$. Similarly, the range measurements between all anchors and agent m have the same agent ranging offsets $b_{t,m}$. Let N_r be the number of anchors and N_t be the number of agents. With these consideration, as shown in Chapter 5, it is possible to estimate the unknown locations of the agents under the presence of the nuisance ranging offsets provided that the number of range measurement $N_r N_t$ is enough. Clearly, the number of range measurements has to be larger than the number of unknown parameters, i.e. $N_r N_t > 4N_t + N_r$. For a given number of anchors, this condition is equivalent to $N_t > \left\lceil \frac{N_r}{N_r - 4} \right\rceil$, if $N_r > 4$, where the ceiling operator $\lceil x \rceil$ denotes the smallest integer larger than x.

However, for a fixed number of anchors N_r, to achieve accurate location estimates the number of agents N_t has to be large, which makes the localization problem complex and hence, leads to a slow update rate. But most importantly, one of the key feature of the proposed human posture capturing system is that it should not rely on external infrastructure. One of the implications of this requirement is that the system should be able to calibrate itself, i.e. determine the anchor locations and ranging offsets based on the range measurements between the agents and the anchors. As discussed in Chapter 5, with the additional unknown locations of the anchors, the calibration problem is a more complex than the localization problem, which requires larger number of agents N_t to achieve accurate calibration performance. The other downside of this system setup, on top of the system and computational complexity, is that the ranging offsets of the anchors is time variant. This implies that the estimated ranging offsets of the anchors from the calibration phase can not be used during the localization phase.

For this reason, we consider the setup where the clocks of the anchors are frequency synchronous with each other. However, the clocks of the agents can still be asynchronous. For this synchronization case, the ranging offset of the anchors $b_{\mathrm{r},n}$ is unknown but constant overtime. As discussed in Chapter 5, the anchor ranging offsets are estimated during the calibration phase and can be subtracted from the range measurements in the localization phase.

Hence, for the case when the anchors are frequency synchronized but the agents are asynchronous, the range measurement between anchor n and agent m after calibrating out the anchor ranging offsets can be written as

$$d_{mn} = \|\boldsymbol{t}_m - \boldsymbol{r}_n\| + b_{\mathrm{t},m} + e_{mn}, \tag{2.9}$$

where e_{mn} is a term that accounts the range measurement error due to noise.

We assume that the effective bandwidth β and/or the signal-to-noise-ratio (SNR) are sufficiently large such that the range measurement error conforms to a Gaussian distribution $\mathcal{N}(\varepsilon_{mn}, \sigma_{mn}^2)$, as discussed in [44]. For the case when anchor n is in a LOS of agent m, the error has a zero mean ($\varepsilon_{mn} = 0$) and its variance is given by [44]

$$\sigma_{mn}^2 = \frac{c_0^2}{4\pi^2\beta_m^2\gamma_{mn}}, \tag{2.10}$$

where $\beta_m = \frac{\int f^2|S_m(f)|^2 \mathrm{d}f}{\int |S_m(f)|^2 \mathrm{d}f}$ is the effective bandwidth of the transmit signal, $S_m(f)$ is the Fourier transform of the transmit signal $s_m(t)$ and γ_{mn} is the SNR of the link.

On the other hand when anchor n and agent m are in a NLOS, the range measurement error takes the distribution $\mathcal{N}(\varepsilon_{mn}, \sigma_{mn}^2)$ with a variance σ_{mn}^2 as in the LOS case (given in (2.10)) but with an unknown mean $\varepsilon_{mn} \geq 0$ [82].

If unaccounted, the unknown range measurement bias ε_{mn} in NLOS situation can severely degrade the posture capturing performance. The problem of NLOS situation in TOA based localization is a known problem and several methods have been proposed to mitigate its effect. The methods can be grouped into three main categories.

The first approach is to consider NLOS bias as perturbation of the true range measurement [83,84] . This approach assumes that the bias due to NLOS is small compared to the true range and hence its impact on the localization performance is not substantial. However, the NLOS bias depends on the environment and can be much larger than the true range measurement. For example, consider an indoor environment where the transmitter and the receiver are located close to each other but their LOS is blocked. The received signal (which is NLOS) is the superposition of the reflections from the walls, the ceiling or the ground, which may have a NLOS bias that is larger than the true distance. Hence, for such cases, accounting it as a small perturbation does not compensate the NLOS induced localization error [85]. Similarly, for the considered on-body propagation channel on the other hand the NLOS bias (which is mainly caused by the diffraction effect of the body) can be in the order of the true range measurement. With the accuracy requirement of the application we are considering in mind, taking such a bias as ranging error will lead to a considerable degradation in the localization performance.

Another method is to treat the NLOS biases as unknown nuisance parameters and estimate them jointly with the agent locations [82, 86–88]. A statistical model for the bias is developed based on range measurements from a set of pre-defined anchor and agent positions (both LOS and NLOS situations). This statistical model is then integrated into the localization algorithm such that the range measurements both from LOS and NLOS situations are utilized for localization. However, accurate modeling of the NLOS bias statistics needs a very detailed knowledge about the environment, which is difficult to get in practice .

The third approach is to detect NLOS situation and discard them from the location estimation process [89–91]. The main motivation for this approach is the fact that if no *a priori* information is available about the NLOS bias, which is difficult to get in practice, then the NLOS range measurements do not improve the localization performance, as shown in [82, 85, 92].

In this thesis, we follow the third approach, i.e. to detect NLOS situation and discard them from the posture capturing process. The next section discuss a NLOS identification method which is based on the statistics of the received signal parameters.

2.4. NLOS Identification

A detailed survey of NLOS identification methods is discussed in [93,94]. Nevertheless, for the sake of completeness, a brief summary of the different methods is provided here. Based on the parameters they use, NLOS identification methods can be divided into three different categories: based on range estimates [94–96], based on position estimates [97, 98] and based on channel statistics [99–102].

For the methods that are based on range estimates, a series of training ranges under LOS conditions are gathered and their variance is calculated. Let σ^2_{LOS} be the variance of the LOS ranges gathered in the training phase. Then during the localization phase, for a given agent to anchor link, the variance of the range estimates from time series of measurements is calculated. If this variance is larger than σ^2_{LOS}, the link is regarded as NLOS. This approach assumes that both the agent and the anchor are stationary. Its extension for moving agent and/or anchor, which accounts the velocity of the moving node, is considered in [93]. Although it is simple to implement, the main bottleneck of this approach is its latency due to the time series of range estimates it requires to classify a link as LOS or NLOS.

The methods based on the estimated positions, on the other hand, assume the map of the environment to be known. Then given the agent position estimate, a Ray-tracing algorithm is run to determine if the links between the anchors and the agent are in a LOS or NLOS. The draw backs of this approach is that accurately modeling the environment (accounting each scattering, reflection and diffraction) is challenging, which limits its practicability. Moreover, the Ray-tracing algorithm is computationally intensive [93].

Channel statistics based methods, as the name implies, use channel parameters that are extracted from the received signal as a metric to detect NLOS situation. The parameters include amplitude of the received signal [102], power and TOA of the first detected path [100], mean excess delay [99], RMS delay spread [99,101] and kurtosis [99, 101,102]. The main advantage of this approach is that acquiring the statistics of channel parameters is relatively easy and by applying a simple likelihood ratio test a reasonably good classification performance can be achieved. In this thesis, we follow this approach and adapt it to the system under consideration to identify NLOS situations.

2.4.1. Channel Parameters Relevant for NLOS Identification

Consider the channel impulse response between agent m and anchor n $h_{mn}(t)$, its estimate is as in (2.5). Given $h_{mn}(t)$, the most valuable information one can use to classify the channel as LOS or NLOS is the statistics of the path amplitudes $\{a^{(l)}_{mn}\}$ and path delays $\{\tau^{(l)}_{mn}\}$ [102]. However, such statistical knowledge requires a TOA estimator that accurately estimates the path amplitudes and path delays. For this reason, we instead consider channel parameters that capture the statistics of $\{a_{mn}^{(l)}\}$ and $\{\tau_{mn}^{(l)}\}$ but can directly be calculated from the channel impulse response without prior pre-processing. Specifically, we use the mean excess delay, the RMS delay spread, kurtosis and SNR of the channel, which are defined in Table 2.1.

Table 2.1.: Definition of channel parameters.

Channel parameter	Definition
Mean excess delay (MED)	$\tau_{mn}^{\text{MED}} = \frac{\int_{\mathbb{R}} t\lvert h_{mn}(t)\rvert^2 \mathrm{d}\,t}{\int_{\mathbb{R}} \lvert h_{mn}(t)\rvert^2 \mathrm{d}\,t}$
RMS delay spread (RMS-DS)	$\tau_{mn}^{\text{RMS}} = \frac{\int_{\mathbb{R}} \left(t-\tau_{mn}^{\text{MED}}\right)^2 \lvert h_{mn}(t)\rvert^2 \mathrm{d}\,t}{\int_{\mathbb{R}} \lvert h_{mn}(t)\rvert^2 \mathrm{d}\,t}$
SNR	$\gamma_{mn} = \frac{\int_{\mathbb{R}} \lvert h_{mn}(t)\rvert^2 \mathrm{d}\,t}{N_0}$
Kurtosis	$\kappa_{mn} = \frac{1/(t_2-t_1)\int_{t_1}^{t_2} (\lvert h_{mn}(t)\rvert - \mu_{mn})^4 \mathrm{d}\,t}{\rho_{mn}^4}$, with $\mu_{mn} = \int_{t_1}^{t_2} \lvert h_{mn}(t)\rvert \,\mathrm{d}\,t$, $\rho_{mn}^2 = \int_{t_1}^{t_2} (\lvert h_{mn}(t)\rvert - \mu_{mn})^2 \mathrm{d}\,t$, and $[t_1, t_2]$ is the considered time window.

2.4.2. NLOS Identification based on Likelihood Ratio Test

The statistics of the channel parameters are constructed from channel impulse response measurements conducted on (and around) the body. The agents transmit a PN sequence, more specifically M-Sequence, with length $2^{13} - 1$. The chip rate of the transmit signals is $f_{\text{chip}} = 2.4375\,\text{GHz}$ and the signal spans the frequency band between 2.5 GHz and 7.5 GHz. The received signals at the anchors are sampled simultaneously with a sampling frequency of 11.3 GHz.

A total of 6 anchors are placed on (and around) the torso: 2 on the front torso, 2 on the back torso, 1 in front (but outside) of the torso and 1 on the side (but outside) of the torso. Two agents are placed on the right arm: one at the elbow and another at the wrist. The arm is moved to different topologies, and at each arm topology, the channel impulse responses between all the agents and all the anchors are recorded. Since the goal of this short exposition is to show how a simple likelihood ratio test based on the channel parameters can be used for NLOS identification, the details of the measurement campaign are omitted. For the detailed description of the measurement setup, the reader is referred to [103].

The histograms of the extracted channel parameters (both for LOS and NLOS situation) are fitted to several known distribution functions and those which provide the best fit are chosen for each parameter. The considered distribution functions are normal distributions, Nakagami distribution, gamma distribution, generalized extreme value (GEV) distribution and t-location-scale distribution. The distribution functions are defined in Appendix A. The best fitting distribution function for each channel parameter and the corresponding parameters of the distribution function are given in Table 2.2, both for LOS and NLOS channels.

Table 2.2.: Fitted PDFs of the channel parameters for LOS and NLOS channels.

Channel parameter	LOS Distribution	LOS Parameter	NLOS Distribution	NLOS Parameter
MED	GEV	$k = 0.10$, $\sigma = 0.55$ $\mu = 1.41$	GEV	$k = 0.06$ $\sigma = 2.07$ $\mu = 5.14$
RMS-DS	GEV	$k = -0.16$ $\sigma = 0.82$ $\mu = 2.83$	Normal	$\sigma = 0.21$ $\mu = 27.92$
Kurtosis	Normal	$\sigma = 9.55$ $\mu = 39.00$	GEV	$k = 0.08$ $\sigma = 3.63$ $\mu = 7.95$
SNR (in dB)	t-location-scale	$k = 31.24$ $\sigma = 3.16$ $\mu = 22.94$	t location-scale	$k = 25.22$ $\sigma = 5.68$ $\mu = 5.11$

As an example, the PDFs of the SNR both for LOS and NLOS scenarios are shown in Figure 2.5. We notice that the mean SNR for the case of LOS is approximately 20 dB larger than the NLOS case. As can be seen the statistics of the SNR for two case are distinct and hence, a simple likelihood ration test can be applied to detect if a channel is LOS or NLOS.

Given the PDFs of the different channel parameters in Table 2.2, the likelihood ratio test for classifying LOS from NLOS situations is straightforward. For example, the likelihood ratio test based on the SNR is given by [104]

$$\frac{p_{\mathrm{SNR}}^{\mathrm{NLOS}}(\gamma)}{p_{\mathrm{SNR}}^{\mathrm{LOS}}(\gamma)} \underset{\mathrm{LOS}}{\overset{\mathrm{NLOS}}{\gtrless}} \frac{P_0(C_{10} - C_{00})}{P_1(C_{01} - C_{11})}, \tag{2.11}$$

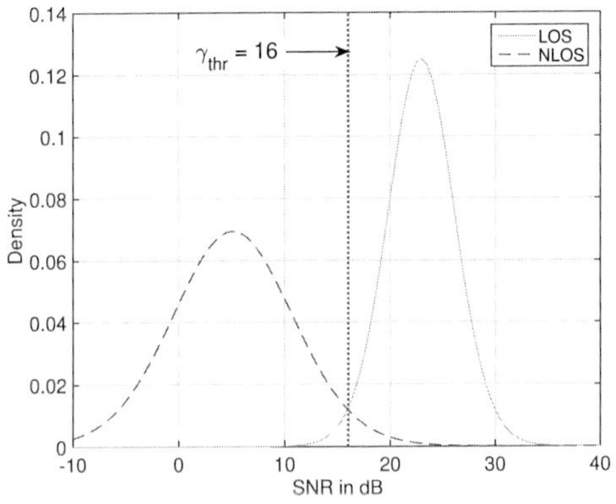

Figure 2.5.: PDFs of the SNR for LOS and NLOS scenarios.

where γ is the SNR, $p_{\mathrm{SNR}}^{\mathrm{LOS}}(\gamma)$ and $p_{\mathrm{SNR}}^{\mathrm{NLOS}}(\gamma)$ are the PDFs of the SNR for the case of LOS and NLOS, respectively, P_0 and P_1 denote the a prior probabilities of LOS and NLOS, respectively. Furthermore, C_{00}, C_{10}, C_{01} and C_{11} denote the costs of decision, e.g. C_{10} denotes the cost of wrongly deciding in favor of NLOS while the link was LOS.

Let η denote the right hand side of (2.11), which is termed as the threshold of the likelihood ratio test [104]. We see that the detection rate of the likelihood ratio test is dependent on the choice of η. For example, if we choose $\eta = +\infty$, the test always decides for LOS. This means the false alarm probability (decide NLOS while LOS was true) is zero. However, the detection rate (decide NLOS while NLOS was true) is also zero. The false alarm probability and the detection probability are dependent on each other, decreasing on also decreases the other. So the threshold η needs to be chosen such that the requirement of the considered application is met.

For our case, no prior probability about the occurrence of NLOS situation is assumed and hence, both LOS and NLOS are assumed to be equally probable. Furthermore, the costs of correct decisions are set to zero. This leads to an intuitive choice of the threshold, which is given by $\eta = C_{10}/C_{01}$. For example, if number of anchors is "large enough", the cost wrongly deciding for LOS while it is NLOS (C_{01}) is much more dire compared to the cost of deciding for NLOS while it LOS (C_{10}). This corresponds to a threshold $\eta > 1$. On the other hand, if the number of anchors is "too few", a threshold $\eta < 1$ might be preferred.

Since it led to a satisfactory result, we chose the cost assignment where the cost of both wrong decisions are the same, i.e. $C_{10} = C_{01}$. This implies that threshold is set to $\eta = 1$. As can be clearly seen from the plot of the two PDFs in Figure 2.5, with this choice of the threshold, the likelihood ratio test in (2.11) is equivalent to comparing the SNR to a threshold $\gamma_{\text{thr}} = 16$ dB. If the measured SNR is larger than γ_{thr}, then the channel is classified as LOS. Otherwise, it is classified as NLOS.

Table 2.3.: LOS and NLOS detection rate in percent (%).

Decided | True Hypothesis	MED	RMS-DS	Kurtosis	SNR
LOS | LOS	88.55	88.19	95.03	91.83
LOS | NLOS	14.22	11.25	25.56	0.76
NLOS | LOS	11.45	11.81	4.97	8.17
NLOS | NLOS	85.78	88.75	74.44	99.24
Total error	12.84	11.53	15.26	4.46

The performances of the likelihood ratio tests for different channel parameters are evaluated. The detection rate (in %) of the different likelihood ratio tests is given in Table 2.3. We notice that the MED and RMS-DS based schemes have correct detection rates ("say LOS while LOS" and "say NLOS while NLOS") between 85 % and 88 %. However, both have a false alarm rate ("say NLOS while LOS") of around 11 %. The test which is based on the kurtosis, on the other hand, has a false alarm rate of about 5 % however this comes at a cost of a bad miss rate (about 25 %). The approach that provides a good compromise between the miss rate and false alarm rate is the one based on the SNR. We see that the SNR based scheme has a false alarm rate of around 8 % and a miss rate of 0.76 %. We also note that the SNR based scheme has the lowest total error.

From the detection performance in Table 2.3, we see that the simple likelihood ratio test which is based on the SNR provides a remarkable NLOS detection rate while having a moderate miss rate. In light of this result, for the human posture capturing system, we propose to detect NLOS using this scheme. And if NLOS situation is detected, the corresponding range measurement is discarded from the posture capturing process.

2.5. Summary

The TOA based human posture capturing system setup, which consists of agent nodes, anchor nodes and a cluster head, is presented. The multiple accessing scheme that is employed by the system and the signal model of the transmission system is discussed. The TOA based range measurement model that takes into account the clock asynchronism between the agents and the anchors is presented. A simple and effective NLOS identification method, which is realized as a likelihood ratio of the received signal SNR, is presented. It is shown that the presented method is able to accurately identify NLOS situation (with a detection rate of 99.24 % and false alarm rate of 8.17 %).

3. Localization of Asynchronous Agents with Position Constraints

In this chapter[1], the TOA based human posture capturing system, described in Chapter 2, is abstracted to the general problem of wireless sensor network localization. The motivation for this twofold. On one hand, known methods from wireless sensor network localization can be applied to the considered problem. On the other hand, the algorithms that are proposed in this thesis can be easily applied to other systems which have similar type of problems.

We consider the setup where the clocks of the anchors are phase synchronized with each other. And the locations of the anchors are assumed to be known. The clocks of the agents, on the other hand, are asynchronous with each other and with that of the anchors. Furthermore, the agents may have position constraints, e.g. due to the kinematic constraints of the body. A localization method that accounts the clock asynchronicity and the position constraints of the agents is proposed. The application of the proposed localization method to the specific case of human posture capturing is discussed in Chapter 6.

3.1. Introduction

The TOA based human posture capturing system described in Section 2.1 can be abstracted to the general problem of wireless sensor network localization shown in Figure 3.1. We assume that a calibration step has been performed and hence, the locations of the N_r anchors $\boldsymbol{r}_1, \ldots, \boldsymbol{r}_{N_\mathrm{r}}$ are assumed to be known and fixed. The clocks of the anchors are also phase synchronized with each other.[2]

[1] Parts of this chapter have been published in [105, 106].

[2] A calibration method which estimates the locations of the anchors and synchronizes the clocks of the anchors is discussed in Chapter 5.

However, the clocks of the agents are considered to be asynchronous with each other and with that of the anchors. We further note that the N_{t} agents, which are located at $\boldsymbol{t}_1, \ldots, \boldsymbol{t}_{N_{\mathrm{t}}}$, may have a distance constraint between them due to the kinematic constraints of the body. For example, if agent 1 is located at the elbow joint and agent 2 is located at the wrist joint, the distance between them is constrained by the length of the forearm.

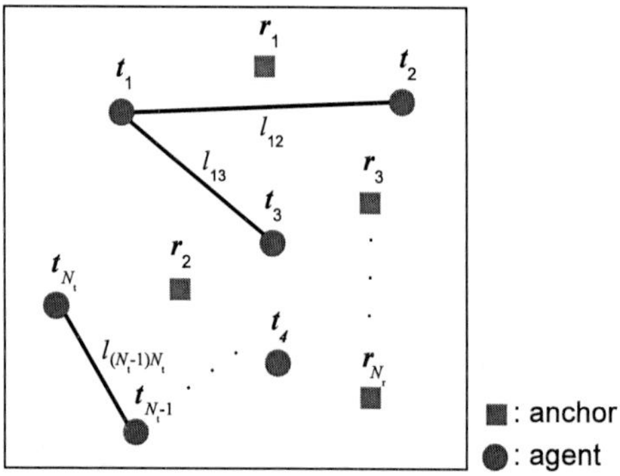

Figure 3.1.: Wireless sensor network with N_{r} anchors and N_{t} agents.

The localization problem that we are considering is hence, to estimate the unknown locations of the agents based on the TOA measurements between the agents and the anchors, while fulfilling the location constraints of the agents. Here we make a remark that, as discussed in Section 2.3, the unknown transmit times of the agents lead to TOA measurements with unknown timing offsets. Hence, the localization method should also deal with this artifact.

A common approach to deal with the unknown transmit time of the agents is to take time difference of arrival (TDOA) measurements, where the TOA measurement at a reference anchor is subtracted from the TOA measurements of all the other anchors. Localization methods that are based on TDOA measurements have been studied in [107–109]. The work in [107] proposes a suboptimal solution of the TDOA based localization problem that tightly approximates the maximum likelihood (ML) solution when the TDOA measurement errors are small. In [108, 109], on the other hand, the relaxation of the ML solution (which is a non-convex optimization problem) to a convex optimization problem is proposed, namely to second order cone programming (SOCP) problem and semi-definite programming (SDP) problem. The shortcomings of TDOA based methods are however, the subtraction of pairwise TOA measurements leads to correlated noise and noise enhancement by 3 dB [76], which degrade localization performance.

Inspired by the drawbacks of TDOA based approaches, in this thesis, we propose a localization method which jointly estimates the locations and the unknown timing offsets of the agents based on the TOA measurements. Hence, no pre-processing of the TOA measurements is required. The localization system also takes into account the location constraints of the agents, e.g. due to the kinematic constraints of the body.

We show that the ML solution of the localization problem is a non-convex optimization problem, with a non-linear non-convex objective function that admits multiple local minima. Hence, common local search methods (e.g. brut-force gradient search) may be trapped in a local minimum if the initialization is not "close enough" to the global minimum. A practically appealing approach to deal with this problem, which has received considerable attention in the wireless sensor network localization community, is to relax the ML solution to a convex optimization problem. The two commonly used convex relaxation techniques are: relaxation to SOCP problem and relaxation to SDP problem [110]. The two approaches are a trade-off between computational complexity and the tightness of the relaxed version to the original problem (which relates to localization accuracy). SOCP is computationally simpler but it is less tight than the SDP counterpart [110], and vice versa.

Considering phase synchronous anchors and agents (i.e. no clock offset between all nodes in the system), in [67], a localization method that relaxes the ML solution to SOCP problem is presented. A distributed algorithm for solving the SOCP problem is presented in [68]. As shown in Section 3.4 however, for the case when the agents are asynchronous, the relaxation of the ML solution is too loose. In fact, the solution of the relaxed SOCP problem does not have a unique solution. Hence, although it might be computationally simple, the approach of relaxing the ML solution to SOCP problem is not suitable for the case when the agents are asynchronous with the anchors, which is the case for our considered system.

Localization methods that are based on SDP relaxation, but still consider phase synchronous anchors and agents, are proposed by Biswas *et. al.* in [64, 65, 111]. In these works, the problem of estimating agents based on the TOA measurements is formulated as finding agent locations that minimizes the weighted sum of the absolute value of the error between the squared range measurements and the squared trial ranges, where the weights correspond to the accuracy of the range measurement. However, as shown in Section 3.3, the ML solution of the TOA based localization problem takes a different form. And most importantly, comparing it to our system setup, the impact of the clock offsets between the agents and the anchors is not considered. Moreover, the agent location constraints that are imposed by the kinematic constraints of the body are not taken into account.

Previous related works that apply convex relaxation techniques while considering phase synchronous anchors but asynchronous agents, similar to our considered system setup, are presented in [112, 113]. To cope with the unknown transmit times of the agents, a localization method that is based on the TDOA measurements is considered. The ML solution of the TDOA based localization problem is then relaxed to SDP problem. However, the cons of these methods, as in any TDOA based localization method, are that the subtraction of pairwise TOA measurements leads to correlated noise and noise enhancement by 3 dB [76]. Furthermore, when comparing it to the problem we are considering, the agent location constraints are not considered.

In this chapter, we propose a TOA based localization method that takes into account the unknown transmit time and the location constraints of the agents. The ML solution of the localization problem is formulated and shown to be non-convex. To cope with the non-convexity problem of the ML estimator, we propose a two-step localization method. In the first step, the ML is relaxed to a SDP, which is convex and can be efficiently solved by standard convex optimization algorithms. In the second step, the accuracy of the SDP solution is improved by performing a local search around it using the ML estimator. The Cramér-Rao Lower Bound (CRLB) of the localization problem that takes into account the agent location constraints is derived. Simulation results confirm that the proposed localization method meets the CRLB and hence, is an optimal location estimator.

The rest of the chapter is organized as follows. The localization problem is formally stated in Section 3.2. The ML solution of the localization problem is stated in Section 3.3. The relaxation of the ML estimator to a convex optimization problem is discussed in Section 3.4. The theoretical performance bound of the proposed localization method is discussed in Section 3.5. Simulation results that assess the performance of the localization method is discussed in Section 3.6.

3.2. Formulation of the Localization Problem

The N_r anchor are located at $\boldsymbol{r}_n = [r_n^{(x)}, r_n^{(y)}, r_n^{(z)}]^T$, for $n = 1, \ldots, N_\mathrm{r}$. The N_t agents are located at $\boldsymbol{t}_m = [t_m^{(x)}, t_m^{(y)}, t_m^{(z)}]$, for $m = 1, \ldots, N_\mathrm{t}$. Noting that the clocks of the anchors are phase synchronized, the range measurement between the anchors and the agents can be depicted as in Figure 3.2. The measured range between anchor n and agent m is modeled as

$$d_{mn} = \|\boldsymbol{t}_m - \boldsymbol{r}_n\| + b_{\mathrm{t},m} + e_{mn}, \tag{3.1}$$

where $b_{\mathrm{t},m}$ is the ranging offset of agent m due to the asynchronocity of its clock to that of the anchors and e_{mn} is the range measurement error. Agent m is assumed to be in a LOS with anchor n and hence, the ranging error conforms a Gaussian distribution $\mathcal{N}(0, \sigma_{mn}^2)$. As discussed in Section 2.3, the ranging error variance is given by $\sigma_{mn}^2 = c_0^2/(4\pi^2\beta_m^2\gamma_{mn})$, where β_m is the effective bandwidth of the transmitted signal and γ_{mn} is SNR of the link.

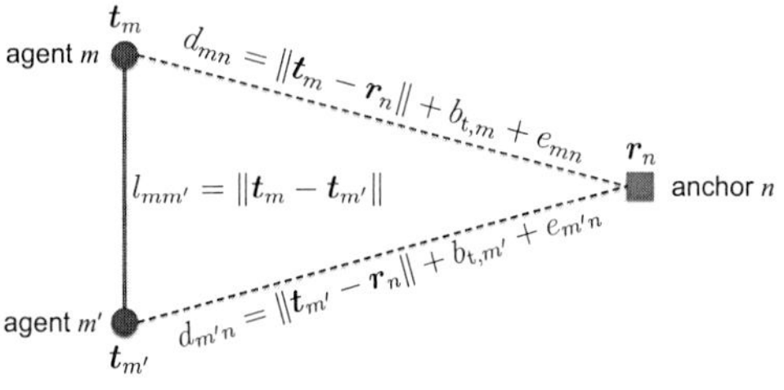

Figure 3.2.: Range measurement at anchor n from agent m and agent m'.

Here, it should be noted that if anchor n and agent m are in a NLOS, the range measurement error e_{mn} takes a non-zero mean. We assume that such a NLOS condition is detected using the method discussed in Section 2.4 and the corresponding range measurement is not taken into account for the estimation of the agent location. For the sake of simplifying the exposition and understanding of the localization method however, we consider the case where the anchors and the agents are in a LOS.

From Figure 3.2, we further note that the distance of agent m and agent m' is constrained by the length $l_{mm'}$. This constraint can equivalently be expressed as

$$\|\boldsymbol{t}_m - \boldsymbol{t}_{m'}\|^2 - l_{mm'}^2 = 0. \tag{3.2}$$

Define $\boldsymbol{v}(\boldsymbol{t}) = [\|\boldsymbol{t}_1 - \boldsymbol{t}_2\|^2, \|\boldsymbol{t}_1 - \boldsymbol{t}_3\|^2, \ldots, \|\boldsymbol{t}_{N_t-1} - \boldsymbol{t}_{N_t}\|^2]^T$ and $\bar{\boldsymbol{l}} = [l_{12}^2, l_{13}^2, \ldots l_{(N_t-1)N_t}^2]^T$. The distance constraint on the agents locations can then be expressed in a generic form as

$$\boldsymbol{c}(\boldsymbol{t}) = \boldsymbol{\omega} \odot \left(\boldsymbol{v}(\boldsymbol{t}) - \bar{\boldsymbol{l}}\right) = \boldsymbol{0}, \tag{3.3}$$

where $\boldsymbol{a} \odot \boldsymbol{b}$ denotes element-wise product of the vectors $\boldsymbol{a}$ and $\boldsymbol{b}$, and $\boldsymbol{\omega}$ is an indictor whose elements are 1 if the corresponding constraint between the agents exists and 0 otherwise.

To this end, the localization problem that we are considering can be described as follows. Given the range measurements $\boldsymbol{d} = [d_{11}, d_{12}, \ldots, d_{N_t N_r}]^T$ and the anchor locations $\boldsymbol{r} = \left[\boldsymbol{r}_1^T, \ldots, \boldsymbol{r}_{N_r}^T\right]^T$, we want to estimate the unknown agent locations $\boldsymbol{t} = \left[\boldsymbol{t}_1^T, \ldots, \boldsymbol{t}_{N_t}^T\right]^T$, which fulfill the constraint in (3.3), under the presence of the unknown nuisance ranging offsets $\boldsymbol{b}_t = [b_{t,1}, \ldots, b_{t,m}]^T$.

Here, we make a remark that for the case when the agents are phase synchronous with the anchors, all the ranging offsets are zero and known. Hence, the only unknown parameters to be estimated are the agent locations $\boldsymbol{t}$. As discussed later, this case can be easily fit into the localization framework and hence the proposed localization method also applies for this synchronization case.

3.3. Maximum Likelihood (ML) Solution

The $N_r N_t$ range measurements given in (3.1) can be rewritten in a vector form as

$$\boldsymbol{d} = \boldsymbol{g} + \boldsymbol{\Gamma}_t \boldsymbol{b}_t + \boldsymbol{e}, \tag{3.4}$$

where $\boldsymbol{g} = [\|\boldsymbol{t}_1 - \boldsymbol{r}_1\|, \ldots, \|\boldsymbol{t}_{N_t} - \boldsymbol{r}_{N_r}\|]^T$, $\boldsymbol{\Gamma}_t$ is a known $N_r N_t \times N_t$ matrix and $\boldsymbol{e} = [e_{11}, \ldots, e_{N_t N_r}]^T$ is the ranging error vector. The matrix $\boldsymbol{\Gamma}_t$ is defined as

$$\boldsymbol{\Gamma}_t = \left[\boldsymbol{E}_{N_r \times N_t}^{(1)\ T}, \ldots, \boldsymbol{E}_{N_r \times N_t}^{(N_t)\ T}\right]^T, \tag{3.5}$$

where $\boldsymbol{E}_{M \times N}^{(i)}$ is a $M \times N$ matrix with all zero elements except the ith column which contains all ones.

Note that for the case when the agents are phase synchronous with the anchors, the ranging offsets are zero and known. The range measurement model in (3.4) also fits for this synchronization case by setting $\boldsymbol{b}_{\mathrm{t}} = [\,]$ and $\boldsymbol{\Gamma}_{\mathrm{t}} = [\,]$.[3]

The joint probability density function (PDF) of the range measurements conditioned on the unknown parameters then takes the form

$$p\left(\boldsymbol{d}|\,\boldsymbol{t},\boldsymbol{b}_{\mathrm{t}}\right) = \frac{|\boldsymbol{\Sigma}|^{-\frac{1}{2}}}{(2\pi)^{\frac{N_{\mathrm{r}}N_{\mathrm{t}}}{2}}} \exp\left(-\frac{1}{2}\left(\boldsymbol{d}-\boldsymbol{g}-\boldsymbol{\Gamma}_{\mathrm{t}}\boldsymbol{b}_{\mathrm{t}}\right)^T \boldsymbol{\Sigma}^{-1}\left(\boldsymbol{d}-\boldsymbol{g}-\boldsymbol{\Gamma}_{\mathrm{t}}\boldsymbol{b}_{\mathrm{t}}\right)\right), \tag{3.6}$$

where $\boldsymbol{\Sigma}$ is the covariance matrix of the range measurement error $\boldsymbol{e}$.

Hence, the joint ML estimate of all the unknown parameters, subject to the constraints in (3.3), is given by

$$\left\{\hat{\boldsymbol{t}},\hat{\boldsymbol{b}}_{\mathrm{t}}\right\} = \arg\max_{\boldsymbol{t},\boldsymbol{b}_{\mathrm{t}}} p\left(\boldsymbol{d}|\,\boldsymbol{t},\boldsymbol{b}_{\mathrm{t}}\right), \quad \text{s.t. } \boldsymbol{c}(\boldsymbol{t}) = \boldsymbol{0}.$$

We note that, given the joint PDF in (3.6), the ML estimator can be written an equivalent form of

$$\left\{\hat{\boldsymbol{t}},\hat{\boldsymbol{b}}_{\mathrm{t}}\right\} = \arg\min_{\boldsymbol{t},\boldsymbol{b}_{\mathrm{t}}} \left(\boldsymbol{d}-\boldsymbol{g}-\boldsymbol{\Gamma}_{\mathrm{t}}\boldsymbol{b}_{\mathrm{t}}\right)^T \boldsymbol{\Sigma}^{-1}\left(\boldsymbol{d}-\boldsymbol{g}-\boldsymbol{\Gamma}_{\mathrm{t}}\boldsymbol{b}_{\mathrm{t}}\right), \qquad \text{s.t. } \boldsymbol{c}(\boldsymbol{t}) = \boldsymbol{0}. \tag{3.7}$$

For a given trial agent locations $\boldsymbol{t}'$, the cost function of the estimator in (3.7) can be expressed as

$$\Psi(\boldsymbol{b}_{\mathrm{t}}) = \left(\boldsymbol{d}-\boldsymbol{g}'-\boldsymbol{\Gamma}_{\mathrm{t}}\boldsymbol{b}_{\mathrm{t}}\right)^T \boldsymbol{\Sigma}^{-1}\left(\boldsymbol{d}-\boldsymbol{g}'-\boldsymbol{\Gamma}_{\mathrm{t}}\boldsymbol{b}_{\mathrm{t}}\right),$$

where $\boldsymbol{g}'$ denotes the vector $\boldsymbol{g}$ for a trial agent locations $\boldsymbol{t}'$. Note that the objective function $\Psi(\boldsymbol{b}_{\mathrm{t}})$ is only a function of $\boldsymbol{b}_{\mathrm{t}}$. Hence, the ML estimate of $\boldsymbol{b}_{\mathrm{t}}$ that minimizes the objective function in (3.7) satisfies $\left.\frac{\partial\Psi(\boldsymbol{b}_{\mathrm{t}})}{\partial\boldsymbol{b}_{\mathrm{t}}}\right|_{\boldsymbol{b}_{\mathrm{t}}=\hat{\boldsymbol{b}}_{\mathrm{t}}} = \boldsymbol{0}$. To this end, we use the relation: If $\boldsymbol{W}$ is a symmetric matrix, then [114]

$$\frac{\partial}{\partial\boldsymbol{s}}(\boldsymbol{x}-\boldsymbol{A}\boldsymbol{s})^T\boldsymbol{W}(\boldsymbol{x}-\boldsymbol{A}\boldsymbol{s}) = -2(\boldsymbol{x}-\boldsymbol{A}\boldsymbol{s})^T\boldsymbol{W}\boldsymbol{A}.$$

Using this relation, we see that

$$\left.\frac{\partial\Psi(\boldsymbol{b}_{\mathrm{t}})}{\partial\boldsymbol{b}_{\mathrm{t}}}\right|_{\boldsymbol{b}_{\mathrm{t}}=\hat{\boldsymbol{b}}_{\mathrm{t}}} = -2\left(\boldsymbol{d}-\boldsymbol{g}'-\boldsymbol{\Gamma}_{\mathrm{t}}\hat{\boldsymbol{b}}_{\mathrm{t}}\right)^T \boldsymbol{\Sigma}^{-1}\boldsymbol{\Gamma}_{\mathrm{t}} = \boldsymbol{0}.$$

[3]For notational convenience, if $\boldsymbol{A}$ is an empty matrix, we assume the following relations hold: $\boldsymbol{A}+\boldsymbol{B} = \boldsymbol{B}-\boldsymbol{A} = \boldsymbol{B}$ and $\boldsymbol{A}\boldsymbol{B} = \boldsymbol{A}^{-1}\boldsymbol{B} = [\,]$.

Rearranging terms and solving for $\hat{\boldsymbol{b}}_{\mathrm{t}}$ leads to

$$\hat{\boldsymbol{b}}_{\mathrm{t}} = \left(\boldsymbol{\Gamma}_{\mathrm{t}}^T \boldsymbol{\Sigma}^{-1} \boldsymbol{\Gamma}_{\mathrm{t}}\right)^{-1} \boldsymbol{\Gamma}_{\mathrm{t}}^T \boldsymbol{\Sigma}^{-1} (\boldsymbol{d} - \boldsymbol{g}'). \tag{3.8}$$

Inserting (3.8) into (3.7) gives us an equivalent ML estimator for the agent locations $\boldsymbol{t}$ that can be expressed as

$$\hat{\boldsymbol{t}} = \arg\min_{\boldsymbol{t}} \left(\bar{\boldsymbol{d}} - \bar{\boldsymbol{g}}\right)^T \boldsymbol{\Sigma}^{-1} \left(\bar{\boldsymbol{d}} - \bar{\boldsymbol{g}}\right), \quad \text{s.t. } \boldsymbol{c}(\boldsymbol{t}) = \boldsymbol{0}, \tag{3.9}$$

where $\bar{\boldsymbol{d}} = \boldsymbol{d} - \boldsymbol{\Lambda} \boldsymbol{d}$, $\bar{\boldsymbol{g}} = \boldsymbol{g} - \boldsymbol{\Lambda} \boldsymbol{g}$ and $\boldsymbol{\Lambda} = \boldsymbol{\Gamma}_{\mathrm{t}} \left(\boldsymbol{\Gamma}_{\mathrm{t}}^T \boldsymbol{\Sigma}^{-1} \boldsymbol{\Gamma}_{\mathrm{t}}\right)^{-1} \boldsymbol{\Gamma}_{\mathrm{t}}^T \boldsymbol{\Sigma}^{-1}$. Note that with the estimator in (3.9), the ranging offset $\boldsymbol{b}_{\mathrm{t}}$ is implicitly estimated. Given the agent locations estimate $\hat{\boldsymbol{t}}$, the ML estimate of $\boldsymbol{b}_{\mathrm{t}}$ can be calculated from (3.8).

To get more intuition about the estimator in (3.9), let us have a closer look at the term $\bar{\boldsymbol{d}} = \boldsymbol{d} - \boldsymbol{\Lambda} \boldsymbol{d}$. Assuming the range measurement errors are statistically independent, and hence a diagonal covariance matrix $\boldsymbol{\Sigma}$, the element of $\bar{\boldsymbol{d}}$ that corresponds to the range measurement between agent m and anchor n is given by

$$\bar{d}_{mn} = d_{mn} - \left(\sum_{n=1}^{N_{\mathrm{r}}} \frac{1}{\sigma_{mn}^2}\right)^{-1} \sum_{n=1}^{N_{\mathrm{r}}} \frac{d_{mn}}{\sigma_{mn}^2} \triangleq d_{mn} - \tilde{d}_m.$$

We note that $\tilde{d}_m$ is a weighted average of the range measurements from all anchors to agent m, where the measurements from the anchors with the smallest error variance is given the largest weight.

If alternatively a TDOA approach would have been used, the ranging offsets are taken out of the estimation process by subtracting the range measurement of a reference anchor from the range measurements of all the other anchors. If, without loss of generality, we choose anchor 1 as the reference anchor, the agent locations are estimated using range differences given by

$$d_{mn}^{\mathrm{TDOA}} = d_{mn} - d_{m1}, \quad \forall m \in \{1, \ldots, N_{\mathrm{t}}\}, \text{ and } \forall n \in \{2, \ldots, N_{\mathrm{r}}\}.$$

Comparing $\bar{d}_{mn}$ and d_{mn}^{TDOA}, we see that the TDOA approach is sensitive to the choice of the reference node. If the range measurement error variance of the reference anchor is large, it will propagate through all the range differences, resulting in a poor localization performance. The ML estimator (3.8), on the other hand, is robust against this problem as the measurements with large error variance are given a small weight.

To this end, let us have a closer look at the objective function of the ML estimator in (3.9). Recall that the trial ranging vector is given by $\boldsymbol{g} = [\|\boldsymbol{t}_1 - \boldsymbol{r}_1\|, \ldots, \|\boldsymbol{t}_{N_t} - \boldsymbol{r}_{N_r}\|]^T$. The elements of $\boldsymbol{g}$ are convex functions. However, the term $\bar{\boldsymbol{g}} = \boldsymbol{g} - \boldsymbol{\Lambda}\boldsymbol{g}$, which is the difference of two convex functions, is not necessarily convex. Furthermore, the cross terms in the product $\left(\bar{\boldsymbol{d}} - \bar{\boldsymbol{g}}\right)^T \Sigma^{-1} \left(\bar{\boldsymbol{d}} - \bar{\boldsymbol{g}}\right)$ make the function non-convex. We also note that the distance constraints $\boldsymbol{c}(\boldsymbol{t}) = \boldsymbol{0}$, which equate convex functions to a constant value, are non-convex constraints. Hence, the estimator in (3.9) is a non-convex optimization problem, which may have multiple locally optimum solutions. This implies that a brut-force gradient search requires an initialization which is "close enough" to the global minimum. Otherwise, it will result in a solution being trapped at a local minimum.

One possible approach to realize the ML estimator in (3.9) is to use stochastic optimization methods such as simulated annealing [115], particle swarm optimization [116] or genetic algorithm [117]. In contrast to classical gradient decent methods, stochastic optimization methods allow a controlled randomness in the search for the minimum of the objective function. Such a randomness gives the search-routine the chance to jump out of local minimum. The drawback of such methods however is that they are computationally intensive with no guarantee of attaining the global minimum [118].

A practically appealing approach, which has got considerable attention in wireless sensor network localization community, is to relax the ML estimator to a convex optimization problem. Although the solution of the relaxed optimization problem is sub-optimal, its main advantage is that it can be efficiently solved by standard convex optimization algorithms. For some applications the accuracy of the sub-optimal solution may be sufficient. However, depending on the requirements of the considered application, the sub-optimal solution can be refined with the ML estimator using a local gradient search to achieve a better localization accuracy.

In this thesis, we follow the approach to relax the ML estimator to a convex optimization problem (more specifically to a SDP problem). The solution of the convex optimization problem is further refined with the ML estimator by performing a local search.

3.4. Convex Relaxation of the ML Solution

In this section, we discuss the relaxation of the ML estimator presented in Section 3.3 into a convex optimization problem. We start with the relaxation of the estimator to a SOCP problem in Section 3.4.1. It is shown that, for the case when the agents are asynchronous with the anchors, the solution of the relaxed SOCP problem is not unique. Hence, this approach is not suitable for the considered localization problem.

The proposed convex relaxation of the ML estimator, which is based on semi-definite relaxation, is then discussed in Section 3.4.2.

3.4.1. Relaxation to SOCP Problem

To facilitate the discussion of the relaxation procedure, we start with the ML estimator in (3.7) which can equivalently be expressed as

$$\left\{\hat{\boldsymbol{t}}, \hat{\boldsymbol{b}}_{\mathrm{t}}\right\} = \arg\min_{\boldsymbol{t},\boldsymbol{b}_{\mathrm{t}}} \sum_{m=1}^{N_{\mathrm{t}}} \sum_{n=1}^{N_{\mathrm{r}}} \frac{1}{\sigma_{mn}^2} \left(d_{mn} - \|\boldsymbol{t}_m - \boldsymbol{r}_n\| - b_{\mathrm{t},m}\right)^2, \qquad (3.10)$$
$$\text{s.t. } \boldsymbol{c}(\boldsymbol{t}) = \boldsymbol{0}.$$

Here, we have used the assumption that the range measurements between different anchors and agents are independent and hence, the ranging error covariance matrix is given by $\boldsymbol{\Sigma} = \mathrm{diag}\{\sigma_{11}^2, \ldots, \sigma_{N_{\mathrm{t}}N_{\mathrm{r}}}^2\}$.

The main steps we follow to relax the ML estimator to a SOCP problem can be summarized as follows.

1. We rewrite the estimator in (3.10) into a form which is close to SOCP problem (see Appendix B). Specifically, we want to rewrite (3.10) to an equivalent optimization problem with a linear objective function and constraints which might be non-convex but are in a form that can easily be relaxed to convex constraints.
2. Relax the non-convex constraints to SOCP constraints, i.e. quadratic inequality constraints and/or linear equality constraints.

To this end, we introduce slack variables $\boldsymbol{y} = [y_{11}, y_{12}, \ldots, y_{N_{\mathrm{t}}N_{\mathrm{r}}}]^T$ and $\boldsymbol{g} = [g_{11}, g_{12}, \ldots, g_{N_{\mathrm{t}}N_{\mathrm{r}}}]^T$, and reformulate (3.10) into an equivalent form

$$\left\{\hat{\boldsymbol{t}}, \hat{\boldsymbol{b}}_{\mathrm{t}}, \hat{\boldsymbol{y}}, \hat{\boldsymbol{g}}\right\} = \arg\min_{\boldsymbol{t},\boldsymbol{b}_{\mathrm{t}},\boldsymbol{y},\boldsymbol{g}} \sum_{m=1}^{N_{\mathrm{t}}} \sum_{n=1}^{N_{\mathrm{r}}} y_{mn}^2,$$
$$\text{s.t. } \frac{1}{\sigma_{mn}} \left|d_{mn} - g_{mn} - b_{\mathrm{t},m}\right| \leq y_{mn}, \ \forall m, n,$$
$$\|\boldsymbol{t}_m - \boldsymbol{r}_n\| = g_{mn}, \ \forall m, n,$$
$$\boldsymbol{c}(\boldsymbol{t}) = \boldsymbol{0}.$$

The objective function of the ML estimator can further be simplified to a linear objective function by introducing a new slack variable u and rewriting it in the following form

$$\left\{\hat{\boldsymbol{t}}, \hat{\boldsymbol{b}}_{\mathrm{t}}, \hat{\boldsymbol{y}}, \hat{\boldsymbol{g}}, \hat{u}\right\} = \arg \min_{\boldsymbol{t}, \boldsymbol{b}_{\mathrm{t}}, \boldsymbol{y}, \boldsymbol{g}, u} u, \tag{3.11a}$$
$$\text{s.t.} \quad \|\boldsymbol{y}\|^2 \leq u, \tag{3.11b}$$
$$\frac{1}{\sigma_{mn}} |d_{mn} - g_{mn} - b_{\mathrm{t},m}| \leq y_{mn}, \; \forall m, n, \tag{3.11c}$$
$$\|\boldsymbol{t}_m - \boldsymbol{r}_n\| = g_{mn}, \; \forall m, n, \tag{3.11d}$$
$$\boldsymbol{c}(\boldsymbol{t}) = \boldsymbol{0}. \tag{3.11e}$$

With the ML estimator written in this form, we see that the objective function in (3.11a) is linear and the constraints in (3.11b) and (3.11c) are convex constraints. The constraints that are non-convex, and hence make the optimization problem non-convex, are those in (3.11d) and (3.11e).[4]

Relaxing the non-convex constraints in (3.11d) and (3.11e), by replacing the equality constraint with inequality constraint, results in a SOCP problem of the form

$$\left\{\hat{\boldsymbol{t}}, \hat{\boldsymbol{b}}_{\mathrm{t}}, \hat{\boldsymbol{y}}, \hat{\boldsymbol{g}}, \hat{u}\right\} = \arg \min_{\boldsymbol{t}, \boldsymbol{b}_{\mathrm{t}}, \boldsymbol{y}, \boldsymbol{g}, u} u, \tag{3.12a}$$
$$\text{s.t.} \quad \|\boldsymbol{y}\|^2 \leq u, \tag{3.12b}$$
$$\frac{1}{\sigma_{mn}} |d_{mn} - g_{mn} - b_{\mathrm{t},m}| \leq y_{mn}, \; \forall m, n, \tag{3.12c}$$
$$\|\boldsymbol{t}_m - \boldsymbol{r}_n\| \leq g_{mn}, \; \forall m, n, \tag{3.12d}$$
$$\boldsymbol{c}(\boldsymbol{t}) \leq \boldsymbol{0}. \tag{3.12e}$$

The optimization problem in (3.12) is now a convex problem which can be efficiently solved by standard optimization algorithms such as interior point method [119].

To minimize the objective function in (3.12a), the term $\|\boldsymbol{y}\|^2$ needs to be minimized. This in turn implies that $(g_{mn} + b_{\mathrm{t},m})$ needs to be chosen as close as possible to d_{mn}, $\forall m, n$. While the choice of g_{mn} is constrained by (3.12d), $b_{\mathrm{t},m}$ can freely take on any value. This means that the solution of the problem in (3.12) is not unique.

[4] Note that the constraint $\boldsymbol{c}(\boldsymbol{t}) = \boldsymbol{0}$, defined in (3.3), represents the distance constraints between agents. E.g., the constraint between agent m and agent m' is given by $\|\boldsymbol{t}_m - \boldsymbol{t}_{m'}\|^2 - l_{mm'}^2 = 0$, which is a non-convex constraint.

Note that for the case when the anchors and the agents are phase synchronous, and hence the ranging offsets $b_{t,m}$ are zero and known, the solution of (3.12) becomes unique by adding a constraint of the form $b_{t,m} = 0$, $\forall m, n$. However, for the case where the agents are asynchronous with the anchors, no *a priori* information is available about the ranging offsets $b_{t,m}$. Hence, the approach of relaxing the ML estimator to SOCP problem is not suitable for this setup.

Another convex relaxation technique that is better suited for the considered setup is semi-definite relaxation, which is the subject of the next sub-section.

3.4.2. Relaxation to SDP Problem

The SDP relaxation procedure that we discuss in this section is also applied for similar type of estimators in Chapter 4 and Chapter 5. The relaxation of the ML estimator in (3.7) involves two main steps. First, we rewrite the estimator into its equivalent form which is as close as possible to a SDP problem (see Appendix C). Then, in the second step, we relax the ML estimator to a SDP problem by applying semi-definite relaxation on the non-convex constraints.

Using the relation that $\boldsymbol{x}^T\boldsymbol{A}\boldsymbol{x} = \mathrm{Tr}\left\{\boldsymbol{A}\boldsymbol{x}\boldsymbol{x}^T\right\}$ and performing simple algebraic manipulations, the ML estimator in (3.7) can be reformulated as[5]

$$\left\{\hat{\boldsymbol{t}}, \hat{\boldsymbol{b}}_{\mathrm{t}}\right\} = \arg\min_{\boldsymbol{t},\boldsymbol{b}_{\mathrm{t}}} \mathrm{Tr}\left\{\boldsymbol{\Sigma}^{-1}\left(\boldsymbol{d}\boldsymbol{d}^T + (\boldsymbol{g}+\boldsymbol{\Gamma}_{\mathrm{t}}\boldsymbol{b}_{\mathrm{t}})(\boldsymbol{g}+\boldsymbol{\Gamma}_{\mathrm{t}}\boldsymbol{b}_{\mathrm{t}})^T - 2\boldsymbol{d}(\boldsymbol{g}+\boldsymbol{\Gamma}_{\mathrm{t}}\boldsymbol{b}_{\mathrm{t}})^T\right)\right\},$$
$$\text{s.t. } \boldsymbol{c}(\boldsymbol{t}) = \boldsymbol{0}.$$

We note the relation that

$$(\boldsymbol{g}+\boldsymbol{\Gamma}_{\mathrm{t}}\boldsymbol{b}_{\mathrm{t}})(\boldsymbol{g}+\boldsymbol{\Gamma}_{\mathrm{t}}\boldsymbol{b}_{\mathrm{t}})^T = [\boldsymbol{I}\ \boldsymbol{\Gamma}_{\mathrm{t}}]\begin{bmatrix}\boldsymbol{g}\boldsymbol{g}^T & \boldsymbol{g}\boldsymbol{b}_{\mathrm{t}}^T\\ \boldsymbol{b}_{\mathrm{t}}\boldsymbol{g}^T & \boldsymbol{b}_{\mathrm{t}}\boldsymbol{b}_{\mathrm{t}}^T\end{bmatrix}\begin{bmatrix}\boldsymbol{I}\\ \boldsymbol{\Gamma}_{\mathrm{t}}^T\end{bmatrix}.$$

Hence, by defining a matrix $\boldsymbol{Q} = [\boldsymbol{I}\ \boldsymbol{\Gamma}_{\mathrm{t}}]$ and introducing slack variables $\boldsymbol{g}$ and $\boldsymbol{Z}$, the ML estimator can be expressed as

$$\left\{\hat{\boldsymbol{t}}, \hat{\boldsymbol{b}}_{\mathrm{t}}, \hat{\boldsymbol{g}}, \hat{\boldsymbol{Z}}\right\} = \arg\min_{\boldsymbol{t},\boldsymbol{b}_{\mathrm{t}},\boldsymbol{g},\boldsymbol{Z}} \mathrm{Tr}\left\{\boldsymbol{\Sigma}^{-1}\left(\boldsymbol{d}\boldsymbol{d}^T + \boldsymbol{Q}\boldsymbol{Z}\boldsymbol{Q}^T - 2\boldsymbol{d}(\boldsymbol{g}+\boldsymbol{\Gamma}_{\mathrm{t}}\boldsymbol{b}_{\mathrm{t}})^T\right)\right\}, \tag{3.13a}$$
$$\text{s.t. } \boldsymbol{Z} = \begin{bmatrix}\boldsymbol{g}\boldsymbol{g}^T & \boldsymbol{g}\boldsymbol{b}_{\mathrm{t}}^T\\ \boldsymbol{b}_{\mathrm{t}}\boldsymbol{g}^T & \boldsymbol{b}_{\mathrm{t}}\boldsymbol{b}_{\mathrm{t}}^T\end{bmatrix}, \tag{3.13b}$$

[5]The reason for considering the ML estimator (3.7) is because it is easier to relax to SDP problem compared to (3.9).

$$g_{mn} = \|\boldsymbol{t}_m - \boldsymbol{r}_n\|, \ \forall m, n, \tag{3.13c}$$

$$\boldsymbol{c}(\boldsymbol{t}) = \boldsymbol{0}. \tag{3.13d}$$

From the relationship between $\boldsymbol{Z}$ and $\boldsymbol{g}$ in (3.13b), we see that

$$\boldsymbol{Z}[l,l] = (g_{mn})^2, \text{ where } l = (m-1)N_\mathrm{r} + n. \tag{3.14}$$

Let us now define a matrix $\boldsymbol{X} = [\boldsymbol{t}_1, \ldots, \boldsymbol{t}_{N_\mathrm{t}}]$, which contains the locations of all the agents. Also define a matrix $\boldsymbol{Y} = \boldsymbol{X}^T\boldsymbol{X}$. Then using the relation in (3.14) and the newly defined matrix $\boldsymbol{Y}$, the constraint in (3.13c) can be equivalently expressed as

$$\begin{aligned}\boldsymbol{Z}[l,l] &= \|\boldsymbol{t}_m - \boldsymbol{r}_n\|^2 = \boldsymbol{t}_m^T\boldsymbol{t}_m + \boldsymbol{r}_n^T\boldsymbol{r}_n - 2\boldsymbol{r}_n^T\boldsymbol{t}_m \\ &= \boldsymbol{Y}[m,m] + \boldsymbol{r}_n^T\boldsymbol{r}_n - 2\boldsymbol{r}_n^T\boldsymbol{X}[:,m].\end{aligned}$$

The ML estimator in (3.13) can therefore be written as

$$\left\{ \begin{smallmatrix}\hat{\boldsymbol{X}},\hat{\boldsymbol{b}}_\mathrm{t},\\ \hat{\boldsymbol{g}},\hat{\boldsymbol{Z}},\hat{\boldsymbol{Y}}\end{smallmatrix} \right\} = \arg\min_{\substack{\boldsymbol{X},\boldsymbol{b}_\mathrm{t},\\ \boldsymbol{g},\boldsymbol{Z},\boldsymbol{Y}}} \mathrm{Tr}\left\{\boldsymbol{\Sigma}^{-1}\left(\boldsymbol{d}\boldsymbol{d}^T + \boldsymbol{Q}\boldsymbol{Z}\boldsymbol{Q}^T - 2\boldsymbol{d}\left(\boldsymbol{g} + \boldsymbol{\Gamma}_\mathrm{t}\boldsymbol{b}_\mathrm{t}\right)^T\right)\right\}, \tag{3.15a}$$

$$\text{s.t. } \boldsymbol{Z} = \begin{bmatrix} \boldsymbol{g}\boldsymbol{g}^T & \boldsymbol{g}\boldsymbol{b}_\mathrm{t}^T \\ \boldsymbol{b}_\mathrm{t}\boldsymbol{g}^T & \boldsymbol{b}_\mathrm{t}\boldsymbol{b}_\mathrm{t}^T \end{bmatrix}, \tag{3.15b}$$

$$\boldsymbol{Y} = \boldsymbol{X}^T\boldsymbol{X}, \tag{3.15c}$$

$$\boldsymbol{Z}[l,l] = \boldsymbol{Y}[m,m] + \boldsymbol{r}_n^T\boldsymbol{r}_n - 2\boldsymbol{r}_n^T\boldsymbol{X}[:,m], \tag{3.15d}$$

$$\text{where } l = (m-1)N_\mathrm{r} + n, \ \forall m, n,$$

$$\boldsymbol{c}(\boldsymbol{t}) = \boldsymbol{0}. \tag{3.15e}$$

We further note that the distance constraints on the agents locations in (3.15e) can be related to the entries of the matrix $\boldsymbol{Y}$. For example, the constraint between agent m and agent m' given in (3.2) can be expressed as follows

$$\begin{gathered}\|\boldsymbol{t}_m - \boldsymbol{t}_{m'}\|^2 - l_{mm'}^2 = 0 \\ \Updownarrow \\ \boldsymbol{Y}[m,m] + \boldsymbol{Y}[m',m'] - 2\boldsymbol{Y}[m,m'] - l_{mm'}^2 = 0.\end{gathered} \tag{3.16}$$

Let $\tilde{\boldsymbol{c}}(\boldsymbol{Y})$ denotes the distance constraints on the agents of the form in (3.2), but now each constraint is replaced by the equivalent form in (3.16). We note the elements of the constraints in $\tilde{\boldsymbol{c}}(\boldsymbol{Y})$ are linear with respect to $\boldsymbol{Y}$.

Hence, by replacing the constraint in (3.15e) by the new constraint, the ML estimator can be re-written as

$$\left\{ \begin{smallmatrix} \hat{\boldsymbol{X}}, \hat{\boldsymbol{b}}_{\mathrm{t}}, \\ \hat{\boldsymbol{g}}, \hat{\boldsymbol{Z}}, \hat{\boldsymbol{Y}} \end{smallmatrix} \right\} = \arg \min_{\substack{\boldsymbol{X}, \boldsymbol{b}_{\mathrm{t}}, \\ \boldsymbol{g}, \boldsymbol{Z}, \boldsymbol{Y}}} \mathrm{Tr} \left\{ \boldsymbol{\Sigma}^{-1} \left(\boldsymbol{d}\boldsymbol{d}^T + \boldsymbol{Q}\boldsymbol{Z}\boldsymbol{Q}^T - 2\boldsymbol{d} \left(\boldsymbol{g} + \boldsymbol{\Gamma}_{\mathrm{t}} \boldsymbol{b}_{\mathrm{t}} \right)^T \right) \right\}, \tag{3.17a}$$

$$\text{s.t.} \quad \boldsymbol{Z} = \begin{bmatrix} \boldsymbol{g}\boldsymbol{g}^T & \boldsymbol{g}\boldsymbol{b}_{\mathrm{t}}^T \\ \boldsymbol{b}_{\mathrm{t}}\boldsymbol{g}^T & \boldsymbol{b}_{\mathrm{t}}\boldsymbol{b}_{\mathrm{t}}^T \end{bmatrix}, \tag{3.17b}$$

$$\boldsymbol{Y} = \boldsymbol{X}^T \boldsymbol{X}, \tag{3.17c}$$

$$\boldsymbol{Z}[l, l] = \boldsymbol{Y}[m, m] + \boldsymbol{r}_n^T \boldsymbol{r}_n - 2\boldsymbol{r}_n^T \boldsymbol{X}[:, m], \tag{3.17d}$$

$$\text{where } l = (m-1)N_{\mathrm{r}} + n, \ \forall m, n,$$

$$\tilde{\boldsymbol{c}}(\boldsymbol{Y}) = \boldsymbol{0}. \tag{3.17e}$$

We now see that the ML estimator in (3.17) has a linear objective function and linear constraints in (3.17d) and (3.17e). However, the constraints in (3.17b) and (3.17c) are non-linear matrix equality constraints, which are non-convex.

The next step is to relax the ML estimator in (3.17) to a convex optimization problem. We do so by replacing the matrix equality constraints with inequality constraints. For example, the constraint in (3.17b) is relaxed to

$$\boldsymbol{Z} \succeq \begin{bmatrix} \boldsymbol{g}\boldsymbol{g}^T & \boldsymbol{g}\boldsymbol{b}_{\mathrm{t}}^T \\ \boldsymbol{b}_{\mathrm{t}}\boldsymbol{g}^T & \boldsymbol{b}_{\mathrm{t}}\boldsymbol{b}_{\mathrm{t}}^T \end{bmatrix}, \tag{3.18}$$

which is convex. It should however be noted that the elements of the matrix on the right hand side of (3.18) are non-linear.

The matrix inequality constraint in (3.18) can be rewritten as

$$\boldsymbol{Z} - \begin{bmatrix} \boldsymbol{g} \\ \boldsymbol{b}_{\mathrm{t}} \end{bmatrix} \begin{bmatrix} \boldsymbol{g}^T & \boldsymbol{b}_{\mathrm{t}}^T \end{bmatrix} \succeq \boldsymbol{0}, \tag{3.19}$$

We note that the left hand side of (3.19) is the Schur complement of $\begin{bmatrix} \boldsymbol{Z} & \begin{smallmatrix} \boldsymbol{g} \\ \boldsymbol{b}_{\mathrm{t}} \end{smallmatrix} \\ \boldsymbol{g}^T \ \boldsymbol{b}_{\mathrm{t}}^T & 1 \end{bmatrix}$. Applying the Schur complement lemma, we note that the non-linear matrix equality constraint of (3.18) can be equivalently expressed as a linear matrix equality constraint of the form [120]

$$\begin{bmatrix} \boldsymbol{Z} & \begin{matrix} \boldsymbol{g} \\ \boldsymbol{b}_{\mathrm{t}} \end{matrix} \\ \boldsymbol{g}^T \ \boldsymbol{b}_{\mathrm{t}}^T & 1 \end{bmatrix} \succeq \boldsymbol{0}. \tag{3.20}$$

By applying a similar relaxation procedure on the constraint of $\boldsymbol{Y}$, the ML estimator in (3.17) is relaxed to a SDP problem of the form

$$\left\{ \begin{matrix} \hat{\boldsymbol{X}}, \hat{\boldsymbol{b}}_{\mathrm{t}}, \\ \hat{\boldsymbol{g}}, \hat{\boldsymbol{Z}}, \hat{\boldsymbol{Y}} \end{matrix} \right\} = \arg \min_{\substack{\boldsymbol{X}, \boldsymbol{b}_{\mathrm{t}}, \\ \boldsymbol{g}, \boldsymbol{Z}, \boldsymbol{Y}}} \mathrm{Tr} \left\{ \boldsymbol{\Sigma}^{-1} \left(\boldsymbol{d}\boldsymbol{d}^T + \boldsymbol{Q}\boldsymbol{Z}\boldsymbol{Q}^T - 2\boldsymbol{d} \left(\boldsymbol{g} + \boldsymbol{\Gamma}_{\mathrm{t}} \boldsymbol{b}_{\mathrm{t}} \right)^T \right) \right\}, \tag{3.21a}$$

$$\text{s.t.} \quad \begin{bmatrix} \boldsymbol{Z} & \begin{matrix} \boldsymbol{g} \\ \boldsymbol{b}_{\mathrm{t}} \end{matrix} \\ \boldsymbol{g}^T \ \boldsymbol{b}_{\mathrm{t}}^T & 1 \end{bmatrix} \succeq \boldsymbol{0}, \tag{3.21b}$$

$$\begin{bmatrix} \boldsymbol{Y} & \boldsymbol{X}^T \\ \boldsymbol{X} & \boldsymbol{I} \end{bmatrix} \succeq \boldsymbol{0}, \tag{3.21c}$$

$$\boldsymbol{Z}[l, l] = \boldsymbol{Y}[m, m] + \boldsymbol{r}_n^T \boldsymbol{r}_n - 2\boldsymbol{r}_n^T \boldsymbol{X}[:, m], \tag{3.21d}$$

$$\text{where } l = (m-1)N_{\mathrm{r}} + n, \ \forall m, n,$$

$$\tilde{\boldsymbol{c}}(\boldsymbol{Y}) = \boldsymbol{0}. \tag{3.21e}$$

The estimator in (3.21) is now a convex problem, which can be efficiently solved by standard convex optimization toolboxes such as SeDuMi and SDPT3 [121].

To get some intuition about the impact of the SDP relaxation, consider the constraint on $\boldsymbol{Z}$ in (3.17b)

$$\boldsymbol{Z} = \begin{bmatrix} \boldsymbol{g}\boldsymbol{g}^T & \boldsymbol{g}\boldsymbol{b}_{\mathrm{t}}^T \\ \boldsymbol{b}_{\mathrm{t}}\boldsymbol{g}^T & \boldsymbol{b}_{\mathrm{t}}\boldsymbol{b}_{\mathrm{t}}^T \end{bmatrix}.$$

The equality constraint forces $\boldsymbol{Z}$ to have a rank of 1. When this matrix equality constraint is relaxed to the inequality constraint in (3.21c), $\boldsymbol{Z}$ is in effect allowed to take on higher dimensions. In fact the solution of (3.21) converges to the maximum rank solution [65]. Note however that $\left[\boldsymbol{g}^T \ \boldsymbol{b}_{\mathrm{t}}^T\right]^T$ is a vector (with a single dimension) and hence the values of $\boldsymbol{Z}$ which are "leaked" to the dimensions higher than 1 are not captured in it.

One approach to cope with this problem is to apply regularization methods. For a problem of similar type, in [65], a regularization term that penalizes a higher dimensional $\boldsymbol{Z}$ is added to the objective function of the estimator. For example, a penalization term

$$\eta \left(\mathrm{Tr} \left\{ \boldsymbol{Z} \left[1 : N_{\mathrm{r}} N_{\mathrm{t}}, 1 : N_{\mathrm{r}} N_{\mathrm{t}} \right] \right\} \right), \tag{3.22}$$

where η is the penalization coefficient, can be added to the objective function of the estimator in (3.21). Note that the matrix $\boldsymbol{Z}\left[1 : N_{\mathrm{r}}N_{\mathrm{t}}, 1 : N_{\mathrm{r}}N_{\mathrm{t}}\right]$ is the outer product of the vector $\boldsymbol{g}$ with itself. This implies that the diagonal elements of the matrix are all non-negative. Hence, adding the penalization term in (3.22) into the objective function will force the diagonal elements of $\boldsymbol{Z}$ to take on small values. The other elements of

$\boldsymbol{Z}$ can also be included in the penalization term. However, as explained later, the optimum choice of the penalization term depends on the knowledge of the parameter to be penalized. As it is difficult to predict the expected value of the ranging offsets, we opt to use the first $N_\mathrm{r}N_\mathrm{t}$ block of $\boldsymbol{Z}$ (which corresponds to the outer product of the trial range $\boldsymbol{g}$).

Figure 3.3 shows the eigenvalue distribution of the estimator output $\hat{\boldsymbol{Z}}$ and the true value $\boldsymbol{Z}$ for different choices of regularization coefficient η. For the simulations, $N_\mathrm{r} = 6$ anchors are placed at $\boldsymbol{r}_1 = [5\,\mathrm{m}, 0, 0]^T$, $\boldsymbol{r}_2 = [0, 5\,\mathrm{m}, 0]^T$, $\boldsymbol{r}_3 = [0, 0, 5\,\mathrm{m}]^T$, $\boldsymbol{r}_4 = [-5\,\mathrm{m}, 0, 0]^T$, $\boldsymbol{r}_5 = [0, -5\,\mathrm{m}, 0]^T$, $\boldsymbol{r}_6 = [0, 0, -5\,\mathrm{m}]^T$. $N_\mathrm{t} = 10$ agents are drawn randomly from a $10\,\mathrm{m} \times 10\,\mathrm{m} \times 10\,\mathrm{m}$ cube, centered at the origin. The range measurements are assumed to be error free.

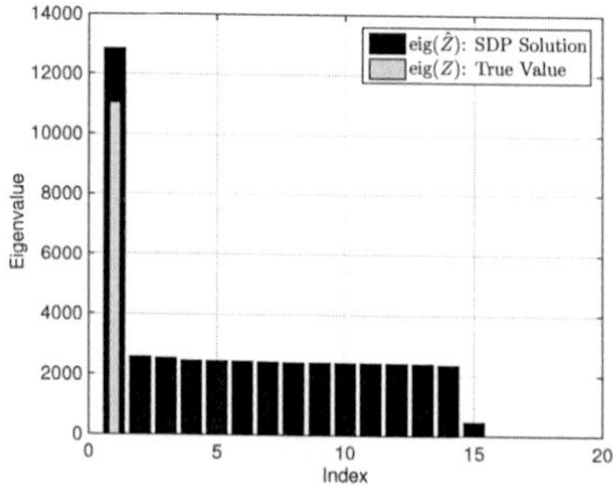

(a) $\eta = 0$

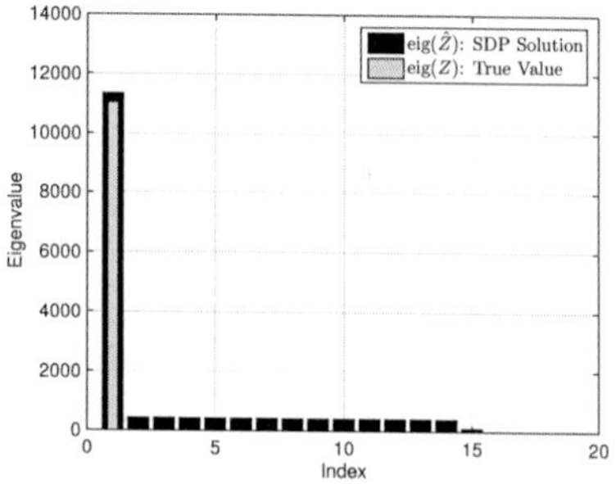

(b) $\eta = 10^{-8}$

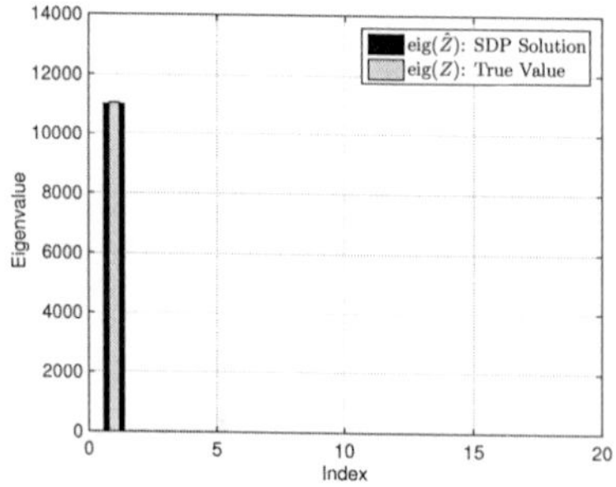

(c) $\eta = 10^{-6}$

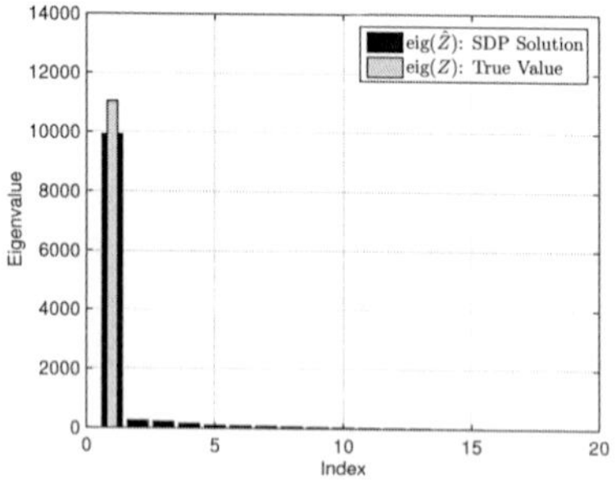

(d) $\eta = 10^{-4}$

Figure 3.3.: Eigen value distribution of the estimator output $\hat{\boldsymbol{Z}}$ for different regularization coefficient η.

From the figure we note that the estimator which does not consider the regularization term (i.e. $\eta = 0$) has around 14 dominant eigenvalues. Introducing a the penalization term improves the eigenvalue distribution of $\hat{\boldsymbol{Z}}$, where the choice $\eta = 10^{-6}$ leads to a distribution that is almost the same as the distribution of the true value $\boldsymbol{Z}$. However, if the regularization coefficient is chosen too high ($\eta = 10^{-4}$), $\boldsymbol{Z}$ is over penalized which degrades the estimator accuracy. Hence, for optimum estimator performance, the penalization coefficient needs to be chosen appropriately.

The choice of η depends on the expected distance between the anchors and the agents. If the anchors and agents are located inside a large volume, η needs to be chosen small such that it gives the estimator enough freedom to take on $\boldsymbol{Z}$ with large elements. On the other hand, if the expected distance is small, a higher penalization is required to discourage $\boldsymbol{Z}$ from taking higher values. Based on the observations of the optimization performance, as a rule of thumb, we propose to choose the penalization coefficient η as

$$\eta = \frac{\alpha}{g_{\max}}, \tag{3.23}$$

where $\alpha \in [10^{-4}, 10^{-5}]$ and $g_{\max}$ is the maximum expected distance between the agents and the anchors.

Here, it is important to make the remark that a poor eigenvalue distribution of $\hat{\boldsymbol{Z}}$ for the case when $\eta = 0$ does not necessarily mean the accuracy of the agent location estimates is similarly poor. Even for the case when no penalization term is considered, the agent location and ranging offset estimates in (3.21) serve as a good initialization for the ML estimator.

To this end, the proposed localization method can be summarized in Algorithm 1.

Algorithm 1 Localization algorithm accounting agent location constraints. Perfect anchor location knowledge assumed.

1: *Known*: anchor locations $\boldsymbol{r}$, range measurements $\boldsymbol{d}$.
2: Add the penalization term in (3.22) to the objective function in (3.21a).
3: Solve the optimization problem in (3.21). For example, using SeDuMi or SDPT3.
4: Reshape $\hat{\boldsymbol{X}}$ to $\hat{\boldsymbol{t}}$.
5: Solve ML estimator in (3.9) with $\hat{\boldsymbol{t}}$ as an initialization. For example, using the Matlab toolbox *lsqnonlin*.

3.5. Performance Bound: Constrained CRLB

In this section, the theoretical performance bound of the localization method discussed in the previous section. As a performance metric, we use the RMSE of the agent location estimates which is defined as

$$\mathrm{RMSE}(\hat{\boldsymbol{t}}) = \sqrt{\frac{1}{N_{\mathrm{t}}}\sum_{m=1}^{N_{\mathrm{t}}} \mathbb{E}\left\{\|\hat{\boldsymbol{t}}_m - \boldsymbol{t}_m\|^2\right\}}. \tag{3.24}$$

For this, we derive the Cramer-Rao lower bound (CRLB) of the estimator for the unknown parameters $\{\boldsymbol{t}, \boldsymbol{b}_{\mathrm{t}}\}$ given the range measurement $\boldsymbol{d}$, under the agent locations constraint in (3.3). First, we consider the unconstrained case and quantify the information about the unknown parameter which is contained in the range measurement $\boldsymbol{d}$. To do so, we calculate the Fisher information matrix (FIM) of the unknown parameters. Then, we account the constraints and derive the constrained CRLB.

Given the joint PDF (also known as the likelihood function) in (3.6), its log-likelihood takes the form

$$\begin{aligned}\mathcal{L}\left(\boldsymbol{d}|\,\boldsymbol{t}, \boldsymbol{b}_{\mathrm{t}}\right) &= \ln\left(p\left(\boldsymbol{d}|\,\boldsymbol{t}, \boldsymbol{b}_{\mathrm{t}}\right)\right) \\ &= \ln\left(\frac{|\boldsymbol{\Sigma}|^{-\frac{1}{2}}}{(2\pi)^{\frac{N_{\mathrm{r}}N_{\mathrm{t}}}{2}}}\right) - \frac{1}{2}\left(\left(\boldsymbol{d} - \boldsymbol{g} - \boldsymbol{\Gamma}_{\mathrm{t}}\boldsymbol{b}_{\mathrm{t}}\right)^T \boldsymbol{\Sigma}^{-1}\left(\boldsymbol{d} - \boldsymbol{g} - \boldsymbol{\Gamma}_{\mathrm{t}}\boldsymbol{b}_{\mathrm{t}}\right)\right).\end{aligned}$$

The FIM of the unknown parameters is then given by [104]

$$\begin{aligned}\boldsymbol{J} &= \begin{bmatrix} \mathbb{E}\left\{\left(\frac{\partial\mathcal{L}}{\partial \boldsymbol{t}}\right)^T\left(\frac{\partial\mathcal{L}}{\partial \boldsymbol{t}}\right)\right\} & \mathbb{E}\left\{\left(\frac{\partial\mathcal{L}}{\partial \boldsymbol{t}}\right)^T\left(\frac{\partial\mathcal{L}}{\partial \boldsymbol{b}_{\mathrm{t}}}\right)\right\} \\ \mathbb{E}\left\{\left(\frac{\partial\mathcal{L}}{\partial \boldsymbol{b}_{\mathrm{t}}}\right)^T\left(\frac{\partial\mathcal{L}}{\partial \boldsymbol{t}}\right)\right\} & \mathbb{E}\left\{\left(\frac{\partial\mathcal{L}}{\partial \boldsymbol{b}_{\mathrm{t}}}\right)^T\left(\frac{\partial\mathcal{L}}{\partial \boldsymbol{b}_{\mathrm{t}}}\right)\right\} \end{bmatrix} \\ &\triangleq \begin{bmatrix} \boldsymbol{J}_1 & \boldsymbol{J}_2 \\ \boldsymbol{J}_2^T & \boldsymbol{J}_3 \end{bmatrix}.\end{aligned} \tag{3.25}$$

The sub-matrices of the FIM $\boldsymbol{J}_1 = \mathbb{E}\{(\frac{\partial\mathcal{L}}{\partial \boldsymbol{t}})^T(\frac{\partial\mathcal{L}}{\partial \boldsymbol{t}})\}$, $\boldsymbol{J}_2 = \mathbb{E}\{(\frac{\partial\mathcal{L}}{\partial \boldsymbol{t}})^T(\frac{\partial\mathcal{L}}{\partial \boldsymbol{b}_{\mathrm{t}}})\}$ and $\boldsymbol{J}_3 = \mathbb{E}\{(\frac{\partial\mathcal{L}}{\partial \boldsymbol{b}_{\mathrm{t}}})^T(\frac{\partial\mathcal{L}}{\partial \boldsymbol{b}_{\mathrm{t}}})\}$ are derived in Appendix D.1.

Note that the FIM $\boldsymbol{J}$ captures the amount of information about both unknown parameters $\boldsymbol{t}$ and $\boldsymbol{b}_{\mathrm{t}}$ that is contained in the range measurement $\boldsymbol{d}$. However, the constraint in (3.3) only applies to $\boldsymbol{t}$ but not to $\boldsymbol{b}_{\mathrm{t}}$. To derive the CRLB of $\boldsymbol{t}$ that accounts for the constraint, we need to calculate the FIM of $\boldsymbol{t}$ from the full FIM $\boldsymbol{J}$, as discussed below.

The covariance matrix of any unbiased estimator of unknown parameters $\{\hat{\boldsymbol{t}}, \hat{\boldsymbol{b}}_{\mathrm{t}}\}$, without accounting the constraints, satisfies the information inequality [104]

$$\begin{bmatrix} \mathbb{E}\left\{(\hat{t}-t)(\hat{t}-t)^T\right\} & \mathbb{E}\left\{(\hat{t}-t)(\hat{b}_t-b_t)^T\right\} \\ \mathbb{E}\left\{(\hat{b}_t-b_t)(\hat{t}-t)^T\right\} & \mathbb{E}\left\{(\hat{b}_t-b_t)(\hat{b}_t-b_t)^T\right\} \end{bmatrix} \succeq \boldsymbol{J}^{-1}. \quad (3.26)$$

In (3.26), the portion of $\boldsymbol{J}^{-1}$ that defines the information inequality for the covariance matrix of the agent location estimates $\hat{\boldsymbol{t}}$ is its first $3N_t \times 3N_t$ block.

Noting that the Schur complement of the matrix $\boldsymbol{J}_3$ in (3.25) is $\boldsymbol{J}_1 - \boldsymbol{J}_2\boldsymbol{J}_3^{-1}\boldsymbol{J}_2^T$, the inverse of the FIM takes the form [122]

$$\boldsymbol{J}^{-1} = \begin{bmatrix} \left(\boldsymbol{J}_1-\boldsymbol{J}_2\boldsymbol{J}_3^{-1}\boldsymbol{J}_2^T\right)^{-1} & \boxtimes \\ \boxtimes & \boxtimes \end{bmatrix}, \quad (3.27)$$

where $\boxtimes$ denotes a block matrix whose value we are not interested in.

Comparing (3.27) and (3.26), we see that the unconstrained agent location estimator $\hat{\boldsymbol{t}}$ satisfies

$$\mathbb{E}\left\{\left(\hat{\boldsymbol{t}}-\boldsymbol{t}\right)\left(\hat{\boldsymbol{t}}-\boldsymbol{t}\right)^T\right\} \succeq \left(\boldsymbol{J}_1 - \boldsymbol{J}_2\boldsymbol{J}_3^{-1}\boldsymbol{J}_2^T\right)^{-1}. \quad (3.28)$$

This implies that the matrix $\boldsymbol{J}_t = \boldsymbol{J}_1 - \boldsymbol{J}_2\boldsymbol{J}_3^{-1}\boldsymbol{J}_2^T$ contains all the information about $\boldsymbol{t}$ that is contained in $\boldsymbol{J}$ and hence, we can call it the FIM of $\boldsymbol{t}$.

The mean squared error (MSE) lower bound of $\boldsymbol{t}$ in (3.28) does not take into account the constraints on $\boldsymbol{t}$. Next, we derive the constrained CRLB of the estimator that takes into account the constrained defined in (3.3). For this, we use the results presented in [123] that can be summarized as follows.

Define a constraint gradient matrix $\boldsymbol{G} = \frac{\partial \boldsymbol{c}(\boldsymbol{t})}{\partial \boldsymbol{t}}$. Assume that the gradient matrix $\boldsymbol{G}$ is full rank for any $\boldsymbol{t}$ satisfying the constraints, which means the constraints are not redundant. Then, given the unconstrained FIM $\boldsymbol{J}_t$, the covariance matrix of the agent locations estimate $\hat{\boldsymbol{t}}$ that takes into account the constraints satisfies [123]

$$\mathbb{E}\left\{\left(\hat{\boldsymbol{t}}-\boldsymbol{t}\right)\left(\hat{\boldsymbol{t}}-\boldsymbol{t}\right)^T\right\} \succeq \boldsymbol{U}\left(\boldsymbol{U}^T\boldsymbol{J}_t\boldsymbol{U}\right)^{-1}\boldsymbol{U}^T, \quad (3.29)$$

where $\boldsymbol{U}$ is a matrix whose columns form the orthonormal basis for the null space of $\boldsymbol{G}$, i.e. $\boldsymbol{G}\boldsymbol{U} = \boldsymbol{0}$.

It is easy to see that, given the agent locations constraint in (3.3), the constraint gradient matrix can be calculated as $\boldsymbol{G} = \frac{\partial \boldsymbol{c}(\boldsymbol{t})}{\partial \boldsymbol{t}} = \mathrm{diag}\left\{\boldsymbol{\omega}\right\} \odot \left(\frac{\partial \boldsymbol{v}(\boldsymbol{t})}{\partial \boldsymbol{t}}\right)$, where $\mathrm{diag}\left\{\boldsymbol{x}\right\}$ denotes a diagonal matrix with the vector $\boldsymbol{x}$ on its diagonal . As an example, the partial derivative of the first element of $\boldsymbol{v}(\boldsymbol{t})$ (which corresponds to the distance constraint between agent 1 and agent 2) with respect to $\boldsymbol{t}$ is given by

$$\frac{\partial \|\boldsymbol{t}_1 - \boldsymbol{t}_2\|^2}{\partial \boldsymbol{t}} = \begin{bmatrix} 2(\boldsymbol{t}_1-\boldsymbol{t}_2)^T & -2(\boldsymbol{t}_1-\boldsymbol{t}_2)^T & \boldsymbol{0} & \dots & \boldsymbol{0} \end{bmatrix}.$$

From the information inequality in (3.29), we see that the root mean squared error (RMSE) of the agent location estimates is lower bounded by

$$\text{RMSE\_LB}(\boldsymbol{t}) = \sqrt{\frac{1}{N_t}\text{Tr}\left\{\boldsymbol{U}\left(\boldsymbol{U}^T\boldsymbol{J}_t\boldsymbol{U}\right)^{-1}\boldsymbol{U}^T\right\}}. \tag{3.30}$$

3.6. Performance Evaluation

In this section, we discuss numerical results that assesses the performance of the proposed localization method under a generic simulation setup. The discussion is extended to the specific case of the human posture capturing setup in Chapter 6.

Consider the two node topologies shown in Figure 3.4. For both topologies, $N_r = 6$ anchors are located at fixed positions $\boldsymbol{r}_1 = [5\,\text{m}, 0, 0]^T$, $\boldsymbol{r}_2 = [0, 5\,\text{m}, 0]^T$, $\boldsymbol{r}_3 = [0, 0, 5\,\text{m}]^T$, $\boldsymbol{r}_4 = [-5\,\text{m}, 0, 0]^T$, $\boldsymbol{r}_5 = [0, -5\,\text{m}, 0]^T$ and $\boldsymbol{r}_6 = [0, 0, -5\,\text{m}]^T$. The range measurements are assumed to be independent and identically distributed (i.i.d.) with a standard deviation $\sigma_r = 1\,\text{cm}$.[6] The $N_t = 10$ agents, on the other hand, are randomly chosen from a $10\,\text{m} \times 10\,\text{m} \times 10\,\text{m}$ cube centered at the origin for Topology 1. And for Topology 2, the agents are chosen randomly from a $10\,\text{m} \times 10\,\text{m} \times 10\,\text{m}$ cube centered at $[10\,\text{m}, 0, 0]$. In oder to analyse the effect the agent location constraints, the agent are chosen with a constraint[7]

$$\|\boldsymbol{t}_m - \boldsymbol{t}_{m+N_t/2}\| = l, \text{ for } m \in \{1, \dots, N_t/2\}, \tag{3.31}$$

with $l = 5\,\text{m}$. The choice of the agents under the constraint in (3.31) implies that the agent locations are drawn in pairs, where the agents in a given pair are l distance apart.

The ranging offsets of the agents are drawn randomly from a uniform distribution in $[-100\,\text{m}, 100\,\text{m}]$. The penalization coefficient η in (3.22) is chosen according to (3.23)

[6] In Section 7.3, using a low-complexity demonstrator system, it is shown that a ranging accuracy in the sub-centimeter range can be achieved based on the TOA estimation of UWB signals.
[7] N_t is assumed to integer multiple of 2.

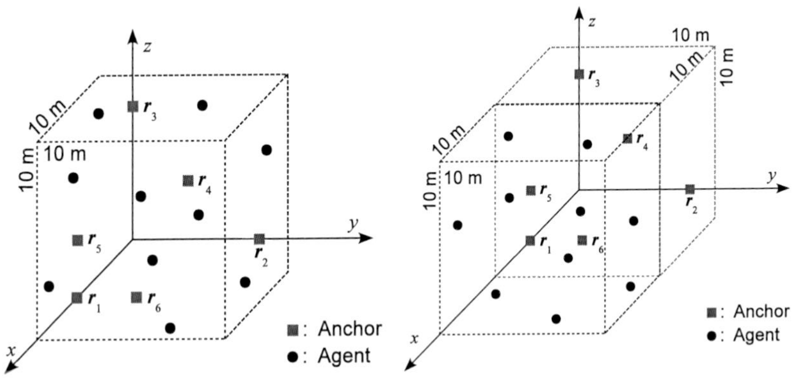

(a) Topology 1

(b) Topology 2

Figure 3.4.: Simulation setup: location of the anchors and agents.

with $\alpha = 5 \times 10^{-5}$, and $g_{\max} = 10\sqrt{3}$ (for Topology 1) and $g_{\max} = 20\sqrt{3}$ (for Topology 2).

Impact of node topology on the localization performance

Figure 3.5 shows the empirical cumulative distribution function (CDF) of the RMSE of the agent location estimates for the case when the clock of the agents are phase synchronous with that of the anchors. For this synchronization case, the ranging offsets of the agents $\boldsymbol{b}_{\mathrm{t}} = \mathbf{0}$ is known and it is taken out of the estimation process by setting $\boldsymbol{\Gamma}_{\mathrm{t}} = [\,]$. The RMSE performance for Topology 1 and Topology 2 are given in Figure 3.5a and Figure 3.5b, respectively.

We first note the ML estimator which is initialized with the SDP solution meets the CRLB both for the case which takes into account the agent location constraints (black solid line) and the case which does not take the constraints into account (red dashed line). This indicates that the proposed location estimator is efficient and the SDP solution serves as a good initialization for ML estimator. We also see that the median (50 %) of the agent location estimates from the SDP solution that takes into account the constraints have an RMSE of less than 1.22 cm (Topology 1) and 1.3 cm (Topology 2). This implies that the SDP solution, although sub-optimum, gives a reasonable accuracy and hence can even serve as a stand-alone location estimator for this synchronization case.

It is also interesting to note that the performance of the location estimator is not sensitive to the choice of the node topology. For example, the median of the constrained ML estimates have an RMSE less than 1.15 cm (Topology 1) and 1.21 cm (Topology 2).

The behavior looks completely different when we consider the case where the clock of the agents are asynchronous with that of the anchors, which is the setup of the posture capturing system. The empirical CDF of the RMSE of the location estimator for the case of asynchronous agents is shown Figure 3.6a (Topology 1) and Figure 3.6b (Topology 2). We see that the ML estimator with and without constraints meet the corresponding CRLB for both topologies. However, although the SDP solution serves as a good initialization for the ML estimator, its RMSE performance is poor and hence the refinement step is necessary.

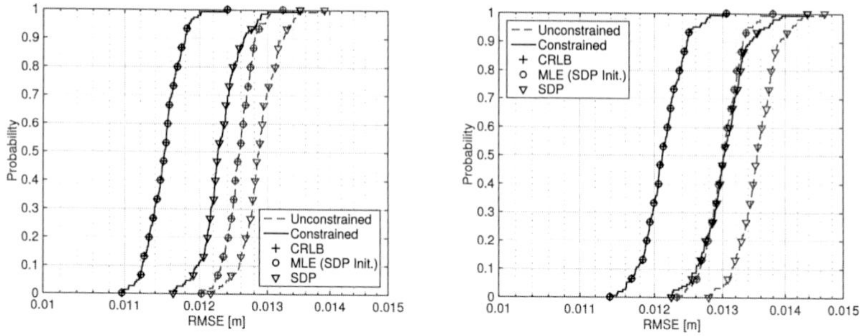

(a) Topology 1

(b) Topology 2

Figure 3.5.: Synchronous agents: Empirical CDF of the RMSE of the agent location estimates.

We further note that, for the unconstrained case, 20 % of the ML estimates of the agent locations have an RMSE larger than 1.5 cm (Topology 1) and 2.25 cm (Topology 2). When taking into account the constraints however, all the agent location estimates have an RMSE less than 1.4 cm (Topology 1) and 1.5 cm (Topology 2). Hence, taking into account the agent location constraints is a key performance enabler for Topology 2. This is because for Topology 2, where the agents are located outside the convex hull of the anchors, the unknown ranging offsets due to the clock asynchronicity of the agents introduce location uncertainties. By taking the constraints into account, the estimator resolves the agent location uncertainties and hence improve performance.

The performance of Topology 2 is of great interest as it is the case for the considered

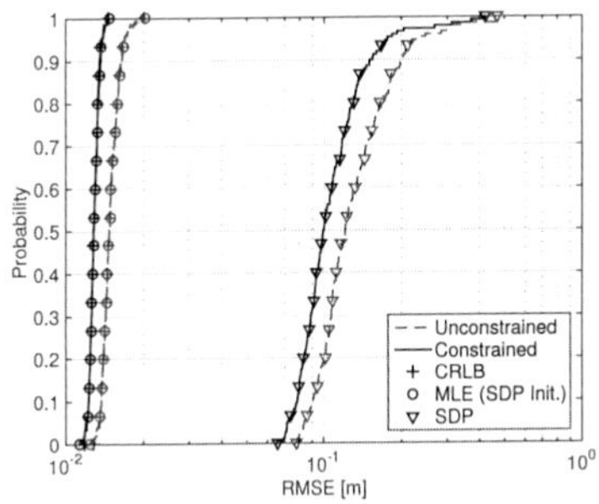

(a) Topology 1

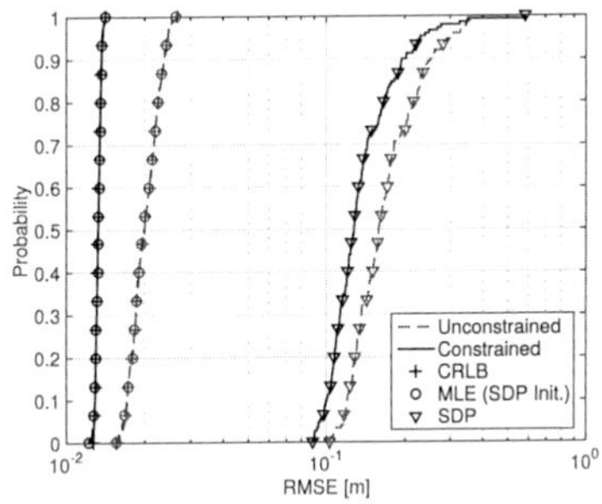

(b) Topology 2

Figure 3.6.: Asynchronous agents: Empirical CDF of the RMSE of the agent location estimates.

human posture capturing setup, where the anchors are located on the torso and the agents are located on the limbs. A detailed analysis of the impact of node topology on the estimator performance for the specific case of the human posture capturing setup is discussed in Chapter 6.

Localization performance for increasing number of agents N_t

To help us better understand the impact of N_t on the localization performance, define another type of constraint on the agents location

$$\|\boldsymbol{t}_m - \boldsymbol{t}_{m-1}\| = l_m, \text{ for } m \in \{2, \ldots, N_t\}, \tag{3.32}$$

where l_m is known.

Figure 3.7 shows the CRLB of the agent location estimates for varying N_t, both for the synchronous and asynchronous setup. The agent locations are drawn from Topology 1. Let us first consider the estimator which accounts the constraint in (3.31). We see that taking into account brings a performance improvement compared to the unconstrained case. However, the estimator performance does not improve for increasing N_t. This is because the joint estimator that takes into account the constraints in (3.31) can be decoupled into $N_t/2$ equivalent estimators, where each of them jointly estimate a pair of agents that are constrained together. Hence, on average, the estimator performance for N_t agents is same as that of 2 agents.

On the other hand, for the estimator that takes into account the constraint in (3.32) the estimates of all the agents are coupled. Hence, the estimator performance improves for increasing N_t.

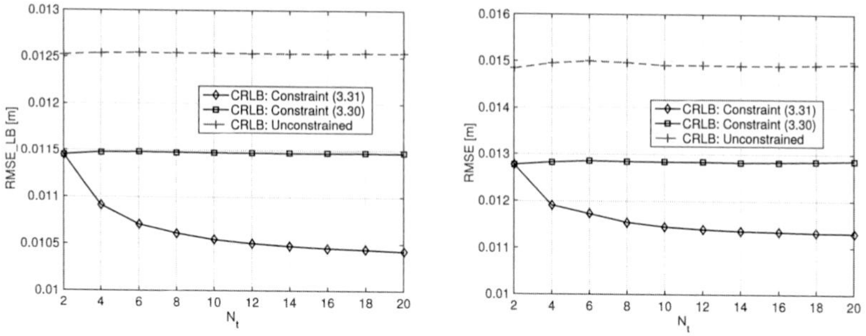

(a) Synchronous agents

(b) Asynchronous agents

Figure 3.7.: CRLB of RMSE of the agent location estimates for varying number of agents under two type of constraints. Node positions are drawn from Topology 1.

It should be mentioned however that for increasing N_t the SDP estimator in (3.21) and the ML estimator in (3.9) become computationally intensive. Although a constraint that couples all the agents leads to an improved estimator performance for increasing N_t, decoupling the joint estimator into smaller equivalent estimators enables a distributed implementation, which is computationally attractive. Hence, in practice, one needs to trade-off between computational complexity and accuracy.

NLOS anchors and localization performance

As discussed in Section 2.4, before the localization step, the signal that is communicated between a given agent and anchor is analysed to detect if the link between the two nodes is LOS or NLOS. If NLOS is detected, the corresponding range measurement is not taken into account for localization. To simplify the discussion, we assume that if an anchor is in a NLOS, it is NLOS to all agents. In Chapter 6, the discussion is extended to a more realistic scenario where the NLOS occurrence for each agent-anchor link is independent.

Consider 12 anchors with locations as given in Table 3.1. The $N_t = 10$ agents are drawn randomly as in Topology 1. Figure 3.8 show the CRLB of the agent location

Table 3.1.: Anchor locations. All values are in meters.

$\boldsymbol{r}_1 = [5,0,0]^T$	$\boldsymbol{r}_2 = [0,5,0]^T$	$\boldsymbol{r}_3 = [0,0,5]^T$	$\boldsymbol{r}_4 = [-5,0,0]^T$
$\boldsymbol{r}_5 = [0,-5,0]^T$	$\boldsymbol{r}_6 = [0,0,-5]^T$	$\boldsymbol{r}_7 = [5,-5,-5]^T$	$\boldsymbol{r}_8 = [-5,5,5]^T$
$\boldsymbol{r}_9 = [-5,-5,5]^T$	$\boldsymbol{r}_{10} = [5,5,-5]^T$	$\boldsymbol{r}_{11} = [-5,-5,-5]^T$	$\boldsymbol{r}_{12} = [5,5,5]^T$

estimates for varying number of LOS anchors N_r. For example, $N_\mathrm{r} = 8$ means anchors $1, 2, \ldots, 8$ are LOS and the others are NLOS.

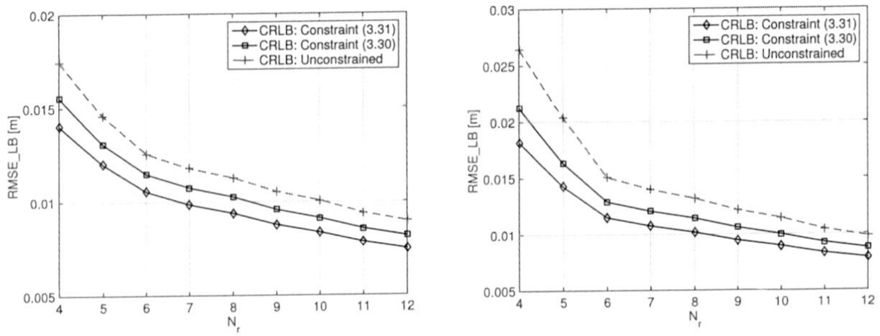

(a) Synchronous agents

(b) Asynchronous agents

Figure 3.8.: CRLB of RMSE of the agent location estimates for varying number of anchors. Node positions are drawn from Topology 1.

Clearly, the accuracy of the agent location estimates improves as the number of LOS anchors increases. What is interesting to note is that the performance gain due to the constraints become more pronounced as the number LOS anchors gets smaller. At $N_\mathrm{r} = 4$, the RMSE of asynchronous agent estimates is lower bounded by 2.6 cm for the unconstrained case. This is reduced to 1.8 cm if the constraints in (3.32) are taken into account.

3.7. Summary

The problem of TOA based human posture capturing is abstracted to the general problem of wireless sensor network localization. The considered localization problem accounts the unknown transmit times of the agents and the constraints on their locations that are imposed by the kinematic constraints of the body. The ML solution of the localization problem is formulated and shown to be a non-convex optimization problem, with a non-convex objective function and non-convex equality constraint. The relaxation of the ML estimator to SOCP and SDP problems, which are convex, is presented. It is shown that for the considered localization problem, where the agents are asynchronous with the anchors, the SOCP relaxation is not suitable as its solution is not unique. The relaxation of the ML estimator to SDP problem on the other hand is tight. Hence, the SDP solution can serve as a good initialization for the ML estimator. Simulation results show that the proposed two-step localization method meets the corresponding CRLB. We also note that accounting the agent location constraints brings a performance gain, notably when the agents are located outside the convex hull of the anchors.

4. Localization Under the Presence of Anchor Position Uncertainties

The localization method in Chapter 3 assumes the positions of the anchors are fixed and perfectly known. However, for the considered application of human posture capturing, the anchors are located on the body. Although they are placed on the relatively static parts of the body (the torso), they can be mobile and hence, their positions are known only up to some uncertainty. Furthermore, the anchor positions are determined from a calibration step (as discussed in Chapter 5), which is prone to errors. If unaccounted, these anchor position errors may lead to considerable performance degradation. In this chapter[1], we extend the localization method in Chapter 3 such that it is robust against anchor position uncertainties.

4.1. Introduction

The common assumption in TOA based wireless sensor network localization systems is that the anchors locations are fixed and perfectly known. However, as discussed above, for the considered TOA based human posture capturing system, the locations of the anchors are known only up to some uncertainties. Similarly, for underwater sensor networks, anchor nodes (which are placed on the water surface) may drift due to the water waves [118]. And in general, before the localization phase in wireless sensor networks, a calibration is performed to determine system parameters which are relevant for localization, including the locations of the anchors. Hence, if the calibration phase is error prone, the measure anchor locations will also have errors. In this chapter, we propose a localization method which is robust against such anchor location errors.

Assuming the clocks of the anchors and the agents are phase synchronous, [110, 118] present localization methods that account the anchor position uncertainties by treating

[1] Parts of this chapter have been published in [106].

the anchor positions as unknowns and estimating them jointly with the agent positions. The ML solution of the localization problem is shown to be a non-convex optimization problem. In [118], the relaxation of the ML estimator to SDP problem is proposed. In [110], on the other hand, the relaxation of the ML estimator to SOCP problem is proposed. Note however that stringent requirement of phase synchronous anchors and agents limits the applicability of such methods for the human posture capturing system, where the agents are considered to be low-complexity transmit-only nodes.

Localization methods that account anchor position uncertainties, while considering asynchronous agents, is presented in [76,108]. To cope with the unknown transmit time of the agents, the method in [108] uses TDOA measurements. The shortcomings of TDOA based methods are that the subtraction of pairwise TOA measurements leads to correlated noise and noise enhancement by 3 dB [76]. Inspired by these drawbacks, the work in [76] proposes an approach which directly utilizes the TOA measurements with unknown transmit times, i.e. the unknown transmit times are jointly estimated with the unknown locations of the agents. Nevertheless, both [108] and [76] assume the anchor location errors to be small. Given this assumption, the unknown anchor locations are taken out of the estimation process by considering an estimator with an objective function in which the ranges between the anchors and the agents are approximated by their first order Taylor-series expansion around the measured anchor positions. As reported in [76] and discussed in the performance comparison in Section 4.6, when the anchor location errors are significant, the proposed approximation incurs a substantial performance loss.

Our proposed localization method considers the system setup, which is inspired by the human posture capturing system, where the anchors are phase synchronized but the agents are asynchronous. Similar to [76], the range measurements from asynchronous agents with unknown transmit times are directly utilized for localization. However, instead of performing prior approximations to eliminate the unknown anchor locations from the estimation process, we take a new approach which jointly estimates the anchor locations along with the unknown locations and transmit times of the agents. The ML solution of the localization problem, which is a non-convex optimization problem is presented. We propose to relax the ML solution to SDP problem, which can be efficiently solved by optimization toolboxes that are readily available in the literature. The SDP solution is then refined by performing a local search with the ML estimator. The comparison of the proposed localization method with the corresponding CRLB shows that the it meets the lower bound for a wide range of anchor location error variance, and hence, it is optimal. It is further shown that the proposed method outperforms the scheme presented in [76], notably when the anchor location errors are more dominant than the range measurement errors.

The rest of this chapter is organized as follows. In Section 4.2, the range measurement model is presented and the localization problem is formally stated. The ML solution of the localization problem is discussed in Section 4.3. The relaxation of the ML estimator to SDP problem is presented in Section 4.4. The theoretical performance bound of the proposed estimator is derived in Section 4.5. Numerical evaluations that assess the performance of the proposed localization method are discussed in Section 4.6.

4.2. Formulation of the Localization Problem

We consider a network which consists of N_r anchors located at $\{\boldsymbol{r}_n\}_{n=1}^{N_\mathrm{r}}$ and N_t agents located at $\{\boldsymbol{t}_m\}_{m=1}^{N_\mathrm{t}}$. The clocks of the anchors are assumed to be phase synchronized with each other but they are asynchronous with that of the agents. Applying the model in (2.9), the range measured at anchor n from agent m and agent m' can be depicted as in Figure 4.1. The range measurement between anchor n and agent m is given by

$$d_{mn} = \|\boldsymbol{t}_m - \boldsymbol{r}_n\| + b_{\mathrm{t},m} + e_{mn},$$

where $b_{\mathrm{t},m}$ is the range measurement offset due to the unknown transmit time of agent m, e_{mn} is the range measurement error. We assume that the agents and the anchors are in a line of sight (LOS), and hence, the range measurement error can be (approximately) modeled as $e_{mn} \sim \mathcal{N}(0, \sigma_{mn}^2)$, where $\sigma_{mn}^2 = c^2/(4\pi^2\beta^2\mathrm{SNR}_{mn})$, β is the effective bandwidth of the transmit signal and SNR_{mn} is the signal to noise ratio of the link [44]. Furthermore, the range measurement errors between different agents and anchors are assumed to be statistically independent.

Note however that for the localization system, the anchor positions are known up to some uncertainties. To account for this, we model the measured position of anchor n by

$$\tilde{\boldsymbol{r}}_n = \boldsymbol{r}_n + \boldsymbol{\delta}_n,$$

where $\boldsymbol{\delta}_n \sim \mathcal{N}(\boldsymbol{0}, \boldsymbol{\Delta}_n)$ is the location error of the nth anchor. We further assume that the location errors of the anchors are statistically independent of each other and of the range measurement errors.

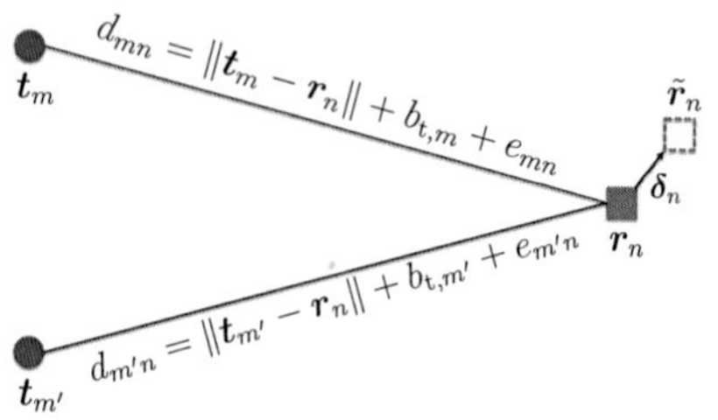

Figure 4.1.: Range measurement model: with anchor position uncertainty.

4.3. Maximum Likelihood (ML) Solution

Noting that the range measurement errors and the anchor location errors are statistically independent, the joint probability density function (PDF) of the observations conditioned on the unknown parameters can be expressed as

$$
\begin{aligned}
p\left(\boldsymbol{d}, \tilde{\boldsymbol{r}} | \boldsymbol{t}, \boldsymbol{b}_{\mathrm{t}}, \boldsymbol{r}\right) &= p\left(\boldsymbol{d} | \boldsymbol{t}, \boldsymbol{b}_{\mathrm{t}}, \boldsymbol{r}\right) p\left(\tilde{\boldsymbol{r}} | \boldsymbol{r}\right) \\
&= \frac{|\boldsymbol{\Sigma}|^{-\frac{1}{2}}}{(2\pi)^{\frac{N_{\mathrm{r}}N_{\mathrm{t}}}{2}}} \exp\left(-\tfrac{1}{2}(\boldsymbol{d} - \boldsymbol{g} - \boldsymbol{\Gamma}_{\mathrm{t}}\boldsymbol{b}_{\mathrm{t}})^T \boldsymbol{\Sigma}^{-1} (\boldsymbol{d} - \boldsymbol{g} - \boldsymbol{\Gamma}_{\mathrm{t}}\boldsymbol{b}_{\mathrm{t}})\right) \\
&\qquad \times \frac{|\boldsymbol{\Delta}|^{-\frac{1}{2}}}{(2\pi)^{\frac{3N_{\mathrm{r}}}{2}}} \exp\left(-\tfrac{1}{2}(\tilde{\boldsymbol{r}} - \boldsymbol{r})^T \boldsymbol{\Delta}^{-1} (\tilde{\boldsymbol{r}} - \boldsymbol{r})\right),
\end{aligned} \tag{4.1}
$$

where $\boldsymbol{\Sigma}$ and $\boldsymbol{\Delta}$ represent the covariance matrices of the range measurements and the anchor location measurements, respectively. The vector $\boldsymbol{g}$ denotes the trial ranges and $\boldsymbol{\Gamma}_{\mathrm{t}}$ is a known $N_{\mathrm{r}}N_{\mathrm{t}} \times N_{\mathrm{t}}$ matrix, as defined in (3.5).

The ML estimator that jointly estimates the unknown parameters is hence given by

$$
\{\hat{\boldsymbol{t}}, \hat{\boldsymbol{b}}_{\mathrm{t}}, \hat{\boldsymbol{r}}\} = \arg\max_{\boldsymbol{t}, \boldsymbol{b}_{\mathrm{t}}, \boldsymbol{r}} p\left(\boldsymbol{d}, \tilde{\boldsymbol{r}} | \boldsymbol{t}, \boldsymbol{b}_{\mathrm{t}}, \boldsymbol{r}\right).
$$

The estimator that maximizes the joint PDF in (4.1) can equivalently be expressed as

$$
\begin{aligned}
\{\hat{\boldsymbol{t}}, \hat{\boldsymbol{b}}_{\mathrm{t}}, \hat{\boldsymbol{r}}\} = \arg\min_{\boldsymbol{t}, \boldsymbol{b}_{\mathrm{t}}, \boldsymbol{r}} & (\boldsymbol{d} - \boldsymbol{g} - \boldsymbol{\Gamma}_{\mathrm{t}}\boldsymbol{b}_{\mathrm{t}})^T \boldsymbol{\Sigma}^{-1} (\boldsymbol{d} - \boldsymbol{g} - \boldsymbol{\Gamma}_{\mathrm{t}}\boldsymbol{b}) \\
& + (\tilde{\boldsymbol{r}} - \boldsymbol{r})^T \boldsymbol{\Delta}^{-1} (\tilde{\boldsymbol{r}} - \boldsymbol{r}).
\end{aligned} \tag{4.2}
$$

We note that the objective function of the ML estimator in (4.2) is a non-convex function, which admits multiple local minima. Hence, a brute-force local search would require a very good initialization which is "close enough" to the global minimum. As an alternative the ML estimator can be realized by stochastic optimization methods such as genetic algorithm and simulated annealing, but they are computationally intensive with no guarantee of attaining the global minimum [118]. The work in [76], on the other hand, assumes the anchor location errors are small and simplifies the objective function in (4.2) by dropping the second term of the objective function and replacing $\boldsymbol{g}$ with its first order Taylor-series approximation around $\tilde{\boldsymbol{r}}$. This way the anchor locations $\boldsymbol{r}$ are taken out of the estimation process.

Instead of performing prior approximation that simplify the objective function of the ML estimator in (4.2), we propose to directly relax the ML estimator to a convex problem. In the next section, we present the relaxation of the ML estimator into a SDP problem, which can be efficiently solved by optimization toolboxes that are readily available in the literature.

4.4. Relaxation of the ML Estimator to SDP Problem

We relax the ML estimator in (4.2) to a SDP problem by applying a similar procedure as in Section 3.4.2. Those who have read the convex relaxation procedure in Section 3.4.2 can skip this discussion and continue from the SDP problem in (4.6), which is the relaxation of the ML estimator.

To make the discussion of this chapter self-contained however, the steps of relaxing the ML estimator to SDP problem is discussed next. First, we re-write the ML estimator into an equivalent form which is easier to relax to a SDP problem (see Appendix C). Then we relax the ML estimator to a SDP problem by replacing the non-convex constraints with convex constraints.

Using the relation $\boldsymbol{x}^T\boldsymbol{A}\boldsymbol{x} = \mathrm{Tr}\{\boldsymbol{A}\boldsymbol{x}\boldsymbol{x}^T\}$ and performing some algebraic manipulation, the ML estimator in (4.2) can equivalently be expressed as

$$\{\hat{\boldsymbol{t}}, \hat{\boldsymbol{b}}_\mathrm{t}, \hat{\boldsymbol{r}}\} = \arg\min_{\boldsymbol{t}, \boldsymbol{b}_\mathrm{t}, \boldsymbol{r}} \mathrm{Tr}\left\{\boldsymbol{\Sigma}^{-1}\left(\boldsymbol{d}\boldsymbol{d}^T + (\boldsymbol{g}+\boldsymbol{\Gamma}_\mathrm{t}\boldsymbol{b}_\mathrm{t})(\boldsymbol{g}+\boldsymbol{\Gamma}_\mathrm{t}\boldsymbol{b}_\mathrm{t})^T - 2\boldsymbol{d}(\boldsymbol{g}+\boldsymbol{\Gamma}_\mathrm{t}\boldsymbol{b}_\mathrm{t})^T\right)\right\}$$
$$+ \mathrm{Tr}\left\{\boldsymbol{\Delta}^{-1}\left(\tilde{\boldsymbol{r}}\tilde{\boldsymbol{r}}^T + \boldsymbol{r}\boldsymbol{r}^T - 2\tilde{\boldsymbol{r}}\boldsymbol{r}^T\right)\right\}. \quad (4.3)$$

We note that $(\boldsymbol{g}+\boldsymbol{\Gamma}_\mathrm{t}\boldsymbol{b}_\mathrm{t})(\boldsymbol{g}+\boldsymbol{\Gamma}_\mathrm{t}\boldsymbol{b}_\mathrm{t})^T = \left[\boldsymbol{I}\ \boldsymbol{\Gamma}_\mathrm{t}\right]\begin{bmatrix}\boldsymbol{g}\boldsymbol{g}^T & \boldsymbol{g}\boldsymbol{b}_\mathrm{t}^T \\ \boldsymbol{b}_\mathrm{t}\boldsymbol{g}^T & \boldsymbol{b}_\mathrm{t}\boldsymbol{b}_\mathrm{t}^T\end{bmatrix}\begin{bmatrix}\boldsymbol{I} \\ \boldsymbol{\Gamma}_\mathrm{t}^T\end{bmatrix}$. Defining $\boldsymbol{Q} = \left[\boldsymbol{I}\ \boldsymbol{\Gamma}_\mathrm{t}\right]$ and introducing some slack variables, the estimator in (4.3) can equivalently be formulated as

$$\left\{\begin{matrix}\hat{t},\hat{b}_{\rm t},\hat{r},\\ \hat{g},\hat{Z},\hat{R}\end{matrix}\right\} = \arg\min_{\substack{t,r,b_{\rm t}\\ g,Z,R}} \operatorname{Tr}\left\{\Sigma^{-1}\left(dd^T + QZQ^T - 2d(g+\Gamma_{\rm t}b_{\rm t})^T\right)\right\}$$

$$+\operatorname{Tr}\left\{\Delta^{-1}\left(\tilde{r}\tilde{r}^T + R - 2\tilde{r}r^T\right)\right\}, \tag{4.4a}$$

$$\text{s.t.}\quad Z = \begin{bmatrix} gg^T & gb_{\rm t}^T \\ b_{\rm t}g^T & b_{\rm t}b_{\rm t}^T \end{bmatrix}, \tag{4.4b}$$

$$R = rr^T, \tag{4.4c}$$

$$g_{mn} = \|t_m - r_n\|, \tag{4.4d}$$

where g_{mn} represents the element of g that corresponds to the trial range between agent m and anchor n.

Noting the relation between Z and g, we see that the diagonal element of Z can be expressed as

$$Z[l,l] = (g_{mn})^2 = r_n^T r_n + t_m^T t_m - 2t_m^T r_n, \text{ where } l = (m-1)N_{\rm r} + n.$$

Let us further define $X = [r_1, \ldots, r_{N_{\rm r}}, t_1, \ldots, t_{N_{\rm t}}]$ and $Y = X^T X$. We see that the lth diagonal element of Z is related to the elements of Y by

$$Z[l,l] = Y[n,n] + Y[N_{\rm r}+m, N_{\rm r}+m] - 2Y[n, N_{\rm r}+m].$$

From the definition of Y and R, we further note that

$$\operatorname{Tr}\{R\} = \operatorname{Tr}\{Y[1:N_{\rm r}, 1:N_{\rm r}]\},$$

where $Y[1:N_{\rm r}, 1:N_{\rm r}]$ represents a submatrix that consist of the first $N_{\rm r}$ rows and $N_{\rm r}$ columns of Y.

Using the newly defined variables and applying the above relationships, the estimator in (4.4) can be expressed as

$$\left\{\begin{matrix}\hat{X},\hat{b}_{\rm t},\\ \hat{g},\hat{Z},\hat{R},\hat{Y}\end{matrix}\right\} = \arg\min_{\substack{X,b_{\rm t}\\ g,Z,R,Y}} \operatorname{Tr}\left\{\Sigma^{-1}\left(dd^T + QZQ^T - 2d(g+\Gamma_{\rm t}b_{\rm t})^T\right)\right\}$$

$$+\operatorname{Tr}\left\{\Delta^{-1}\left(\tilde{r}\tilde{r}^T + R - 2\tilde{r}r^T\right)\right\}, \tag{4.5a}$$

$$\text{s.t.}\quad Z = \begin{bmatrix} gg^T & gb_{\rm t}^T \\ b_{\rm t}g^T & b_{\rm t}b_{\rm t}^T \end{bmatrix}, \tag{4.5b}$$

$$\boldsymbol{R} = \boldsymbol{r}\boldsymbol{r}^T, \tag{4.5c}$$

$$\boldsymbol{Y} = \boldsymbol{X}^T\boldsymbol{X}, \tag{4.5d}$$

$$\mathrm{Tr}\{\boldsymbol{R}\} = \mathrm{Tr}\{\boldsymbol{Y}[1:N_\mathrm{r}, 1:N_\mathrm{r}]\}, \tag{4.5e}$$

$$\boldsymbol{Z}[l,l] = \boldsymbol{Y}[n,n] + \boldsymbol{Y}[N_\mathrm{r}+m, N_\mathrm{r}+m] - 2\boldsymbol{Y}[n, N_\mathrm{r}+m], \quad \text{with } l = (m-1)N_\mathrm{r} + n, \forall m, \forall n, \tag{4.5f}$$

where, for the sake of notational simplicity, we have not included the trivial relationship between $\boldsymbol{r}$ and $\boldsymbol{X}$. We note that the first three non-linear matrix equality constraints in (4.5) are non-convex, and hence the optimization problem is non-convex.

We now relax (4.5) to a convex optimization problem by applying semi-definite relaxation. As an example, the non-convex constraint $\boldsymbol{Y}$ in (4.5d) can be relaxed to a convex constraint by replacing the equality constraint with inequality constraint as follow

$$\boldsymbol{Y} \succeq \boldsymbol{X}^T\boldsymbol{X}.$$

This constraint on $\boldsymbol{Y}$ is now a convex constraint, but it is non-linear. The constraint can equivalently be expressed as a linear matrix equality constraint of the form [120]

$$\begin{bmatrix} \boldsymbol{Y} & \boldsymbol{X}^T \\ \boldsymbol{X} & \boldsymbol{I} \end{bmatrix} \succeq \boldsymbol{0}.$$

Applying a similar relaxation to the other matrix equality constraints, the ML estimator in (4.5) can be relaxed to a SDP problem of the form

$$\left\{ \substack{\hat{\boldsymbol{X}}, \hat{\boldsymbol{b}}_\mathrm{t}, \\ \hat{\boldsymbol{g}}, \hat{\boldsymbol{Z}}, \hat{\boldsymbol{R}}, \hat{\boldsymbol{Y}}} \right\} = \arg \min_{\substack{\boldsymbol{X}, \boldsymbol{b}_\mathrm{t} \\ \boldsymbol{g}, \boldsymbol{Z}, \boldsymbol{R}, \boldsymbol{Y}}} \mathrm{Tr}\left\{\boldsymbol{\Sigma}^{-1}\left(\boldsymbol{d}\boldsymbol{d}^T + \boldsymbol{Q}\boldsymbol{Z}\boldsymbol{Q}^T - 2\boldsymbol{d}(\boldsymbol{g} + \boldsymbol{\Gamma}_\mathrm{t}\boldsymbol{b}_\mathrm{t})^T\right)\right\}$$
$$+ \mathrm{Tr}\left\{\boldsymbol{\Delta}^{-1}\left(\tilde{\boldsymbol{r}}\tilde{\boldsymbol{r}}^T + \boldsymbol{R} - 2\tilde{\boldsymbol{r}}\boldsymbol{r}^T\right)\right\}, \tag{4.6a}$$

$$\text{s.t.} \quad \begin{bmatrix} \boldsymbol{Z} & & \boldsymbol{g} \\ & & \boldsymbol{b}_\mathrm{t} \\ \boldsymbol{g}^T & \boldsymbol{b}_\mathrm{t}^T & 1 \end{bmatrix} \succeq \boldsymbol{0}, \tag{4.6b}$$

$$\begin{bmatrix} \boldsymbol{R} & \boldsymbol{r} \\ \boldsymbol{r}^T & 1 \end{bmatrix} \succeq \boldsymbol{0}, \quad \begin{bmatrix} \boldsymbol{Y} & \boldsymbol{X}^T \\ \boldsymbol{X} & \boldsymbol{I} \end{bmatrix} \succeq \boldsymbol{0}, \tag{4.6c}$$

$$\mathrm{Tr}\{\boldsymbol{R}\} = \mathrm{Tr}\{\boldsymbol{Y}[1:N_\mathrm{r}, 1:N_\mathrm{r}]\}, \tag{4.6d}$$

$$\boldsymbol{Z}[l,l] = \boldsymbol{Y}[n,n] + \boldsymbol{Y}[N_\mathrm{r}+m, N_\mathrm{r}+m] - 2\boldsymbol{Y}[n, N_\mathrm{r}+m], \quad \text{with } l = (m-1)N_\mathrm{r} + n, \forall m, \forall n, \tag{4.6e}$$

The estimator in (4.6) is now a convex problem which can be efficiently solved by standard convex optimization algorithms such as SeDuMi and SDPT3 [121]. To this end, the proposed localization method that accounts the anchor position uncertainties and also takes into account the agent position constraints is summarized in Algortithm 2.

Algorithm 2 Localization algorithm accounting agent location constraints. Anchor positions are known only up to some uncertainty.

1: Known: measured anchor positions $\tilde{\boldsymbol{r}}$, range measurements $\boldsymbol{d}$.
2: Solve the optimization problem in (4.6). For example, using SeDuMi or SDPT3.
3: Reshape $\hat{\boldsymbol{X}}$ to $\hat{\boldsymbol{t}}$ and $\hat{\boldsymbol{r}}$.
4: Solve ML estimator in (4.2) with $\hat{\boldsymbol{t}}$, $\hat{\boldsymbol{r}}$ and $\hat{\boldsymbol{b}}_{\mathrm{t}}$ as an initialization. For example, using the Matlab toolbox *lsqnonlin*.

4.5. Theoretical Performance Bound

In this section, we present the CRLB of the agent location estimates, which can be used as a benchmark to analyze the performance of the estimator in (4.2). The derivation of the CRLB follows similar steps that are discussed in Section 3.5.

Given the joint PDF of the measurements conditioned on the unknown parameters in (4.1), the corresponding log-likelihood function takes the form

$$\begin{aligned}\mathcal{L}\left(\boldsymbol{d},\tilde{\boldsymbol{r}}|\boldsymbol{t},\boldsymbol{b}_{\mathrm{t}},\boldsymbol{r}\right) &= \ln\left(p\left(\boldsymbol{d},\tilde{\boldsymbol{r}}|\boldsymbol{t},\boldsymbol{b}_{\mathrm{t}},\boldsymbol{r}\right)\right)\\ &= -\tfrac{1}{2}(\boldsymbol{d}-\boldsymbol{g}-\boldsymbol{\Gamma}_{\mathrm{t}}\boldsymbol{b}_{\mathrm{t}})^T\boldsymbol{\Sigma}^{-1}(\boldsymbol{d}-\boldsymbol{g}-\boldsymbol{\Gamma}_{\mathrm{t}}\boldsymbol{b}_{\mathrm{t}}) - \tfrac{1}{2}(\tilde{\boldsymbol{r}}-\boldsymbol{r})^T\boldsymbol{\Delta}^{-1}(\tilde{\boldsymbol{r}}-\boldsymbol{r})\\ &\quad + \ln\left(\frac{|\boldsymbol{\Sigma}|^{-\frac{1}{2}}}{(2\pi)^{\frac{N_{\mathrm{r}}N_{\mathrm{t}}}{2}}} \times \frac{|\boldsymbol{\Delta}|^{-\frac{1}{2}}}{(2\pi)^{\frac{3N_{\mathrm{r}}}{2}}}\right) \end{aligned} \tag{4.7}$$

From the unknown parameters $\{\boldsymbol{t},\boldsymbol{b}_{\mathrm{t}},\boldsymbol{r}\}$, we are interested in the estimation accuracy of the agent locations $\boldsymbol{t}$. To quantify the CRLB of the agent locations estimates, from the joint estimator of all the unknown parameters, we follow a procedure similar to Section 3.5.

Given the log-likelihood function in (4.7), the Fisher information matrix (FIM) of the unknown parameters $\{\boldsymbol{t},\boldsymbol{b}_{\mathrm{t}},\boldsymbol{r}\}$ can be calculated as

$$\boldsymbol{J} = \left[\begin{array}{c|cc} \mathbb{E}\left\{\left(\frac{\partial\mathcal{L}}{\partial\boldsymbol{t}}\right)^T\left(\frac{\partial\mathcal{L}}{\partial\boldsymbol{t}}\right)\right\} & \mathbb{E}\left\{\left(\frac{\partial\mathcal{L}}{\partial\boldsymbol{t}}\right)^T\left(\frac{\partial\mathcal{L}}{\partial\boldsymbol{b}_{\mathrm{t}}}\right)\right\} & \mathbb{E}\left\{\left(\frac{\partial\mathcal{L}}{\partial\boldsymbol{t}}\right)^T\left(\frac{\partial\mathcal{L}}{\partial\boldsymbol{r}}\right)\right\} \\ \hline \mathbb{E}\left\{\left(\frac{\partial\mathcal{L}}{\partial\boldsymbol{b}_{\mathrm{t}}}\right)^T\left(\frac{\partial\mathcal{L}}{\partial\boldsymbol{t}}\right)\right\} & \mathbb{E}\left\{\left(\frac{\partial\mathcal{L}}{\partial\boldsymbol{b}_{\mathrm{t}}}\right)^T\left(\frac{\partial\mathcal{L}}{\partial\boldsymbol{b}_{\mathrm{t}}}\right)\right\} & \mathbb{E}\left\{\left(\frac{\partial\mathcal{L}}{\partial\boldsymbol{b}_{\mathrm{t}}}\right)^T\left(\frac{\partial\mathcal{L}}{\boldsymbol{r}}\right)\right\} \\ \mathbb{E}\left\{\left(\frac{\partial\mathcal{L}}{\partial\boldsymbol{r}}\right)^T\left(\frac{\partial\mathcal{L}}{\partial\boldsymbol{t}}\right)\right\} & \mathbb{E}\left\{\left(\frac{\partial\mathcal{L}}{\partial\boldsymbol{r}}\right)^T\left(\frac{\partial\mathcal{L}}{\partial\boldsymbol{b}_{\mathrm{t}}}\right)\right\} & \mathbb{E}\left\{\left(\frac{\partial\mathcal{L}}{\partial\boldsymbol{r}}\right)^T\left(\frac{\partial\mathcal{L}}{\partial\boldsymbol{r}}\right)\right\} \end{array}\right]$$

$$\triangleq \begin{bmatrix} \boldsymbol{J}_1 & \boldsymbol{J}_2 \\ \boldsymbol{J}_2^T & \boldsymbol{J}_3 \end{bmatrix}, \tag{4.8}$$

where we have defined the sub-matrices of the FIM as

$$\begin{aligned} \boldsymbol{J}_1 &= \mathbb{E}\{(\tfrac{\partial \mathcal{L}}{\partial \boldsymbol{t}})^T \tfrac{\partial \mathcal{L}}{\partial \boldsymbol{t}}\}, \\ \boldsymbol{J}_2 &= \begin{bmatrix} \mathbb{E}\{(\tfrac{\partial \mathcal{L}}{\partial \boldsymbol{t}})^T \tfrac{\partial \mathcal{L}}{\partial \boldsymbol{b}_{\mathrm{t}}}\} & \mathbb{E}\{(\tfrac{\partial \mathcal{L}}{\partial \boldsymbol{t}})^T \tfrac{\partial \mathcal{L}}{\partial \boldsymbol{r}}\} \end{bmatrix}, \text{ and} \\ \boldsymbol{J}_3 &= \begin{bmatrix} \mathbb{E}\{(\tfrac{\partial \mathcal{L}}{\partial \boldsymbol{b}_{\mathrm{t}}})^T \tfrac{\partial \mathcal{L}}{\partial \boldsymbol{b}_{\mathrm{t}}}\} & \mathbb{E}\{(\tfrac{\partial \mathcal{L}}{\partial \boldsymbol{b}_{\mathrm{t}}})^T \tfrac{\partial \mathcal{L}}{\partial \boldsymbol{r}}\} \\ \mathbb{E}\{(\tfrac{\partial \mathcal{L}}{\partial \boldsymbol{r}})^T \tfrac{\partial \mathcal{L}}{\partial \boldsymbol{b}_{\mathrm{t}}}\} & \mathbb{E}\{(\tfrac{\partial \mathcal{L}}{\partial \boldsymbol{r}})^T \tfrac{\partial \mathcal{L}}{\partial \boldsymbol{r}}\} \end{bmatrix}. \end{aligned}$$

The sub-matrices $\boldsymbol{J}_1$, $\boldsymbol{J}_2$ and $\boldsymbol{J}_3$ are calculated in Appendix D.2.

From the result in (3.28), we note that the information about $\boldsymbol{t}$ that is contained in $\boldsymbol{J}$ is also contained in $\boldsymbol{J}_t = \boldsymbol{J}_1 - \boldsymbol{J}_2\boldsymbol{J}_3^{-1}\boldsymbol{J}_2^T$. Hence, the covariance matrix of any unbiased estimate of $\boldsymbol{t}$ (without taking into account the constraints) satisfies the information inequality

$$\mathbb{E}\left\{\left(\hat{\boldsymbol{t}} - \boldsymbol{t}\right)\left(\hat{\boldsymbol{t}} - \boldsymbol{t}\right)^T\right\} \succeq \boldsymbol{J}_t^{-1}. \tag{4.9}$$

Let $\hat{\boldsymbol{t}}$ be an unbiased estimate of $\boldsymbol{t}$ that fulfills the constraint $\boldsymbol{c}(\boldsymbol{t}) = \boldsymbol{0}$. Furthermore, let $\boldsymbol{G} = \frac{\partial(\boldsymbol{c}(\boldsymbol{t}))}{\partial \boldsymbol{t}}$ be the constraint gradient matrix. Then using the result in Section 3.5, the covariance matrix of the agent location estimates that fulfills the constraints is given by

$$\mathbb{E}\left\{\left(\hat{\boldsymbol{t}} - \boldsymbol{t}\right)\left(\hat{\boldsymbol{t}} - \boldsymbol{t}\right)^T\right\} \succeq \boldsymbol{U}\left(\boldsymbol{U}^T\boldsymbol{J}_t\boldsymbol{U}\right)^{-1}\boldsymbol{U}^T, \tag{4.10}$$

where $\boldsymbol{U}$ is a matrix whose columns form the orthonormal basis for the null space of $\boldsymbol{G}$, i.e. $\boldsymbol{G}\boldsymbol{U} = \boldsymbol{0}$. From (3.29), we see that the root mean squared error (RMSE) of the agent location estimates is lower bounded by

$$\text{RMSE\_LB}(\boldsymbol{t}) = \sqrt{\frac{1}{N_{\mathrm{t}}}\mathrm{Tr}\left\{\boldsymbol{U}\left(\boldsymbol{U}^T\boldsymbol{J}_t\boldsymbol{U}\right)^{-1}\boldsymbol{U}^T\right\}}. \tag{4.11}$$

4.6. Performance Evaluation

In this section, we evaluate the performance of the localization method presented in Section 4.3 and Section 4.4. As a performance metric, we use the RMSE of the agent location estimates and the corresponding CRLB given in (4.11).

We consider a network consisting of $N_\mathrm{r} = 6$ anchors and $N_\mathrm{t} = 10$ agents. The anchors and the agents are located as shown in Figure 3.4. The $N_\mathrm{r} = 6$ anchors are located at fixed positions $\boldsymbol{r}_1 = [5\,\mathrm{m}, 0, 0]^T$, $\boldsymbol{r}_2 = [0, 5\,\mathrm{m}, 0]^T$, $\boldsymbol{r}_3 = [0, 0, 5\,\mathrm{m}]^T$, $\boldsymbol{r}_4 = [-5\,\mathrm{m}, 0, 0]^T$, $\boldsymbol{r}_5 = [0, -5\,\mathrm{m}, 0]^T$ and $\boldsymbol{r}_6 = [0, 0, -5\,\mathrm{m}]^T$. For the agent locations, as in Chapter 3, we consider two topologies. For Topology 1, the agents are drawn randomly from a $10\,\mathrm{m} \times 10\,\mathrm{m} \times 10\,\mathrm{m}$ cube centered at $[0, 0, 0]^T$, as shown in Figure 3.4a. For Topology 2, on the other hand, the agents are drawn from a $10\,\mathrm{m} \times 10\,\mathrm{m} \times 10\,\mathrm{m}$ cube centered at $[5\,\mathrm{m}, 0, 0]^T$, as shown in Figure 3.4b.

The range measurement errors are assumed to be i.i.d. zero-mean Gaussian random variables with a standard deviation of σ_range. The anchor position errors are also i.i.d. random vectors, where each element is zero-mean Gaussian distributed with standard deviation σ_anchor. The ranging offsets of the agents are drawn randomly from a uniform distribution in $[-100\,\mathrm{m}, 100\,\mathrm{m}]$.

Impact of unaccounted anchor position errors

The standard deviation of the range measurement errors is set to $\sigma_\mathrm{range} = 1\,\mathrm{cm}$. Considering the fact that the anchor position errors are due to the estimation error in the calibration phase and the movement of anchor nodes, we set $\sigma_\mathrm{anchor} = 5\,\mathrm{cm}$. The performance of the localization method for a varying σ_anchor is discussed afterwards.

Figure 4.2 shows the RMSE of the agent location estimates for both agent topologies. The figure compares the performance of the estimators (SDP and MLE) that take into account the anchor position uncertainties and those that do not. As it can be clearly seen from the figure, unaccounted anchor position errors lead to a considerable performance degradation. For example, for Topology 1, when the anchor position errors are not taken into account, only 20 % of the ML estimates of the agent locations have a RMSE less than 5 cm. However, when the anchor position errors are taken into account, almost all of the ML estimates of the agent locations have a RMSE less than 5 cm. The performance degradation due to unaccounted anchor position errors is even more pronounced for Topology 2. For Topology 2, when the anchor position errors are not accounted 30 % of the ML estimates have a RMSE above 10 cm. But when they are taken into account, 90 % of the ML estimates have a RMSE less than 6 cm.

From this observation, we may therefore conclude that the estimator that takes into account the anchor position errors brings a considerable performance improvement.

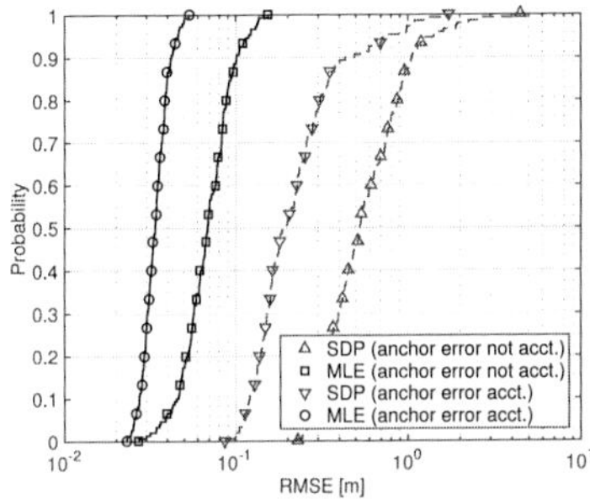

(a) Topology 1

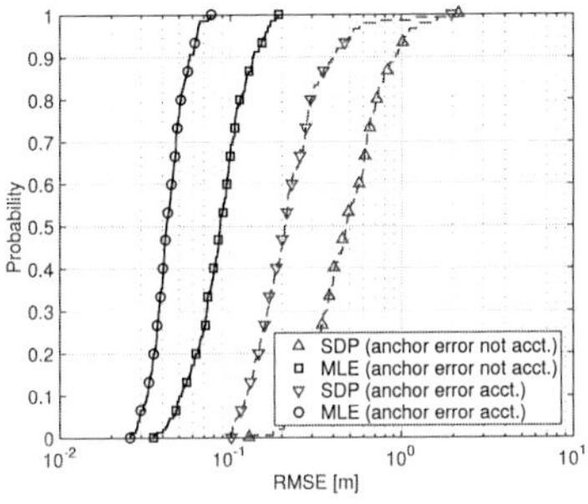

(b) Topology 2

Figure 4.2.: Empirical CDF of RMSE of the agent location estimates in the presence of anchor location uncertainties.

Localization performance for varying σ_{anchor}

The RMSE performance in Figure 4.2 is only for a specific choice of σ_{anchor}. Next we evaluate the performance of the localization method for varying anchor position accuracy. The accuracy of the ML estimates of the agent locations is compared with the CRLB. Furthermore, the proposed SDP relaxation is compared with the SDP relaxation reported in [76]. Here, we make a remark that, in [76], two SDP based localization methods were presented. Namely, robust 2-step least squares (R2LS) and robust min-max algorithm (RMMA). Since in our system model we assume independent and Gaussian distributed range measurement errors, we chose the R2LS algorithm for comparison, which is reported as the method that shows a better performance for the considered error model.

Fig. 4.3 shows RMSE performance of the proposed SDP solution and the R2LS algorithm presented in [76] for varying ratio of $\sigma_{\text{anchor}}/\sigma_{\text{range}}$. Also shown in the figure are RMSE performance of the proposed ML estimator (initialized with the SDP solution) and the corresponding CRLB. The ratio $\sigma_{\text{anchor}}/\sigma_{\text{range}}$ is varied by fixing $\sigma_{\text{range}} = 1\,\text{cm}$ and increasing σ_{anchor} from $0.5\,\text{cm}$ to $10\,\text{cm}$.

We first observe that, for both topologies, the ML estimator tightly matches the CRLB for a wide range of $\sigma_{\text{anchor}}/\sigma_{\text{range}}$, which confirms that the proposed estimator is efficient. We further see that the proposed SDP performs close to the R2LS algorithm when the ranging errors are the dominant source of error, i.e. small $\sigma_{\text{anchor}}/\sigma_{\text{range}}$. However, when the anchor position errors become more dominant, i.e. increasing

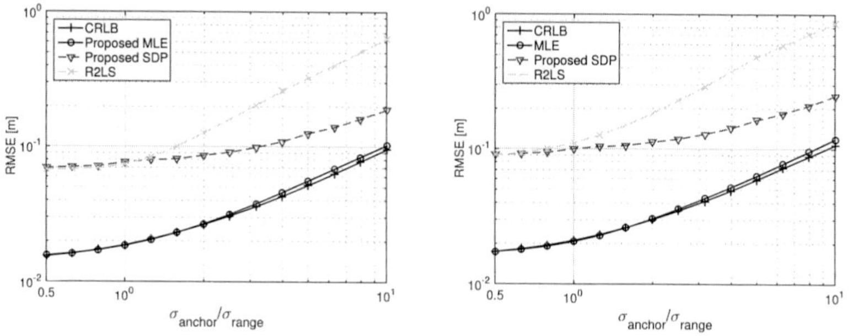

(a) Topology 1 (b) Topology 2

Figure 4.3.: Performance comparison of the proposed SDP and the R2LS method from [76].

$\sigma_{\mathrm{anchor}}/\sigma_{\mathrm{range}}$, the proposed estimator considerably outperforms the R2LS algorithm. This is because when the anchor position errors increase, the objective function in (4.2) is dominated by the second term. And hence, the R2LS algorithm, which approximates the objective function with its first order Taylor series approximation, incurs a big performance loss.

Localization performance for varying N_r and N_t

If the anchor locations are perfectly known, the second term of the objective function in (4.2) is zero and hence the joint ML estimator can be decoupled into N_t equivalent estimators that estimate each agent location and ranging offset independently. However, in the presence of anchor position uncertainty, the second term couples the estimates of the agent locations and hence the estimator accuracy can be improved for increasing N_t. Next, we study the impact of N_r and N_t on the localization performance.

The CRLB of the agent location estimates for varying N_r and N_t is shown in Figure 4.4a. The colormap denotes a RMSE_LB from 3 cm (dark blue) to 13.5 cm (light yellow). The corresponding contour plot is shown in Figure 4.4b. $\sigma_{\mathrm{range}} = 1$ cm and $\sigma_{\mathrm{anchor}} = 5$ cm. The N_t agents are drawn from Topology 1. The $N_\mathrm{r} = 12$ anchors and their order of choice is given in Table 4.1.

From the figure, we observe that when $N_\mathrm{r} = 4$, the accuracy of the agent location estimates is poor (around 13 cm for any choice of N_t). This is because for 3D localization with asynchronous agent and with anchor position uncertainties, the range measurements from 4 anchors do not provide sufficient information to accurately estimate the

Table 4.1.: Anchor locations. All values are in meters.

$r_1 = [5,0,0]^T$	$r_2 = [0,5,0]^T$	$r_3 = [0,0,5]^T$	$r_4 = [-5,0,0]^T$
$r_5 = [0,-5,0]^T$	$r_6 = [0,0,-5]^T$	$r_7 = [5,-5,-5]^T$	$r_8 = [-5,5,5]^T$
$r_9 = [-5,-5,5]^T$	$r_{10} = [5,5,-5]^T$	$r_{11} = [-5,-5,-5]^T$	$r_{12} = [5,5,5]^T$

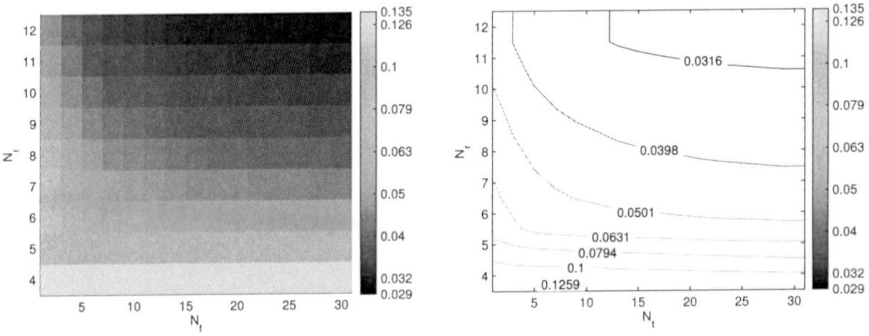

(a) Surface plot (b) Contour plot

Figure 4.4.: CRLB of the agent location estimates for varying N_r and N_t.

agent locations. For $N_\mathrm{r} > 5$ however, the accuracy of the agent location estimates is improved for increasing N_t. For example, for $N_\mathrm{r} = 5$ the RMSE_LB of 6.5 cm ($N_\mathrm{t} = 5$) is reduced to around 5.5 cm ($N_\mathrm{t} = 20$).

What is also interesting to note is that there exist multiple $(N_\mathrm{t}, N_\mathrm{r})$ tuples that achieve a given target of accuracy. For example, as shown in Figure 4.4b, RMSE_LB = 5 cm can be achieved with $(N_\mathrm{t}, N_\mathrm{r}) = (5, 8)$ or $(N_\mathrm{t}, N_\mathrm{r}) = (15, 6)$. This implies that the performance loss due to potential NLOS anchors can be compensated by increasing the number of agents that we estimate jointly. Clearly, the number of agents that we can estimate jointly is limited by the computational capability of the system. Hence, in practice, a trade-off between the achievable accuracy and computational complexity need to be considered.

4.7. Summary

The localization problem considered in Chapter 3 is extended to account anchor location errors. The ML solution of the localization problem, which jointly estimates the unknown anchor locations along with the unknown locations and ranging offsets of the anchors, is formulated. The relaxation of the ML estimator, which is a non-convex optimization problem, to a SDP problem is presented. To benefit from the computational tractability of the SDP problem and the accuracy of the ML estimator, the proposed localization method follows a two-step approach where the SDP solution is refined with the ML estimator. The comparison of the proposed localization method with the CRLB shows that the SDP solution serves as a good initialization for the ML estimator even when the ranging error variance is large. It is also shown that the proposed method outperforms the R2LS method proposed in [76], notably when the anchor location errors are the dominant source of error.

5. Self-calibration Method

The localization methods discussed in the previous chapters assume a perfect knowledge (Chapter 3) or an imperfect knowledge of the anchor locations (Chapter 4). Furthermore, the clock of all the anchors are assumed to be phase synchronized. However, in practice, a calibration phase is required to synchronize the clocks of the anchors and determine their locations. In this chapter[1], we present a practically appealing calibration method that enables wireless sensor networks to calibrate themselves based on the TOA measurements gathered by the nodes in the system, i.e. no external infrastructure is required to perform calibration.

5.1. Introduction

TOA based localization methods, including those presented in Chapter 3 and 4, assume *a priori* knowledge of the anchors locations and clock synchronized anchors. One possible approach to calibrate the anchors locations is to use an additional system that estimates the anchors locations. For example, reflective markers can be attached to the anchors and their locations can be estimated using cameras, by applying a principle similar to the vision based systems described in Section 1.2.1. However, this would mean that an external infrastructure is required to perform calibration, which increases system complexity and cost. In this chapter, we consider a calibration method which estimates the locations and clock offsets of the anchors based on the TOA measurements between the nodes in the system. The calibration method does not assume the agent locations to be surveyed and hence, multiple agent locations can be realized by a single moving agent, which makes the calibration process simple and cost effective.

As discussed in Section 2.3, we make three distinctions for clock synchronization between two nodes: 1) *Phase synchronous (PS)*: both the phase and frequency of

[1]Parts of this chapter has been presented in [124].

the clocks of the two nodes are perfectly synchronized, and hence, there is no clock offset between them. 2) *Frequency synchronous (FS)*: the clocks of the two nodes are frequency synchronized but they may have an unknown phase shift, which is constant over time. 3) *Asynchronous (Async.)*: the clocks of the two nodes are neither phase nor frequency synchronized and hence, they may experience a phase shift that changes over time. Depending on the scheme that is used to synchronize the clocks of the anchors (among themselves) and the clocks of the anchors to the clock of the agent, several cases may arise which are explained in Section 5.2.

Previous related works considered only a specific clock synchronization scheme that suits a certain application scenario. A self-calibration method that assumes phase synchronized anchors and agents is presented in [125]. The work in [126] on the other hand, assumes a phase synchronized anchors but asynchronous agents. The case of frequency synchronized anchors and asynchronous agents is considered in [127]. All these works have presented the maximum likelihood (ML) solution of the corresponding calibration problem and it was shown that it is a non-convex optimization problem which admits multiple local minima. Hence, standard gradient search methods require an initialization which is close enough to the global minimum. In [125], the TOA measurements are assumed to be error free and the ML solution is approximated to a simpler non-linear least squares problem by rewriting the TOA measurement equations in a linear form. The work in [127] on the other hand, proposes a heuristic initialization method in which the agents are first placed close to the anchors and the TOA measurements gathered between them are used to get an initial estimate of the anchor locations and their clock offsets. Another set of TOA measurements are then taken to get an initial estimate of the locations and clock offsets of the agents.

Instead of concentrating on a specific scenario, we develop and analyze a framework which generalizes the calibration problem to all practically relevant clock synchronization classes. The ML solution of the calibration problem under generic clock synchronization requirements is derived and shown to be a non-convex optimization problem. To solve, the initialization problem of the ML estimator, we propose to relax it to a semi-definite programming (SDP) problem, which can be efficiently solved by convex optimization toolboxes that are readily available in the literature. Simulation results show that the output of the relaxed optimization problem have a reasonable accuracy which can serve as a good initialization for the ML estimator.

The rest of the paper is structured as follows. In Section 5.2, the systematic classification of the different synchronization classes is discussed and the calibration problem is formally stated. The ML solution of the calibration problem is presented in Section 5.4. The ML estimator is relaxed to a SDP problem in Section 5.5. The performance of the proposed calibration method is then assessed in Section 5.8.

5.2. Systematic Classification of Synchronization Classes

The main goal of the calibration method is to estimate the positions and clock offsets of the N_r anchors, which are located at $\boldsymbol{r}_n = [r_n^{(x)}, r_n^{(y)}, r_n^{(z)}]^T, n \in \{1, 2, \ldots, N_\mathrm{r}\}$. The agent, which periodically emits a ranging signal, is moved to N_t locations $\boldsymbol{t}_m = [t_m^{(x)}, t_m^{(y)}, t_m^{(z)}]^T, m \in \{1, 2, \ldots, N_\mathrm{t}\}$. The anchors gather the TOA measurements between themselves and the agent (from all the N_t locations). The range measurement gathered between agent m, anchor n and anchor n' is depicted in Figure 5.1.

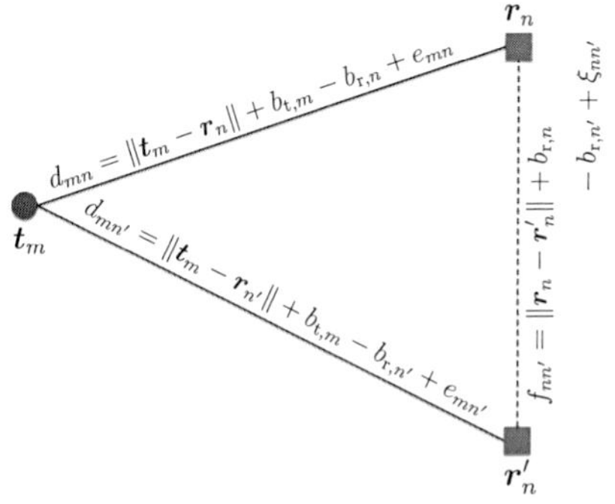

Figure 5.1.: Range measurement model: anchor-to-agent and anchor-to-anchor ranges.

Assume the agent and the anchors are in a line-of-sight (LOS). Then following a similar procedure that lead to (2.8), the measured range between anchor n and the agent when at location $\boldsymbol{t}_m$ can be modeled as

$$d_{mn} = \|\boldsymbol{t}_m - \boldsymbol{r}_n\| + b_{\mathrm{t},m} - b_{\mathrm{r},n} + e_{mn},$$

where $b_{\mathrm{t},m}$ is the ranging offset of agent when at location $\boldsymbol{t}_m$, $b_{\mathrm{r},n}$ is the ranging offset of anchor n. The ranging error e_{mn} is modeled as $e_{mn} \sim \mathcal{N}(0, \sigma_{mn}^2)$, where $\sigma_{mn}^2 = c_0^2/(4\pi^2\beta^2\mathrm{SNR}_{mn})$, β is the effective bandwidth of the transmit signal and SNR_{mn} is the SNR of the received signal [44].

Table 5.1.: Ranging offsets for different synchronization classes.

Synchronization: (anchor-to-anchor) – (anchor-to-agent)	Vector of unknown ranging offsets $\boldsymbol{b}_\mathrm{r}$ and $\boldsymbol{b}_\mathrm{t}$	Matrices $\boldsymbol{\Gamma}_\mathrm{r}$, $\boldsymbol{\Gamma}_\mathrm{t}$ and $\boldsymbol{\Lambda}$
PS-PS	$\boldsymbol{b}_\mathrm{r} = [\,]$, $\boldsymbol{b}_\mathrm{t} = [\,]$	$\boldsymbol{\Gamma}_\mathrm{r} = [\,]$, $\boldsymbol{\Gamma}_\mathrm{t} = [\,]$, $\boldsymbol{\Lambda} = [\,]$
PS-FS	$\boldsymbol{b}_\mathrm{r} = [\,]$, $\boldsymbol{b}_\mathrm{t} = b \in \boldsymbol{R}$	$\boldsymbol{\Gamma}_\mathrm{r} = [\,]$, $\boldsymbol{\Gamma}_\mathrm{t} = \mathbf{1}_{N_\mathrm{t}N_\mathrm{r}\times 1}$, $\boldsymbol{\Lambda} = [\,]$
FS-FS	$\boldsymbol{b}_\mathrm{r} = [b_{\mathrm{r},1}, \ldots, b_{\mathrm{r},N_\mathrm{r}}]^T$, $\boldsymbol{b}_\mathrm{t} = [\,]$	$\boldsymbol{\Gamma}_\mathrm{r} = \begin{bmatrix} -\boldsymbol{I}_{N_\mathrm{r}\times N_\mathrm{r}} \\ \vdots \\ -\boldsymbol{I}_{N_\mathrm{r}\times N_\mathrm{r}} \end{bmatrix}$, $\boldsymbol{\Gamma}_\mathrm{t} = [\,]$, $\boldsymbol{\Lambda} = \begin{bmatrix} \boldsymbol{E}^{(1)}_{N_\mathrm{r}\times N_\mathrm{r}} - \boldsymbol{I}_{N_\mathrm{r}\times N_\mathrm{r}} \\ \vdots \\ \boldsymbol{E}^{(N_\mathrm{r})}_{N_\mathrm{r}\times N_\mathrm{r}} - \boldsymbol{I}_{N_\mathrm{r}\times N_\mathrm{r}} \end{bmatrix}$
PS-Async	$\boldsymbol{b}_\mathrm{r} = [\,]$, $\boldsymbol{b}_\mathrm{t} = [b_{\mathrm{t},1}, \ldots, b_{\mathrm{t},N_\mathrm{t}}]^T$	$\boldsymbol{\Gamma}_\mathrm{r} = [\,]$, $\boldsymbol{\Gamma}_\mathrm{t} = \begin{bmatrix} \boldsymbol{E}^{(1)}_{N_\mathrm{r}\times N_\mathrm{t}} \\ \vdots \\ \boldsymbol{E}^{(N_\mathrm{t})}_{N_\mathrm{r}\times N_\mathrm{t}} \end{bmatrix}$, $\boldsymbol{\Lambda} = [\,]$
FS-Async	$\boldsymbol{b}_\mathrm{r} = [b_{\mathrm{r},1}, \ldots, b_{\mathrm{r},N_\mathrm{r}}]^T$, $\boldsymbol{b}_\mathrm{t} = [b_{\mathrm{t},1}, \ldots, b_{\mathrm{t},N_\mathrm{t}}]^T$	$\boldsymbol{\Gamma}_\mathrm{r} = \begin{bmatrix} -\boldsymbol{I}_{N_\mathrm{r}\times N_\mathrm{r}} \\ \vdots \\ -\boldsymbol{I}_{N_\mathrm{r}\times N_\mathrm{r}} \end{bmatrix}$, $\boldsymbol{\Gamma}_\mathrm{t} = \begin{bmatrix} \boldsymbol{E}^{(1)}_{N_\mathrm{r}\times N_\mathrm{t}} \\ \vdots \\ \boldsymbol{E}^{(N_\mathrm{t})}_{N_\mathrm{r}\times N_\mathrm{t}} \end{bmatrix}$, $\boldsymbol{\Lambda} = \begin{bmatrix} \boldsymbol{E}^{(1)}_{N_\mathrm{r}\times N_\mathrm{r}} - \boldsymbol{I}_{N_\mathrm{r}\times N_\mathrm{r}} \\ \vdots \\ \boldsymbol{E}^{(N_\mathrm{r})}_{N_\mathrm{r}\times N_\mathrm{r}} - \boldsymbol{I}_{N_\mathrm{r}\times N_\mathrm{r}} \end{bmatrix}$

In case the system is able to measure ranges between the anchors, the measured range between anchor n and anchor n' can be modeled as

$$f_{nn'} = \begin{cases} \|\boldsymbol{r}_n - \boldsymbol{r}'_n\| + b_{\mathrm{r},n} - b_{\mathrm{r},n'} + \xi_{nn'}, & \text{if } n \neq n' \\ 0, & \text{if } n = n' \end{cases}$$

where $\xi_{nn'} \sim \mathcal{N}(0, \delta^2_{nn'})$ and $\delta^2_{nn'} = c_0^2/(4\pi^2\beta^2\mathrm{SNR}_{nn'})$. Here, it should be noted that for our TOA based human posture capturing system, the anchors are low-complexity relays which forward the signals they receive from the agents to the cluster head. And hence, the anchor-to-anchor range measurements are not available for this system. Nevertheless, for the sake of completeness, we consider the anchor-to-anchor range measurements in the formulation of the calibration problem. The performance of the calibration problem when the anchor-to-anchor range measurements are absent is discussed in Section 5.8.

To this end, for the different synchronization classes, the vectors of range measurements $\boldsymbol{d} = [d_{11}, d_{12}, \dots, d_{N_\mathrm{t}N_\mathrm{r}}]^T$ and $\boldsymbol{f} = [f_{11}, f_{12}, \dots, f_{N_\mathrm{r}N_\mathrm{r}}]^T$ can be modeled in generic form as

$$\boldsymbol{d} \sim \mathcal{N}\left(\boldsymbol{g} + \boldsymbol{\Gamma}_\mathrm{t}\boldsymbol{b}_\mathrm{t} + \boldsymbol{\Gamma}_\mathrm{r}\boldsymbol{b}_\mathrm{r}, \boldsymbol{\Sigma}_\mathrm{d}\right) \text{ and } \boldsymbol{f} \sim \mathcal{N}\left(\boldsymbol{h} + \boldsymbol{\Lambda}\boldsymbol{b}_\mathrm{r}, \boldsymbol{\Sigma}_\mathrm{f}\right),$$

where $\boldsymbol{\Sigma}_\mathrm{d}$ and $\boldsymbol{\Sigma}_\mathrm{f}$ are the covariance matrices of the corresponding range measurements, the trial vectors $\boldsymbol{g}$ and $\boldsymbol{h}$ are defined as $\boldsymbol{g} = \left[\|\boldsymbol{t}_1 - \boldsymbol{r}_1\|, \dots, \|\boldsymbol{t}_{N_\mathrm{t}} - \boldsymbol{r}_{N_\mathrm{r}}\|\right]^T$, $\boldsymbol{h} = \left[0, \|\boldsymbol{r}_1 - \boldsymbol{r}_2\|, \|\boldsymbol{r}_1 - \boldsymbol{r}_3\|, \dots, \|\boldsymbol{r}_{N_\mathrm{r}} - \boldsymbol{r}_{N_\mathrm{r}-1}\|, 0\right]^T$. The matrices $\boldsymbol{\Gamma}_\mathrm{t}$, $\boldsymbol{\Gamma}_\mathrm{r}$ and $\boldsymbol{\Lambda}$, and the ranging offset vectors $\boldsymbol{b}_\mathrm{t}$ and $\boldsymbol{b}_\mathrm{r}$ are defined in Table 5.1 for the different synchronization classes. For example, for the case when the anchors are phase synchronous with each other but they are asynchronous with the agent (PS-Async), the ranging offsets of the anchors are all known and zero (hence the vector of the unknown ranging offsets of the anchors is set to $\boldsymbol{b}_\mathrm{r} = [\;]$) but the ranging offset of the agent $\boldsymbol{b}_\mathrm{t}$ is unknown. With this formulation, the problem of calibration is hence, given the range measurements $\boldsymbol{d}$ and $\boldsymbol{f}$, estimate the anchor locations $\boldsymbol{r} = \left[\boldsymbol{r}_1^T, \dots, \boldsymbol{r}_{N_\mathrm{r}}^T\right]^T$ and the agent locations $\boldsymbol{t} = \left[\boldsymbol{t}_1^T, \dots, \boldsymbol{t}_{N_\mathrm{t}}^T\right]^T$ along with $\boldsymbol{b}_\mathrm{r}$ and $\boldsymbol{b}_\mathrm{t}$.

The conditional PDF of the range measurements given the unknown parameters can be expressed as

$$\begin{aligned} p(\boldsymbol{d}, \boldsymbol{f} | \boldsymbol{r}, \boldsymbol{t}, \boldsymbol{b}_\mathrm{r}, \boldsymbol{b}_\mathrm{t}) &= p(\boldsymbol{d} | \boldsymbol{r}, \boldsymbol{t}, \boldsymbol{b}_\mathrm{r}, \boldsymbol{b}_\mathrm{t}) p(\boldsymbol{f} | \boldsymbol{r}, \boldsymbol{b}_\mathrm{r}) \\ &= \frac{|\boldsymbol{\Sigma}_\mathrm{d}|^{-\frac{1}{2}}}{(2\pi)^{\frac{N_\mathrm{t}N_\mathrm{r}}{2}}} \exp\Big(-\frac{1}{2}\left(\boldsymbol{d} - \boldsymbol{g} - \boldsymbol{\Gamma}_\mathrm{t}\boldsymbol{b}_\mathrm{t} - \boldsymbol{\Gamma}_\mathrm{r}\boldsymbol{b}_\mathrm{r}\right)^T \boldsymbol{\Sigma}_\mathrm{d}^{-1} \left(\boldsymbol{d} - \boldsymbol{g} - \boldsymbol{\Gamma}_\mathrm{t}\boldsymbol{b}_\mathrm{t} - \boldsymbol{\Gamma}_\mathrm{r}\boldsymbol{b}_\mathrm{r}\right)\Big) \\ &\quad \times \frac{|\boldsymbol{\Sigma}_\mathrm{f}|^{-\frac{1}{2}}}{(2\pi)^{\frac{N_\mathrm{r}N_\mathrm{r}}{2}}} \exp\Big(-\frac{1}{2}\left(\boldsymbol{f} - \boldsymbol{h} - \boldsymbol{\Lambda}\boldsymbol{b}_\mathrm{r}\right)^T \boldsymbol{\Sigma}_\mathrm{f}^{-1} \left(\boldsymbol{f} - \boldsymbol{h} - \boldsymbol{\Lambda}\boldsymbol{b}_\mathrm{r}\right)\Big). \end{aligned} \tag{5.1}$$

The ML estimate of the unknown parameters is then the value that maximizes the conditional PDF. However, it should be noted that the metrics that appear in the PDF are the trial ranges, i.e. $\{\|\boldsymbol{t}_m - \boldsymbol{r}_n\|\}$ and $\{\|\boldsymbol{r}_n - \boldsymbol{r}_{n'}\|\}$. This implies that any 3D-geometric transformation that preserves the distance between any pair of points does not affect the conditional PDF and hence, the ML solution will not be unique. Such transformations are referred to as rigid transformations which are the subject of the next section.

5.3. Rigid Transformations

A rigid transformation is a geometric transformation that preserves the distance between any pair of points [128]. Rigid transformations include translation, rotation and reflection.

Translation and Rotation

The translation of a given point $\boldsymbol{a}$ in the (x, y, z) coordinate system to a new coordinate system (x', y', z') by a translation vector $\boldsymbol{v}$ can be expressed as

$$\boldsymbol{a}' = \boldsymbol{a} + \boldsymbol{v}.$$

The translation operation is depicted in Figure 5.2.

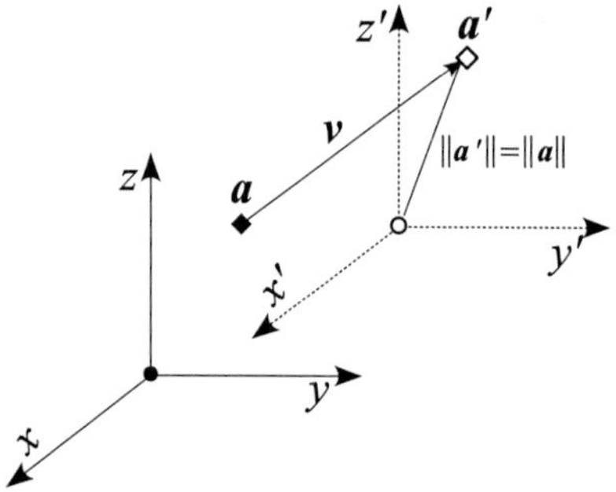

Figure 5.2.: Translation of point $\boldsymbol{a}$ by a translation vector $\boldsymbol{v}$.

A given point $\boldsymbol{a}$ in the (x, y, z) coordinate system after a counter-clockwise rotation by angles ϕ_z, ϕ_y and ϕ_x with respect to the z-axis, y-axis and x-axis, respectively, can be expressed as

$$\boldsymbol{a}' = \boldsymbol{V}\boldsymbol{a},$$

where the rotation matrix is defined as $\boldsymbol{V} = \boldsymbol{V}_z(\phi_z)\boldsymbol{V}_y(\phi_y)\boldsymbol{V}_x(\phi_x)$, with

$$\boldsymbol{V}_z = \begin{bmatrix} \cos(\phi_z) & -\sin(\phi_z) & 0 \\ \sin(\phi_z) & \cos(\phi_z) & 0 \\ 0 & 0 & 1 \end{bmatrix},$$

$$\boldsymbol{V}_y = \begin{bmatrix} \cos(\phi_y) & 0 & \sin(\phi_y) \\ 0 & 1 & 0 \\ -\sin(\phi_y) & 0 & \cos(\phi_y) \end{bmatrix} \quad \text{and}$$

$$\boldsymbol{V}_x = \begin{bmatrix} 1 & 0 & 0 \\ 0 & \cos(\phi_x) & -\sin(\phi_x) \\ 0 & \sin(\phi_x) & \cos(\phi_x) \end{bmatrix}.$$

As an example, the rotation of the (x, y, z) coordinate system by an angle ϕ_x with respect to the x-axis is shown in Figure 5.3.

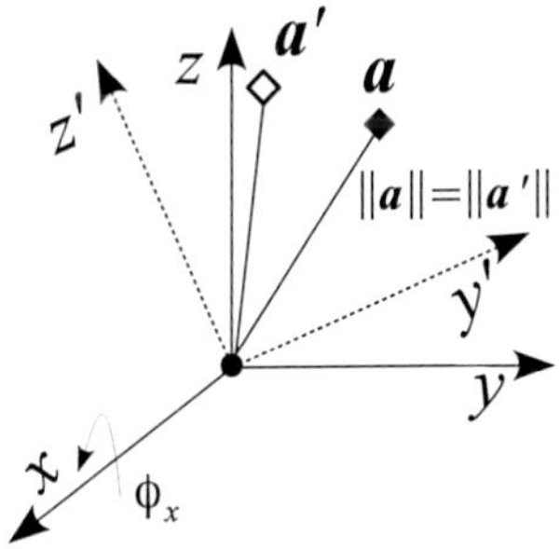

Figure 5.3.: Counter-clockwise rotation of the (x, y, z) coordinate system by ϕ_x with respect to the x-axis.

Reflection

Reflecting the reference coordinate system on a given plane preserves the distance between every pair of points. In a special case, if the reflecting plane is perpendicular to one of the axis of the reference coordinate system, reflection corresponds to sign flipping. For example, reflecting the reference coordinate system with respect to xy-plane corresponds to flipping the sign of the z-coordinates of the reference coordinate system.

To help us relate such a sign flipping reflection with rotation, we define two reference coordinate systems: a right handed (RH) reference coordinate system and a left handed (LH) reference coordinate system. The two reference coordinate systems are depicted in Figure 5.4.

As an example, we see that reflecting the RH reference coordinate system corresponds to rotating the LH reference coordinate system by $-90°$ (counter-clockwise).

(a) Right handed (RH) coordinate system (b) Left handed (LH) coordinate system

Figure 5.4.: Right handed and left handed reference coordinate systems.

Table 5.2.: Sign flipping on RH coordinate system and the corresponding rotation in LH coordinate system.

RH: Sign flip			Equivalent rotation
x	y	z	
-	+	+	LH by $\boldsymbol{V} = \boldsymbol{V}_z(-90°)$
+	-	+	LH by $\boldsymbol{V} = \boldsymbol{V}_z(90°)$
+	+	-	LH by $\boldsymbol{V} = \boldsymbol{V}_z(90°)\boldsymbol{V}_x(180°)$
-	-	+	RH by $\boldsymbol{V} = \boldsymbol{V}_z(180°)$
-	+	-	RH by $\boldsymbol{V} = \boldsymbol{V}_y(180°)$
+	-	-	RH by $\boldsymbol{V} = \boldsymbol{V}_x(180°)$
-	-	-	LH by $\boldsymbol{V} = \boldsymbol{V}_z(180°)$

This is implies that sign flipping the x-coordinate of the RH reference coordinate system is equivalent to multiplying all points in the LH reference coordinate system by $\boldsymbol{V}_z(-90°)$. Other sign flipping combinations on the RH reference coordinate system and the corresponding rotation operation in the LH coordinate system is listed in Table 5.2.

Noting that the sign flipping in a given reference coordinate system can equivalently be expressed by rotation of the LH or RH coordinate system, here after we only consider the effect of translation and rotation on the ML solution.

5.4. Maximum Likelihood (ML) Solution

The ML solution of the calibration problem that jointly estimates all the unknown parameters is the value of $\{\boldsymbol{r}, \boldsymbol{t}, \boldsymbol{b}_\mathrm{r}, \boldsymbol{b}_\mathrm{t}\}$ that minimizes the PDF in (5.1). We note see that any translation (by $\boldsymbol{v}$) and rotation (by $\boldsymbol{V}$) of all the node positions

$$\boldsymbol{r}'_n = \boldsymbol{V}\boldsymbol{r}_n + \boldsymbol{v}, \quad \boldsymbol{t}'_m = \boldsymbol{V}\boldsymbol{t}_m + \boldsymbol{v}, \quad \forall n, m,$$

does not affect the ML estimates. This can be easily seen from the relation

$$\begin{aligned}\|\boldsymbol{t}'_m - \boldsymbol{r}'_n\| &= \|(\boldsymbol{V}\boldsymbol{t}_m + \boldsymbol{v}) - (\boldsymbol{V}\boldsymbol{r}_n + \boldsymbol{v})\| \\ &= \left((\boldsymbol{t}_m - \boldsymbol{r}_n)^T \boldsymbol{V}^T \boldsymbol{V} (\boldsymbol{t}_m - \boldsymbol{r}_n)\right)^{1/2} \\ &= \|\boldsymbol{t}_m - \boldsymbol{r}_n\|,\end{aligned}$$

where have used the property $\boldsymbol{V}^T\boldsymbol{V} = \boldsymbol{I}$, as the rotation matrix is an orthogonal matrix. This implies that we can not establish a global reference coordinate system based on the measured distances.

Without loss of generality, we can make the maximum likelihood solution unique by considering a coordinate system relative to anchor 1, anchor 2 and anchor 3. All other equivalent solutions then follow by translation and rotation. Specifically we define a reference coordinate system by constraining the locations of anchors 1, 2 and 3 as follows

$$\boldsymbol{r}_1 = [0,0,0]^T, \ \left[r_2^{(y)}, r_2^{(z)}\right]^T = [0,0]^T, \text{ and } r_3^{(z)} = 0. \tag{5.2}$$

This constraint forms a reference coordinate system where the origin is at $\boldsymbol{r}_1$, the x-axis is the line connecting $\boldsymbol{r}_1$ and $\boldsymbol{r}_2$, and the xy-plane is the plane formed by the points $\boldsymbol{r}_1$, $\boldsymbol{r}_2$ and $\boldsymbol{r}_3$, as shown in Figure 5.5.

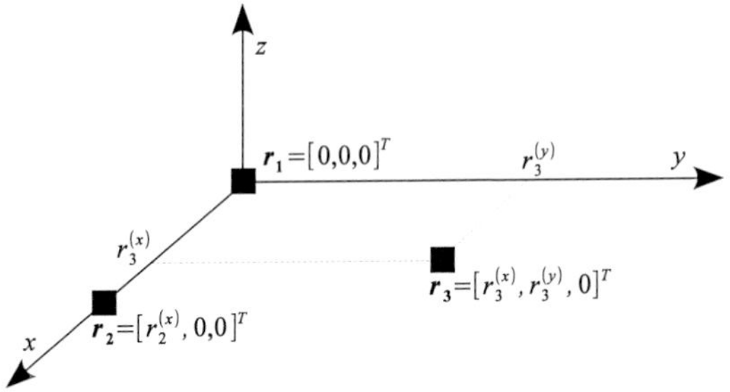

Figure 5.5.: A reference coordinate system defined by constraining the locations of anchor 1, anchor 2 and anchor 3.

We further note that for the case when both the anchor ranging offsets and the agent ranging offsets are non-zero and unknown (i.e. for the cases of FS-Async), an arbitrary constant term can be added to all the ranging offsets without changing the measured ranges. To avoid this ambiguity, without loss of generality, we choose the clock of anchor 1 as a central clock from which the clock offsets of the other nodes is measured.

An equality constraint that captures the above two issues can hence be defined as

$$c_{\text{ref}}(\boldsymbol{r}, \boldsymbol{b}_{\text{r}}) = \begin{cases} [\boldsymbol{r}_1^T, r_2^{(y)}, r_2^{(z)}, r_3^{(z)}, b_{\text{r},1}]^T = \boldsymbol{0}, & \text{for FS-Async} \\ [\boldsymbol{r}_1^T, r_2^{(y)}, r_2^{(z)}, r_3^{(z)}]^T = \boldsymbol{0}, & \text{for others.} \end{cases} \tag{5.3}$$

The ML estimate of the unknown parameters that accounts these constraints hence is given by

$$\left\{\hat{\boldsymbol{r}}, \hat{\boldsymbol{t}}, \hat{\boldsymbol{b}}_{\text{r}}, \hat{\boldsymbol{b}}_{\text{t}}\right\} = \arg \min_{\boldsymbol{r},\boldsymbol{t},\boldsymbol{b}_{\text{r}},\boldsymbol{b}_{\text{t}}} (\boldsymbol{d} - \boldsymbol{g} - \boldsymbol{\Gamma}_{\text{t}}\boldsymbol{b}_{\text{t}} - \boldsymbol{\Gamma}_{\text{r}}\boldsymbol{b}_{\text{r}})^T \boldsymbol{\Sigma}_{\text{d}}^{-1} (\boldsymbol{d} - \boldsymbol{g} - \boldsymbol{\Gamma}_{\text{t}}\boldsymbol{b}_{\text{t}} - \boldsymbol{\Gamma}_{\text{r}}\boldsymbol{b}_{\text{r}})$$

$$+ (\boldsymbol{f} - \boldsymbol{h} - \boldsymbol{\Lambda}\boldsymbol{b}_{\text{r}}) \boldsymbol{\Sigma}_{\text{f}}^{-1} (\boldsymbol{f} - \boldsymbol{h} - \boldsymbol{\Lambda}\boldsymbol{b}_{\text{r}}), \tag{5.4a}$$

$$\text{s.t. } c_{\text{ref}}(\boldsymbol{r}, \boldsymbol{b}_{\text{r}}) = \boldsymbol{0}. \tag{5.4b}$$

Since the elements of $\boldsymbol{g}$ and $\boldsymbol{h}$ are non-linear non-convex functions, one can easily see that the ML estimator in (5.4) is a non-convex optimization problem with an objective function that admits multiple local minima. Standard gradient descent algorithms hence require a very good initialization which is "close enough" to the global minimum. Note that the number of unknown parameters is very large and hence applying methods such as grid search to get an initialization value is impractical. In the next section, we present the relaxation of the ML estimator to a SDP problem which can be efficiently solved by convex optimization toolboxes that are readily available in the literature. The solution of the SDP problem can then be refined by a gradient descent algorithm which implements the ML estimator.

5.5. Relaxation of the ML Estimator to a SDP Problem

The first step in relaxing the ML solution to a convex optimization problem is to rewrite the estimator in (5.4) into an equivalent form which is close to a SDP problem, i.e. an optimization problem with a linear objective function and a constraint which includes a linear matrix inequality constraint and a linear equality constraint, see Appendix C.

To this end, we follow a similar SDP relaxation procedure that is discussed in Section 3.4.2. Readers who are familiar with the relaxation procedure can skip this discussion and directly continue from the SDP problem in (5.8), which is the semi-definite relaxation of the ML estimator in (5.4). Here, however, we make a remark that the ML estimator in (5.4) is relatively complex as the locations and ranging offsets of both the anchors and the agents are unknown. And hence, the relaxed problem may not be unique, which requires further refinement as discussed later in this section.

Using the relation that $\boldsymbol{x}^T\boldsymbol{A}\boldsymbol{x} = \mathrm{Tr}\{\boldsymbol{A}\boldsymbol{x}\boldsymbol{x}^T\}$, the estimator in (5.4) can be written in a form

$$\begin{aligned}\left\{\hat{\boldsymbol{r}}, \hat{\boldsymbol{t}}, \hat{\boldsymbol{b}}_{\mathrm{r}}, \hat{\boldsymbol{b}}_{\mathrm{t}}\right\} = \arg\min_{\boldsymbol{r},\boldsymbol{t},\boldsymbol{b}_{\mathrm{r}},\boldsymbol{b}_{\mathrm{t}}} &\mathrm{Tr}\left\{\Sigma_{\mathrm{d}}^{-1}\left(\boldsymbol{d}\boldsymbol{d}^T + (\boldsymbol{g}+\boldsymbol{\Gamma}_{\mathrm{t}}\boldsymbol{b}_{\mathrm{t}}+\boldsymbol{\Gamma}_{\mathrm{r}}\boldsymbol{b}_{\mathrm{r}})(\boldsymbol{g}+\boldsymbol{\Gamma}_{\mathrm{t}}\boldsymbol{b}_{\mathrm{t}}+\boldsymbol{\Gamma}_{\mathrm{r}}\boldsymbol{b}_{\mathrm{r}})^T\right.\right.\\ &\left.\left.-2\boldsymbol{d}(\boldsymbol{g}+\boldsymbol{\Gamma}_{\mathrm{t}}\boldsymbol{b}_{\mathrm{t}}+\boldsymbol{\Gamma}_{\mathrm{r}}\boldsymbol{b}_{\mathrm{r}})^T\right)\right\}\\ &+\mathrm{Tr}\left\{\Sigma_{\mathrm{f}}^{-1}\left(\boldsymbol{f}\boldsymbol{f}^T + (\boldsymbol{h}+\boldsymbol{\Lambda}\boldsymbol{b}_{\mathrm{r}})(\boldsymbol{h}+\boldsymbol{\Lambda}\boldsymbol{b}_{\mathrm{r}})^T\right.\right.\\ &\left.\left.-2\boldsymbol{f}(\boldsymbol{h}+\boldsymbol{\Lambda}\boldsymbol{b}_{\mathrm{r}})^T\right)\right\}, \qquad (5.5a)\\ &\text{s.t. } \boldsymbol{c}_{\mathrm{ref}}(\boldsymbol{r},\boldsymbol{b}_{\mathrm{r}}) = \boldsymbol{0}. \qquad (5.5b)\end{aligned}$$

Defining $\boldsymbol{Q} = [\,\boldsymbol{I}\ \boldsymbol{\Gamma}_{\mathrm{t}}\ \boldsymbol{\Gamma}_{\mathrm{r}}\,]$ and $\boldsymbol{P} = [\,\boldsymbol{I}\ \boldsymbol{\Lambda}\,]$, one can show that (5.5) can equivalently be expressed as

$$\begin{aligned}\left\{\begin{matrix}\hat{\boldsymbol{r}},\hat{\boldsymbol{t}},\hat{\boldsymbol{b}}_{\mathrm{r}},\hat{\boldsymbol{b}}_{\mathrm{t}},\\ \hat{\boldsymbol{g}},\hat{\boldsymbol{h}},\hat{\boldsymbol{Z}},\hat{\boldsymbol{S}}\end{matrix}\right\} = \arg\min_{\substack{\boldsymbol{r},\boldsymbol{t},\boldsymbol{b}_{\mathrm{r}},\boldsymbol{b}_{\mathrm{t}},\\ \boldsymbol{g},\boldsymbol{h},\boldsymbol{Z},\boldsymbol{S}}} &\mathrm{Tr}\left\{\Sigma_{\mathrm{d}}^{-1}\left(\boldsymbol{d}\boldsymbol{d}^T + \boldsymbol{Q}\boldsymbol{Z}\boldsymbol{Q}^T - 2\boldsymbol{d}(\boldsymbol{g}+\boldsymbol{\Gamma}_{\mathrm{t}}\boldsymbol{b}_{\mathrm{t}}+\boldsymbol{\Gamma}_{\mathrm{r}}\boldsymbol{b}_{\mathrm{r}})^T\right)\right\}\\ &+\mathrm{Tr}\left\{\Sigma_{\mathrm{f}}^{-1}\left(\boldsymbol{f}\boldsymbol{f}^T + \boldsymbol{P}\boldsymbol{S}\boldsymbol{P}^T - 2\boldsymbol{f}(\boldsymbol{h}+\boldsymbol{\Lambda}\boldsymbol{b}_{\mathrm{r}})^T\right)\right\} \qquad (5.6a)\\ \text{s.t. } \boldsymbol{Z} &= \begin{bmatrix}\boldsymbol{g}\boldsymbol{g}^T & \boldsymbol{g}\boldsymbol{b}_{\mathrm{t}}^T & \boldsymbol{g}\boldsymbol{b}_{\mathrm{r}}^T\\ \boldsymbol{b}_{\mathrm{t}}\boldsymbol{g}^T & \boldsymbol{b}_{\mathrm{t}}\boldsymbol{b}_{\mathrm{t}}^T & \boldsymbol{b}_{\mathrm{t}}\boldsymbol{b}_{\mathrm{r}}^T\\ \boldsymbol{b}_{\mathrm{r}}\boldsymbol{g}^T & \boldsymbol{b}_{\mathrm{r}}\boldsymbol{b}_{\mathrm{t}}^T & \boldsymbol{b}_{\mathrm{r}}\boldsymbol{b}_{\mathrm{r}}^T\end{bmatrix}, \qquad (5.6b)\\ \boldsymbol{S} &= \begin{bmatrix}\boldsymbol{h}\boldsymbol{h}^T & \boldsymbol{h}\boldsymbol{b}_{\mathrm{r}}^T\\ \boldsymbol{b}_{\mathrm{r}}\boldsymbol{g}^T & \boldsymbol{b}_{\mathrm{r}}\boldsymbol{b}_{\mathrm{r}}^T\end{bmatrix}, \qquad (5.6c)\\ g_{mn} &= \|\boldsymbol{t}_m - \boldsymbol{r}_n\|, \quad \forall m,n, \qquad (5.6d)\\ h_{nn'} &= \|\boldsymbol{r}_n - \boldsymbol{r}_{n'}\|, \quad \forall n,n', \qquad (5.6e)\\ \boldsymbol{c}_{\mathrm{ref}}(\boldsymbol{r},\boldsymbol{b}_{\mathrm{r}}) &= \boldsymbol{0}, \qquad (5.6f)\end{aligned}$$

where g_{mn} denotes the element of $\boldsymbol{g}$ that corresponds to the trial range between agent m and anchor n, and $h_{nn'}$ is the element of $\boldsymbol{h}$ that corresponds to the trial range between anchor n and anchor n'. We see that the ML estimator in (5.6) has a linear objective function. However, except the constraint in (5.6f), all the constraints are non-convex.

Noting the relationship between $\boldsymbol{Z}$ and $\boldsymbol{g}$, the constraint in (5.6d) can be equivalently be expressed as

$$\boldsymbol{Z}[l,l] = (g_{mn})^2 = \boldsymbol{r}_n^T\boldsymbol{r}_n + \boldsymbol{t}_m^T\boldsymbol{t}_m - 2\boldsymbol{r}_n^T\boldsymbol{t}_m,$$

where $l = (m-1)N_\mathrm{r} + n$.

Similarly, the constraint in (5.6e) can be replaced by

$$\boldsymbol{S}[k,k] = (h_{nn'})^2 = \boldsymbol{r}_n^T\boldsymbol{r}_n + \boldsymbol{r}_{n'}^T\boldsymbol{r}_{n'} - 2\boldsymbol{r}_n\boldsymbol{r}_{n'},$$

where $k = (n-1)N_\mathrm{r} + n'$.

Next, we use the above relationships to rewrite the constraints in (5.6d) and (5.6e) into a form which is easier to relax to a convex constraint. To do so, we define $\boldsymbol{X} = [\boldsymbol{r}_1, \ldots, \boldsymbol{r}_{N_\mathrm{r}}, \boldsymbol{t}_1, \ldots, \boldsymbol{t}_{N_\mathrm{t}}]$ and $\boldsymbol{Y} = \boldsymbol{X}^T\boldsymbol{X}$. We then see that the ML estimator can be expressed as

$$\begin{aligned}
\left\{\begin{smallmatrix}\hat{\boldsymbol{X}},\hat{\boldsymbol{Y}},\hat{\boldsymbol{b}}_\mathrm{r},\hat{\boldsymbol{b}}_\mathrm{t},\\ \hat{\boldsymbol{g}},\hat{\boldsymbol{h}},\hat{\boldsymbol{Z}},\hat{\boldsymbol{S}}\end{smallmatrix}\right\} = \arg \min_{\substack{\boldsymbol{X},\boldsymbol{Y},\boldsymbol{b}_\mathrm{r},\boldsymbol{b}_\mathrm{t},\\ \boldsymbol{g},\boldsymbol{h},\boldsymbol{Z},\boldsymbol{S}}} \ & \mathrm{Tr}\left\{\Sigma_\mathrm{d}^{-1}(\boldsymbol{d}\boldsymbol{d}^T + \boldsymbol{Q}\boldsymbol{Z}\boldsymbol{Q}^T - 2\boldsymbol{d}(\boldsymbol{g} + \boldsymbol{\Gamma}_\mathrm{t}\boldsymbol{b}_\mathrm{t} + \boldsymbol{\Gamma}_\mathrm{r}\boldsymbol{b}_\mathrm{r})^T)\right\} \\
& + \mathrm{Tr}\left\{\Sigma_\mathrm{f}^{-1}(\boldsymbol{f}\boldsymbol{f}^T + \boldsymbol{P}\boldsymbol{S}\boldsymbol{P}^T - 2\boldsymbol{f}(\boldsymbol{h} + \boldsymbol{\Lambda}\boldsymbol{b}_\mathrm{r})^T)\right\} && (5.7a)\\
\text{s.t.}\ & \boldsymbol{Z} = \begin{bmatrix} \boldsymbol{g}\boldsymbol{g}^T & \boldsymbol{g}\boldsymbol{b}_\mathrm{t}^T & \boldsymbol{g}\boldsymbol{b}_\mathrm{r}^T \\ \boldsymbol{b}_\mathrm{t}\boldsymbol{g}^T & \boldsymbol{b}_\mathrm{t}\boldsymbol{b}_\mathrm{t}^T & \boldsymbol{b}_\mathrm{t}\boldsymbol{b}_\mathrm{r}^T \\ \boldsymbol{b}_\mathrm{r}\boldsymbol{g}^T & \boldsymbol{b}_\mathrm{r}\boldsymbol{b}_\mathrm{t}^T & \boldsymbol{b}_\mathrm{r}\boldsymbol{b}_\mathrm{r}^T \end{bmatrix}, && (5.7b)\\
& \boldsymbol{S} = \begin{bmatrix} \boldsymbol{h}\boldsymbol{h}^T & \boldsymbol{h}\boldsymbol{b}_\mathrm{r}^T \\ \boldsymbol{b}_\mathrm{r}\boldsymbol{g}^T & \boldsymbol{b}_\mathrm{r}\boldsymbol{b}_\mathrm{r}^T \end{bmatrix}, && (5.7c)\\
& \boldsymbol{Y} = \boldsymbol{X}^T\boldsymbol{X}, && (5.7d)\\
& \boldsymbol{Z}[l,l] = \boldsymbol{Y}[n,n] + \boldsymbol{Y}[N_\mathrm{r}+m, N_\mathrm{r}+m] \\
& \qquad - 2\boldsymbol{Y}[n, N_\mathrm{r}+m], && (5.7e)\\
& \boldsymbol{S}[k,k] = \boldsymbol{Y}[n,n] + \boldsymbol{Y}[n',n'] - 2\boldsymbol{Y}[n,n'], && (5.7f)\\
& c_\mathrm{ref}(\boldsymbol{r}, \boldsymbol{b}_\mathrm{r}) = \boldsymbol{0}. && (5.7g)
\end{aligned}$$

If not for the constraints in (5.7b) and (5.7c), the ML estimator is now a convex optimization problem. To relax the constraints in (5.7b) and (5.7c) into a convex constraint, we apply a semi-definite relaxation and replace the matrix equality constraints with inequality constraints. Furthermore, using the relation that [120]

$$\boldsymbol{Y} \succeq \boldsymbol{X}^T\boldsymbol{X} \Leftrightarrow \left[\begin{smallmatrix}\boldsymbol{Y} & \boldsymbol{X}^T \\ \boldsymbol{X} & \boldsymbol{I}\end{smallmatrix}\right] \succeq \boldsymbol{0},$$

and applying the same relation to the other matrix inequality constraints, the ML estimator can be relaxed to a SDP problem of the following form

$$\begin{Bmatrix} \hat{\boldsymbol{X}},\hat{\boldsymbol{Y}},\hat{\boldsymbol{b}}_{\mathrm{r}},\hat{\boldsymbol{b}}_{\mathrm{t}}, \\ \hat{\boldsymbol{g}},\hat{\boldsymbol{h}},\hat{\boldsymbol{Z}},\hat{\boldsymbol{S}} \end{Bmatrix} = \arg \min_{\substack{\boldsymbol{X},\boldsymbol{Y},\boldsymbol{b}_{\mathrm{r}},\boldsymbol{b}_{\mathrm{t}}, \\ \boldsymbol{g},\boldsymbol{h},\boldsymbol{Z},\boldsymbol{S}}} \mathrm{Tr}\left\{\Sigma_{\mathrm{d}}^{-1}\left(\boldsymbol{d}\boldsymbol{d}^T + \boldsymbol{Q}\boldsymbol{Z}\boldsymbol{Q}^T - 2\boldsymbol{d}(\boldsymbol{g} + \boldsymbol{\Gamma}_{\mathrm{t}}\boldsymbol{b}_{\mathrm{t}} + \boldsymbol{\Gamma}_{\mathrm{r}}\boldsymbol{b}_{\mathrm{r}})^T\right)\right\}$$

$$+ \mathrm{Tr}\left\{\Sigma_{\mathrm{f}}^{-1}\left(\boldsymbol{f}\boldsymbol{f}^T + \boldsymbol{P}\boldsymbol{S}\boldsymbol{P}^T - 2\boldsymbol{f}(\boldsymbol{h} + \boldsymbol{\Lambda}\boldsymbol{b}_{\mathrm{r}})^T\right)\right\}$$

$$\text{s.t.} \begin{bmatrix} & & & \boldsymbol{g} \\ & \boldsymbol{Z} & & \boldsymbol{b}_{\mathrm{t}} \\ & & & \boldsymbol{b}_{\mathrm{r}} \\ \boldsymbol{g}^T & \boldsymbol{b}_{\mathrm{t}}^T & \boldsymbol{b}_{\mathrm{r}}^T & 1 \end{bmatrix} \succeq \boldsymbol{0}, \tag{5.8a}$$

$$\begin{bmatrix} \boldsymbol{S} & & \boldsymbol{h} \\ & & \boldsymbol{b}_{\mathrm{r}} \\ \boldsymbol{h}^T & \boldsymbol{b}_{\mathrm{r}}^T & 1 \end{bmatrix} \succeq \boldsymbol{0}, \tag{5.8b}$$

$$\begin{bmatrix} \boldsymbol{Y} & \boldsymbol{X}^T \\ \boldsymbol{X} & \boldsymbol{I} \end{bmatrix} \succeq \boldsymbol{0}, \tag{5.8c}$$

$$\boldsymbol{Z}[l,l] = \boldsymbol{Y}[n,n] + \boldsymbol{Y}[N_{\mathrm{r}}+m, N_{\mathrm{r}}+m] - 2\boldsymbol{Y}[n, N_{\mathrm{r}}+m], \tag{5.8d}$$

$$\boldsymbol{S}[k,k] = \boldsymbol{Y}[n,n] + \boldsymbol{Y}[n',n'] - 2\boldsymbol{Y}[n,n'], \tag{5.8e}$$

$$c_{\mathrm{ref}}(\boldsymbol{r}, \boldsymbol{b}_{\mathrm{r}}) = \boldsymbol{0}. \tag{5.8f}$$

The estimator in (5.8) is now a convex optimization problem which can be efficiently solved by standard convex optimization toolboxes such as SeDuMi and SDPT3 [121]. However, the solution of (5.8) may not be unique and the following issue need to be addressed such that it converges to the right solution.

Rank relaxation of Z and S

Due to the semidefinite relaxation, the rank constraints of the matrices $\boldsymbol{Z}$ and $\boldsymbol{S}$ (which are supposed to be of rank 1) are lifted. And hence, they can take on any rank value. In fact, the solution always converges to the maximum rank case and chooses the corresponding $\boldsymbol{g}$, $\boldsymbol{b}_{\mathrm{t}}$ and $\boldsymbol{b}_{\mathrm{r}}$ such that the objective function is minimized. To discourage the estimator from converging to a solution with higher dimensions, we add the following penalty term in the objective function

$$\eta(\mathrm{Tr}\{\tilde{\boldsymbol{Z}}\} + \mathrm{Tr}\{\tilde{\boldsymbol{S}}\}), \tag{5.9}$$

where $\tilde{\boldsymbol{Z}}$ represents the first $N_{\mathrm{r}}N_{\mathrm{t}}$ block matrix of $\boldsymbol{Z}$ and $\tilde{\boldsymbol{S}}$ represents the first $N_{\mathrm{r}}N_{\mathrm{r}}$ block matrix of $\boldsymbol{S}$. The choice of the penalization term η depends on the expected range between the nodes in the network. If the agents and the anchors are placed in a large volume, then η need to be chosen small such that the estimator has enough freedom to chose $\boldsymbol{Z}$ and $\boldsymbol{S}$ which can have higher dimensions. On the other hand, if they are placed in a small confined volume, η needs to be chosen small. Here, it is worth to make a remark that the other elements of $\boldsymbol{Z}$ and $\boldsymbol{S}$ can be included in the penalization term. However, one needs to have knowledge of the ranging offset values to choose the right penalization coefficient. As it is difficult in practice to get this knowledge, we opt to use the penalization term in (5.9).

Ambiguous solution for the synchronization classes PS-Async and FS-Async

As it is discussed in the simulation results in Section 5.8, the estimator in (5.8) including the penalization term in (5.9) provides a reasonable accuracy except for synchronization classes PS-Async and FS-Async (where $\boldsymbol{b}_{\mathrm{t}}$ is unknown). However, for the synchronization classes PS-Async and FS-Async, the solution is not unique. The reason behind this ambiguity can be explained as follows.

Consider the first term of the objective function in (5.8), i.e. $\mathrm{Tr}\left\{\boldsymbol{\Sigma}_{\mathrm{d}}^{-1}\left(\boldsymbol{d}\boldsymbol{d}^{T}+\boldsymbol{Q}\boldsymbol{Z}\boldsymbol{Q}^{T}-2\boldsymbol{d}(\boldsymbol{g}+\boldsymbol{\Gamma}_{\mathrm{t}}\boldsymbol{b}_{\mathrm{t}}+\boldsymbol{\Gamma}_{\mathrm{r}}\boldsymbol{b}_{\mathrm{r}})^{T}\right)\right\}$. We note that, for a given objective function value, any arbitrary value that is added on $\boldsymbol{b}_{\mathrm{t}}$ can be compensated by subtracting the right value on $\boldsymbol{g}$ without affecting the objective function value and the constraints of the estimator. This means that the solution of the SDP problem in (5.8) is not unique and hence, further information is required to avoid this ambiguity.

We propose to take a "rough" distance measurement (which is free from ranging offsets) between one of the anchors and the N_{t} agent locations. Such measurement can be taken by any distance measurement tool (e.g. measurement tape). Let, $\boldsymbol{\gamma}$ be such N_{t} distance measurements between anchor 1 and the N_{t} agent locations. Then, the following constraint can be included in (5.8) to avoid this ambiguity

$$(\boldsymbol{g}[mN_{\mathrm{r}}+1]-\boldsymbol{\gamma}[m])^{2}\leq\rho^{2},\quad\forall m, \tag{5.10}$$

where ρ is chosen proportional to the error of the distance measurements.

As discussed in the simulation results, the calibration result (which is the SDP solution refined with the ML estimator) is less sensitive to the errors in the rough distance measurement $\boldsymbol{\gamma}$. This is because the ML estimator does not have the aforementioned ambiguity problem. One can easily see this from the equivalent expression of the ML estimator in (5.7). We see that the values of $\boldsymbol{b}_\mathrm{t}$ and $\boldsymbol{g}$ in the objective function can not be chosen arbitrary as they are constrained by the equality constraint in (5.7b).

X is loosely constrained

Due to the semidefinite relaxation, in (5.8), we note that the variable $\boldsymbol{X}$ is loosely constrained. In fact $\boldsymbol{X}$ can be chosen as an all zero matrix and still fulfills its constraints for any value of $\boldsymbol{Y}$. Hence, the estimates of the anchor and the agent locations need to be extracted from $\boldsymbol{Y}$. Let $\hat{\boldsymbol{Y}}$ be the estimate of $\boldsymbol{Y}$ and its eigenvalue decomposition is given by $\hat{\boldsymbol{Y}} = \boldsymbol{U}\boldsymbol{D}\boldsymbol{U}^T$. The corresponding estimate of the anchor and the agent locations $\hat{\boldsymbol{X}}$ is then given by

$$\hat{\boldsymbol{X}} = \tilde{\boldsymbol{D}}\boldsymbol{U}^T, \tag{5.11}$$

where $\tilde{\boldsymbol{D}}$ is defined as a matrix that contains the first 3 rows of $\boldsymbol{D}^{1/2}$. We further note that since the choice of the unitary matrix $\boldsymbol{U}$ is arbitrary, the estimates $\hat{\boldsymbol{X}}$ are described in a coordinate system which is a 3D rotated version of the original coordinate system. Hence, the estimate $\hat{\boldsymbol{X}}$ needs to be rotated to the coordinate system that is described in (5.2), i.e. anchor 1 is on the origin, anchor 2 is on the x-axis, and anchor 1, 2 and 3 form the xy-plane.

Taking into account the above points, the proposed calibration method can be summarized as in Algorithm 3.

Algorithm 3 Calibration algorithm.

1: Gather the range measurements $\boldsymbol{d}$ and $\boldsymbol{f}$.
2: Add the penalization term in (5.9) to the objective function of (5.8) .
3: **if** Synchronization class is PS-Async or FS-Async **then**
4:     Take the distance measurement γ.
5:     Include the constraints in (5.10) to (5.8).
6: **end if**
7: Solve the optimization problem in (5.8).
8: Calculate $\hat{\boldsymbol{X}}$ from $\hat{\boldsymbol{Y}}$ according to (5.11).
9: Rotate the coordinate system of $\hat{\boldsymbol{X}}$ to the coordinate system described in (5.2).
10: Refine the estimates with the ML estimator in (5.4).

5.6. Performance Metric of the ML Estimator

The straight forward metric to quantify the performance of the anchor position estimates of the proposed calibration method is to use the RMSE, defined as

$$\mathrm{RMSE}(\hat{\boldsymbol{r}}) = \sqrt{\frac{1}{N_\mathrm{r}}\mathrm{Tr}\left\{\mathbb{E}\left\{(\boldsymbol{r}-\hat{\boldsymbol{r}})(\boldsymbol{r}-\hat{\boldsymbol{r}})^T\right\}\right\}} = \sqrt{\frac{1}{N_\mathrm{r}}\sum_{n=1}^{N_\mathrm{r}}\mathbb{E}\left\{\|\boldsymbol{r}_n-\hat{\boldsymbol{r}}_n\|^2\right\}}, \tag{5.12}$$

where the expectation is taken across different ranging error realization and different observations of the agent locations.

Note however that the metrics that appear in the objective function of the estimator in (5.4) are the distances between the anchors and the agents and hence, the estimator tries to find distances that minimize the objective function. In other words, the ML estimator in (5.4) estimates a geometric shape which is close to the geometric shape formed by the true anchor and agent locations. The constraint on the anchors ($\boldsymbol{c}_\mathrm{ref}(\boldsymbol{r},\boldsymbol{b}_\mathrm{r}) = \boldsymbol{0}$) then makes sure that the vertices of the estimated shape (which represent either an estimated anchor or agent location) are expressed in 3D coordinate points. Hence, the RMSE of the anchor position estimates defined in (5.12) is dependent on the choice of anchors which are used to define the reference coordinate system. For example, if anchor 1 and anchor 2 are very close to each other, a small estimation error of anchor 2 can considerably divert the x-axis of the reference coordinate system and hence result in a pessimistic RMSE performance even if the other anchors are estimated correctly.

Another performance metric that one can define is a measure of the similarity between the true and the estimated geometric shape of the anchors. For this we rotate and translate the estimated anchor locations such that their shape is aligned as close as possible to the true shape. Mathematically speaking, we want to find a rotation matrix $\boldsymbol{V}$ and a translation vector $\boldsymbol{v}$ which minimize the squared error between the estimated anchor locations and the true anchor locations, i.e.

$$\{\hat{\boldsymbol{V}},\hat{\boldsymbol{v}}\} = \arg\min_{\boldsymbol{V},\boldsymbol{v}}\sum_{n=1}^{N_\mathrm{r}}\|\boldsymbol{r}_n-(\boldsymbol{V}\hat{\boldsymbol{r}}_n+\boldsymbol{v})\|^2. \tag{5.13}$$

For a given trial rotation matrix $\boldsymbol{V}'$, the objective function of the estimator in (5.13) take the form

$$\psi(\boldsymbol{v}) = \sum_{n=1}^{N_\mathrm{r}} \left\| \boldsymbol{r}_n - (\boldsymbol{V}'\hat{\boldsymbol{r}}_n + \boldsymbol{v}) \right\|^2 .$$

Hence, the optimum translation vector $\boldsymbol{v}^*$ that solves (5.13) satisfies

$$\left.\frac{\partial\psi(\boldsymbol{v})}{\partial\boldsymbol{v}}\right|_{\boldsymbol{v}=\boldsymbol{v}^*} = -2\sum_{n=1}^{N_\mathrm{r}} \left(\boldsymbol{r}_n - (\boldsymbol{V}'\hat{\boldsymbol{r}}_n + \boldsymbol{v}^*)\right)^T = \boldsymbol{0}$$

$$\Rightarrow \boldsymbol{v}^* = \frac{1}{N_\mathrm{r}}\sum_{n=1}^{N_\mathrm{r}} (\boldsymbol{r}_n - \boldsymbol{V}'\hat{\boldsymbol{r}}_n) \tag{5.14}$$

Inserting (5.14) into (5.13) results in an equivalent estimator for the optimum rotation matrix $\boldsymbol{V}^*$ (the optimum translation vector is implicitly estimated) which takes the from

$$\boldsymbol{V}^* = \arg\min_{\boldsymbol{V}} \sum_{n=1}^{N_\mathrm{r}} \left\| \left(\boldsymbol{r}_n - \tfrac{1}{N_\mathrm{r}}\sum_{k=1}^{N_\mathrm{r}} \boldsymbol{r}_k\right) - \boldsymbol{V}\left(\hat{\boldsymbol{r}}_n - \tfrac{1}{N_\mathrm{r}}\sum_{k=1}^{N_\mathrm{r}} \hat{\boldsymbol{r}}_k\right) \right\|^2 . \tag{5.15}$$

We now note that the problem in (5.15) is equivalent to Whab's problem presented in [129]. The optimum rotation matrix $\boldsymbol{V}^*$ that solves (5.15) is given by [130]

$$\boldsymbol{V}^* = \boldsymbol{\Pi}\boldsymbol{\Omega}^T,$$

where $\boldsymbol{\Pi}$ and $\boldsymbol{\Omega}$ are orthogonal matrices which form the singular value decomposition of $\sum_{n=1}^{N_\mathrm{r}}(\boldsymbol{r}_n - \frac{1}{N_\mathrm{r}}\sum_{k=1}^{N_\mathrm{r}} \boldsymbol{r}_k)(\hat{\boldsymbol{r}}_n - \frac{1}{N_\mathrm{r}}\sum_{k=1}^{N_\mathrm{r}} \hat{\boldsymbol{r}}_k)^T = \boldsymbol{\Omega}\boldsymbol{\Upsilon}\boldsymbol{\Pi}^T$, with a diagonal matrix $\boldsymbol{\Upsilon}$ that contains the singular values on its diagonal. Given $\boldsymbol{V}^*$, the optimum translation vector $\boldsymbol{v}^*$ can be determined by inserting $\boldsymbol{V}^*$ in (5.14).

Define $\hat{\boldsymbol{r}}_n^{(\mathrm{pp})} = \boldsymbol{V}^*\hat{\boldsymbol{r}}_n + \boldsymbol{v}^*$, which is the location estimate of anchor n after post-processing (rotation and translation). The RMSE of the vector of the post-processed anchor positions estimates $\hat{\boldsymbol{r}}^{(\mathrm{pp})}$ can then be defined as

$$\mathrm{RMSE}\left(\hat{\boldsymbol{r}}^{(\mathrm{pp})}\right) = \sqrt{\frac{1}{N_\mathrm{r}}\sum_{n=1}^{N_\mathrm{r}} \mathbb{E}\left\{\left\|\boldsymbol{r}_n - \hat{\boldsymbol{r}}_n^{(\mathrm{pp})}\right\|^2\right\}}, \tag{5.16}$$

This performance metric can serve as a measure of how well the geometric shape of the anchor is estimated, which is independent of the choice of anchors that are used to define the reference coordinate system. It is however not straightforward to calculate the theoretical lower bound for this performance metric because the rotation matrix $\boldsymbol{V}^*$

depends on the instantaneous anchor positions estimate $\hat{\boldsymbol{r}}$ and hence, the instantaneous realization of the range measurement error.

In Section 5.8, the performance of the ML estimator is evaluated using both metrics. The comparison of the two metrics shows that the metric in (5.12) is more pessimistic than the metric in (5.16). However, Since the derivation of the performance bound using the metric in (5.16) is difficult, in the next section the CRLB of the ML estimator is derived using the performance metric in (5.12).

5.7. Performance Bound

In this section, we derive the performance bound of the ML estimator for the performance metric in (5.12). To this end, we follow the approaches in Section 3.5 and Section 4.5 to derive the constrained CRLB of the wanted parameters for the estimator that jointly estimates both the wanted and unwanted parameters under parameter constraints.

We divide the vector of unknown parameters into two and define a vector of wanted parameters $\boldsymbol{\theta}_1 = \left[\boldsymbol{r}^T, \boldsymbol{b}_{\mathrm{r}}^T\right]^T$ and a vector of nuisance parameters $\boldsymbol{\theta}_2 = \left[\boldsymbol{t}^T, \boldsymbol{b}_{\mathrm{t}}^T\right]^T$. First, we calculate the information about $\boldsymbol{\theta}_1$ that is contained in the range measurement vector, a.k.a. the Fisher information matrix (FIM) of $\boldsymbol{\theta}_1$. Then we incorporate the constraints to derive the constrained CRLB on the RMSE of the wanted parameter estimates.

Given the joint PDF (or the likelihood function) in (5.1), the log-likelihood takes the form

$$\begin{aligned}\mathcal{L}(\boldsymbol{d}, \boldsymbol{f} | \boldsymbol{r}, \boldsymbol{t}, \boldsymbol{b}_{\mathrm{r}}, \boldsymbol{b}_{\mathrm{t}}) &= \ln\left(p(\boldsymbol{d}, \boldsymbol{f} | \boldsymbol{r}, \boldsymbol{t}, \boldsymbol{b}_{\mathrm{r}}, \boldsymbol{b}_{\mathrm{t}})\right) \\ &= -\frac{1}{2}\left(\boldsymbol{d} - \boldsymbol{g} - \boldsymbol{\Gamma}_{\mathrm{t}}\boldsymbol{b}_{\mathrm{t}} - \boldsymbol{\Gamma}_{\mathrm{r}}\boldsymbol{b}_{\mathrm{r}}\right)^T \boldsymbol{\Sigma}_{\mathrm{d}}^{-1}\left(\boldsymbol{d} - \boldsymbol{g} - \boldsymbol{\Gamma}_{\mathrm{t}}\boldsymbol{b}_{\mathrm{t}} - \boldsymbol{\Gamma}_{\mathrm{r}}\boldsymbol{b}_{\mathrm{r}}\right) \\ &\quad - \frac{1}{2}\left(\boldsymbol{f} - \boldsymbol{h} - \boldsymbol{\Lambda}\boldsymbol{b}_{\mathrm{r}}\right)^T \boldsymbol{\Sigma}_{\mathrm{f}}^{-1}\left(\boldsymbol{f} - \boldsymbol{h} - \boldsymbol{\Lambda}\boldsymbol{b}_{\mathrm{r}}\right) \\ &\quad + \ln\left(\frac{|\boldsymbol{\Sigma}_{\mathrm{d}}|^{-\frac{1}{2}}}{(2\pi)^{\frac{N_{\mathrm{t}}N_{\mathrm{r}}}{2}}} \times \frac{|\boldsymbol{\Sigma}_{\mathrm{f}}|^{-\frac{1}{2}}}{(2\pi)^{\frac{N_{\mathrm{r}}N_{\mathrm{r}}}{2}}}\right).\end{aligned} \tag{5.17}$$

The FIM of all the unknown parameters $\boldsymbol{\theta} = \left[\boldsymbol{\theta}_1^T, \boldsymbol{\theta}_2^T\right]^T$ is then given by

$$\boldsymbol{J} = \mathbb{E}\left\{\left(\frac{\partial \mathcal{L}}{\partial \boldsymbol{\theta}}\right)^T \frac{\partial \mathcal{L}}{\partial \boldsymbol{\theta}}\right\} \triangleq \begin{bmatrix} \boldsymbol{J}_1 & \boldsymbol{J}_2 \\ \boldsymbol{J}_2^T & \boldsymbol{J}_3 \end{bmatrix}, \tag{5.18}$$

where we have defined the sub-matrices of the FIM as $\boldsymbol{J}_1 = \mathbb{E}\{(\frac{\partial \mathcal{L}}{\partial \boldsymbol{\theta}_1})^T \frac{\partial \mathcal{L}}{\partial \boldsymbol{\theta}_1}\}$, $\boldsymbol{J}_2 = \mathbb{E}\{(\frac{\partial \mathcal{L}}{\partial \boldsymbol{\theta}_1})^T \frac{\partial \mathcal{L}}{\partial \boldsymbol{\theta}_2}\}$ and $\boldsymbol{J}_3 = \mathbb{E}\{(\frac{\partial \mathcal{L}}{\partial \boldsymbol{\theta}_2})^T \frac{\partial \mathcal{L}}{\partial \boldsymbol{\theta}_2}\}$. The sub-matrices $\boldsymbol{J}_1$, $\boldsymbol{J}_2$ and $\boldsymbol{J}_3$ are are calculated in Appendix D.3.

Using the result in (3.28), we note that the matrix $\boldsymbol{J}_{\boldsymbol{\theta}_1} = \boldsymbol{J}_1 - \boldsymbol{J}_2 \boldsymbol{J}_3^{-1} \boldsymbol{J}_2^T$ contains all the information about $\boldsymbol{\theta}_1$ that is contained in $\boldsymbol{J}$. Hence, the covariance matrix of any unbiased estimate of $\boldsymbol{\theta}_1$ that does not take the constraints into account satisfies

$$\mathbb{E}\left\{\left(\hat{\boldsymbol{\theta}}_1 - \boldsymbol{\theta}_1\right)\left(\hat{\boldsymbol{\theta}}_1 - \boldsymbol{\theta}_1\right)^T\right\} \succeq \boldsymbol{J}_{\boldsymbol{\theta}_1}^{-1}. \tag{5.19}$$

Next we take into account the constraint in (5.3) to derive the constrained CRLB of the wanted parameters $\boldsymbol{\theta}_1$. Define a constraint gradient matrix $\boldsymbol{G} = \frac{\partial(\boldsymbol{c}_{\text{ref}}(\boldsymbol{\theta}_1))}{\partial \boldsymbol{\theta}_1}$. For example, the constraint gradient matrix for the synchronization class FS-Async takes the form[2]

$$\boldsymbol{G} = \frac{\partial(\boldsymbol{c}_{\text{ref}}(\boldsymbol{\theta}_1))}{\partial \boldsymbol{\theta}_1} = \begin{bmatrix} 1\,0\,0\,0\,0\,0\,0\,0\,0 & & 0 & \\ 0\,1\,0\,0\,0\,0\,0\,0\,0 & & 0 & \\ 0\,0\,1\,0\,0\,0\,0\,0\,0 & \mathbf{0}_{7\times(3N_\text{r}-9)} & 0 & \mathbf{0}_{7\times(N_\text{r}-1)} \\ 0\,0\,0\,0\,1\,0\,0\,0\,0 & & 0 & \\ 0\,0\,0\,0\,0\,1\,0\,0\,0 & & 0 & \\ 0\,0\,0\,0\,0\,0\,0\,0\,1 & & 0 & \\ 0\,0\,0\,0\,0\,0\,0\,0\,0 & & 1 & \end{bmatrix}.$$

The covariance matrix of any unbiased estimate of $\boldsymbol{\theta}_1$ that take into account the constraints then satisfies

$$\mathbb{E}\left\{\left(\hat{\boldsymbol{\theta}}_1 - \boldsymbol{\theta}_1\right)\left(\hat{\boldsymbol{\theta}}_1 - \boldsymbol{\theta}_1\right)^T\right\} \succeq \boldsymbol{U}\left(\boldsymbol{U}^T \boldsymbol{J}_{\boldsymbol{\theta}_1} \boldsymbol{U}\right)^{-1} \boldsymbol{U}^T, \tag{5.20}$$

where $\boldsymbol{U}$ is a matrix whose columns form the orthonormal basis for the null space of $\boldsymbol{G}$, i.e. $\boldsymbol{G}\boldsymbol{U} = \mathbf{0}$. From (5.20), we see that the RMSE of the anchor location estimates is lower bounded by

$$\text{RMSE\_LB}(\boldsymbol{r}) = \sqrt{\frac{1}{N_\text{t}} \text{Tr}\left\{\left[\boldsymbol{U}\left(\boldsymbol{U}^T \boldsymbol{J}_{\boldsymbol{\theta}_1} \boldsymbol{U}\right)^{-1} \boldsymbol{U}^T\right]_{3N_\text{r} \times 3N_\text{r}}\right\}}. \tag{5.21}$$

5.8. Performance Evaluation

In this section, we discuss numerical results that assess the performance of the calibration algorithm. We consider the simulation setup where the nodes are placed as shown in Figure 3.4a. The $N_\text{r} = 6$ anchors are located at $\boldsymbol{r}_1 =$

[2]The constraint gradient matrix for the other synchronization case can be calculated similarly.

$[0,0,0]^T, \boldsymbol{r}_2 = [5\,\mathrm{m},0,0]^T, \boldsymbol{r}_3 = [-5\,\mathrm{m},5\,\mathrm{m},0]^T, \boldsymbol{r}_4 = [5\,\mathrm{m},-5\,\mathrm{m},-5\,\mathrm{m}]^T, \boldsymbol{r}_5 = [-5\,\mathrm{m},5\,\mathrm{m},5\,\mathrm{m}]^T$, and $\boldsymbol{r}_6 = [5\,\mathrm{m},5\,\mathrm{m},-5\,\mathrm{m}]^T$. The agent is randomly moved to $N_\mathrm{t} = 30$ agent locations inside a $10\,\mathrm{m} \times 10\,\mathrm{m} \times 10\,\mathrm{m}$ cube centered at the origin. The ranging offsets of the anchors and the agents is chosen randomly from the range $[-100\,\mathrm{m}, 100\,\mathrm{m}]$. Furthermore, the range measurement error of both between the anchors and the agents, and between the anchors themselves are assumed have the same standard deviation of 1 cm.

Comparison of different clock synchronization classes

Figure 5.6 shows the empirical cumulative density function (CDF) of the RMSE of the anchor location estimates with the proposed calibration method. To ease the readability of the plots, we chose a set of representative synchronization classes, namely PS-PS, FS-FS and FS-Async. The penalization coefficient $\eta = 10^{-4}$ is chosen. To understand its impact, the distance measurement $\boldsymbol{\gamma}$ (and hence the constraint in (5.10)), which is required for the synchronization class FS-Async, is not considered for the calibration.

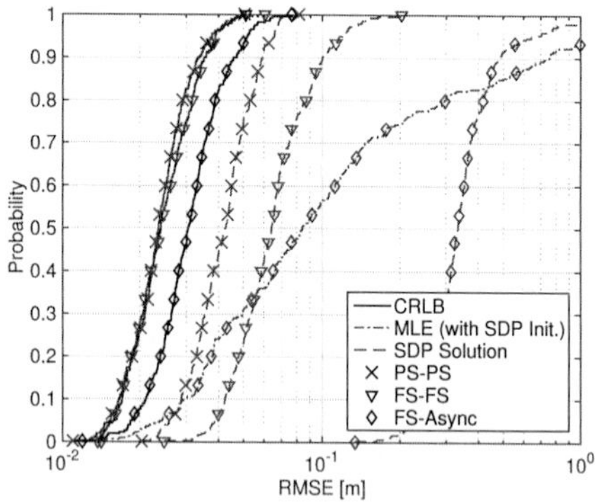

Figure 5.6.: Empirical CDF of the RMSE of the anchor position estimates for a selected set of synchronization classes.

From the figure, we notice that the median (50 %) of the anchor location estimates from the SDP solution have a RMSE of less than 4.5 cm (PS-PS) and 6.5 cm (FS-FS). Refining the SDP solution with the ML estimator reduces the median value of the RMSE to 2.5 cm, which matches the corresponding CRLB. For the case of FS-Async, on the other hand, the SDP solution has a median RMSE of around 33 cm. And the

ML estimator which is initialized with the SDP solution performs poorly compared to the CRLB. This is clearly because, without including the constraint in (5.10), the SDP solution in (5.8) can not uniquely estimate the anchor locations. Hence, the ML estimator which is initialized with this solution may converge to the wrong local minimum.

Figure 5.7 shows the empirical CDF the RMSE of the anchor location estimates for the case of FS-Async when considering the constraint in (5.10). The N_t "rough" distance measurements (from all agent positions to anchor 1) are modeled as the true distance perturbed by a zero mean Gaussian error with variance ρ^2, i.e. $\gamma[m] \sim \mathcal{N}(\boldsymbol{g}[mN_\mathrm{r}+1], \rho^2), \forall m$. As expected, the performance of the SDP solution gets worse as ρ increases. It is interesting to note however that the ML estimates initialized with the respective SDP solutions have a similar performance (a median RMSE of around 3 cm). This indicates that even for the case when $\rho = 20\,\mathrm{cm}$, the SDP solution is close to the parameter value corresponding to the global minimum of the objective function of the ML estimator. Hence, even though the SDP solution is affected by the accuracy of the distance measurement $\boldsymbol{\gamma}$, the final calibration output (which is the ML estimate) is insensitive to the accuracy of $\boldsymbol{\gamma}$.

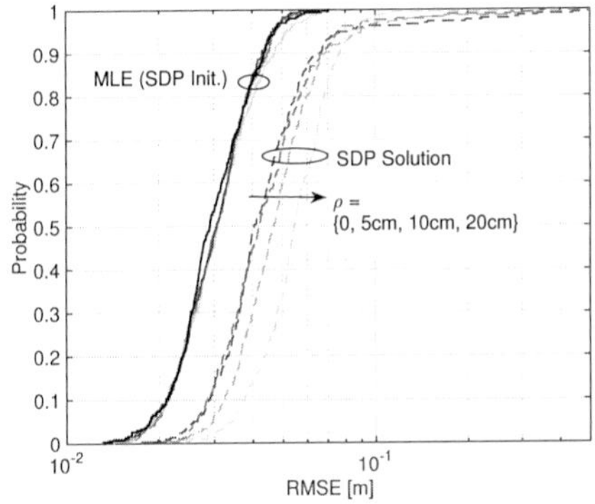

Figure 5.7.: FS-Async: Empirical CDF of the RMSE of the anchor location estimates with distance measurement $\boldsymbol{\gamma}$ having different accuracies.

For the simulation results in Figure 5.6 and Figure 5.7, the performance metric that is used is the RMSE of the anchor location estimates without post-processing, defined in (5.12). However, as discussed in Section 5.6, the ML solution of the calibration problem estimates a geometric shape, where the anchors and the agents are its vertices. The best suited metric that quantifies the similarity between the estimated geometric shape and the true geometric shape of the anchors and the agents is given in (5.16), which corresponds to the RMSE of the anchor position estimates after post-processing.

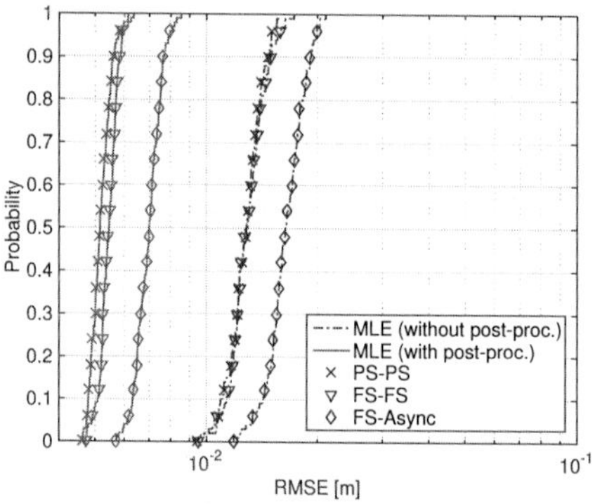

Figure 5.8.: Empirical CDF of the RMSE of the ML estimates of the agents with and without processing.

Figure 5.8 compares the RMSE of the ML estimates of the anchor locations with and without post processing. For the synchronization class FS-Async, the distance measurement γ is considered with $\rho = 20\,\text{cm}$. The blue (dash-dot) lines denote the ML estimator without post-processing, i.e. the RMSE defined in (5.12). The magenta (solid) lines denote the ML estimator with post-processing, i.e. the RMSE defined in (5.16).

We see that the median RMSE of the anchor location estimates without post-processing is 1.3 cm (PS-PS and FS-FS) and 1.6 cm (FS-Async). When post-processing is performed, the median RMSE is reduced to 5 mm (PS-PS and FS-FS) and 7 mm (FS-Async). This shows that the RMSE of the anchor location estimates without post-processing is a pessimistic performance metric. Nevertheless, we use this metric for our analysis as it is easier to derive its corresponding CRLB.

Calibration performance for varying N_r and N_t

The accuracy of the calibration output can be improved by increasing the number of range measurements. This can be achieved by either increasing the number of anchors N_r or by increasing the number of agent locations N_t. Figure 5.9 shows the CRLB of the anchor location estimates for varying N_r and N_t, for synchronization classes PS-PS, FS-FS and FS-Async. The considered anchor locations are given in Table 5.3.

Table 5.3.: Anchor locations. All values are in meters.

$\boldsymbol{r}_1 = [0, 0, 0]^T$	$\boldsymbol{r}_2 = [5, 0, 0]^T$	$\boldsymbol{r}_3 = [-5, 5, 0]^T$
$\boldsymbol{r}_4 = [-5, -5, 5]^T$	$\boldsymbol{r}_5 = [5, 5, -5]^T$	$\boldsymbol{r}_6 = [5, -5, -5]^T$
$\boldsymbol{r}_7 = [-7.5, 0, -7.5]^T$	$\boldsymbol{r}_8 = [7.5, 0, 7.5]^T$	$\boldsymbol{r}_9 = [0, -7.5, 7.5]^T$
$\boldsymbol{r}_{10} = [0, 7.5, -7.5]^T$	$\boldsymbol{r}_{11} = [10, -10, -10]^T$	$\boldsymbol{r}_{12} = [-10, -10, 10]^T$

As an example, consider the synchronization class FS-Async, i.e. Figure 5.9e and Figure 5.9f. A RMSE_LB of 1 cm can be achieved at $N_\mathrm{r} = 8$ and $N_\mathrm{t} = 55$, or at $N_\mathrm{r} = 6$ and $N_\mathrm{t} = 210$. Hence, for a given system setup (where N_r is fixed), a target RMSE of the anchor location estimates can be achieved by gathering range measurements from enough number of agent locations N_t. Although this is true from information theoretic perspective, in practice, the choice of N_t is constrained by the computational capability of the system. As N_t increases, the SDP solution in (5.8) and the ML solution (5.4) become computationally intensive. Hence, a trade-off between the target RMSE and computational complexity need to be made.

Calibration with only "anchor-to-agent" range measurements

The results discussed above all consider both the range measurement between the anchors and the agents, and between the anchors themselves. However, for some applications, where the anchors are implemented as only transmitters or receivers, the range measurements between two anchors is not available. For example, for the considered human posture capturing setup, where the anchors are a low-complexity relays, the range between the anchors can not be measured.

Figure 5.10 shows the empirical CDF of the anchor location estimates when only the range measurement between the anchors and the agents is considered. The RMSE values are calculated without the post-processing step. For the synchronization class FS-Async, the distance measurement γ (with $\rho = 20\,\mathrm{cm}$) is considered.

First consider the synchronization classes PS-PS and FS-FS. We see that the ML estimates of the anchor locations match their corresponding CRLB. Only less 5 % of the estimates for the FS-FS case diverge from the CRLB, which may mean that the SDP initialization is not close enough to the global optimum point for these cases. Comparing this with the corresponding result in Figure 5.6, we note that there is

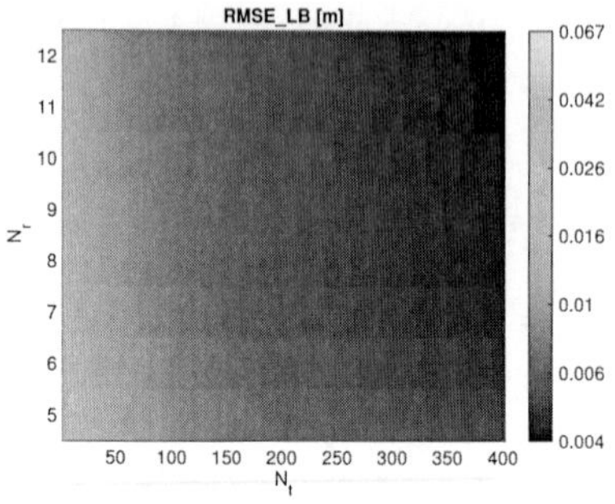

(a) Surface plot: PS-PS

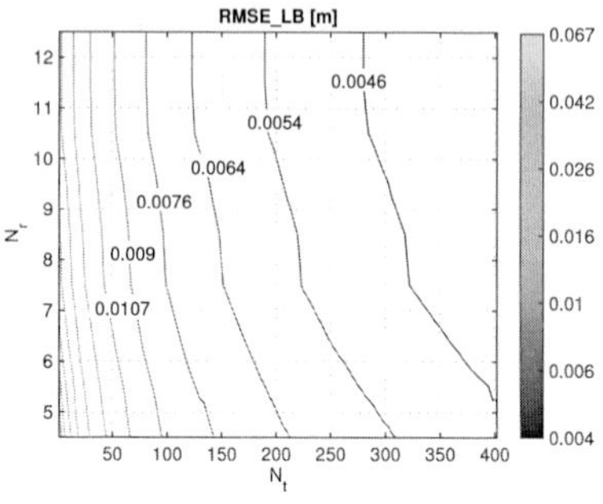

(b) Contour plot: PS-PS

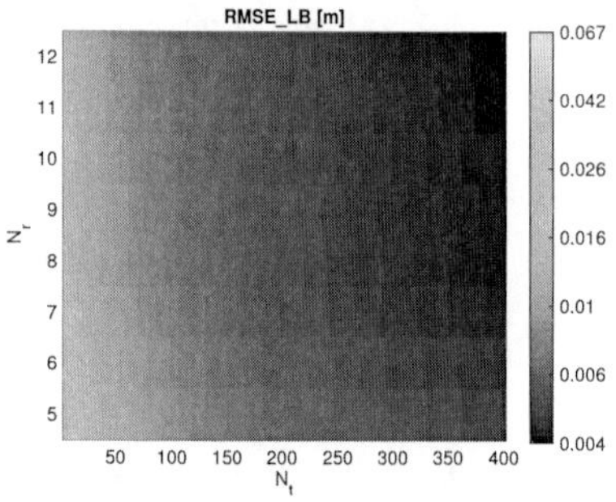

(c) Surface plot: FS-FS

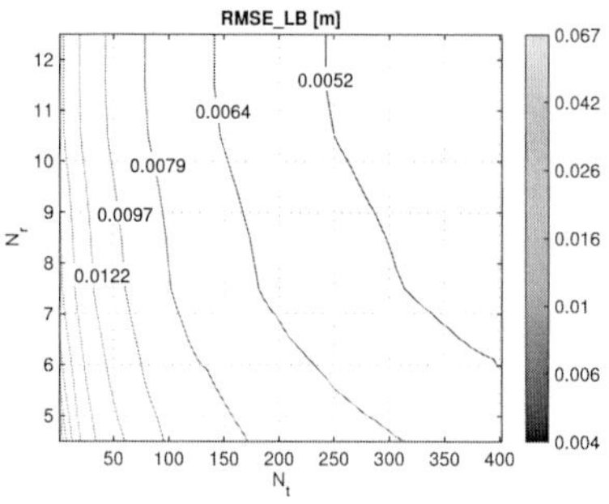

(d) Contour plot: FS-FS

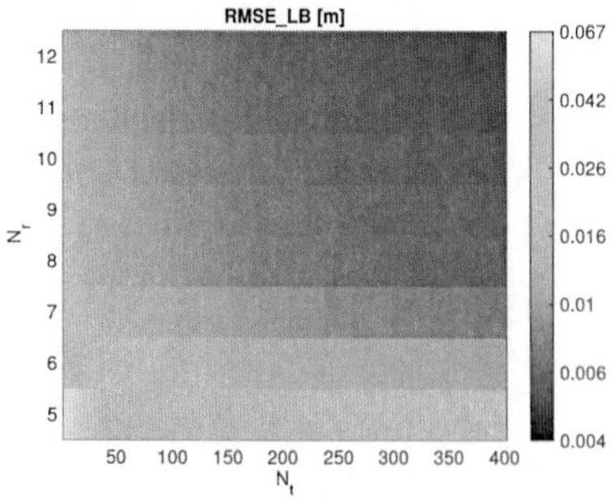

(e) Surface plot: FS-Async

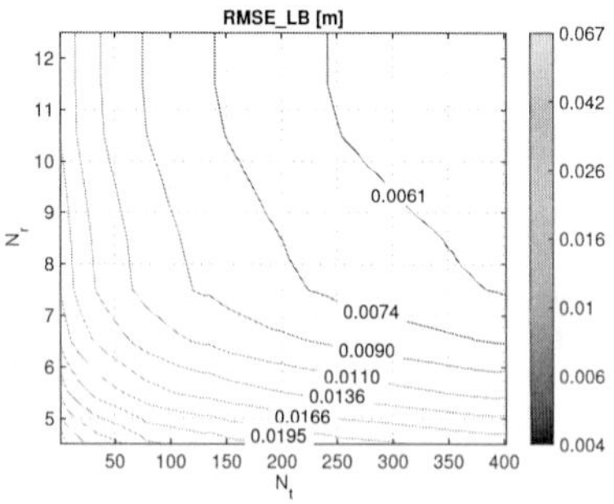

(f) Contour plot: FS-Async

Figure 5.9.: CRLB of the anchor location estimates for varying N_r and N_t.

a drop in the calibration accuracy. This drop in accuracy can be compensated by considering more agent locations in N_t. Hence, for the synchronization classes PS-

PS and FS-FS, accurate calibration can be performed only with range measurements between the agents and the anchors.

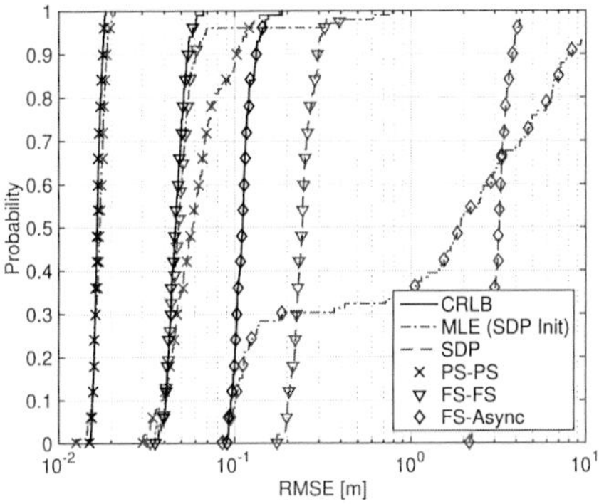

Figure 5.10.: Empirical CDF of the RMSE of the anchor position estimates for a selected synchronization classes. Only range measurements between the anchors and the agents is considered.

For the synchronization class FS-Async however, more than 70 % of the ML estimates completely diverge from the CRLB. Looking at the result in Figure 5.10, it is clear that the calibration output for this synchronization class is unacceptable. The reason behind this is that the location information from the range measurements is not sufficient enough for the SDP estimator to provide a solution which is close to the global minimum of the ML estimator objective function. As shown in Chapter 6, this problem can be alleviated by providing more location information to the calibration algorithm, for example considering agent location constraints.

5.9. Summary

A calibration method that estimates the locations and clock offsets of the anchors based on the range measurements of the localization system is proposed. The locations of the agents are not surveyed. Hence, multiple agent locations can be realized by a single moving agent, which makes the calibration procedure simple and cost effective. The calibration problem is formulated such that different practically relevant clock synchronization cases can fit into the framework. The ML solution of the calibration problem, which is non-convex, is relaxed to SDP problem.

Considering a measurement system that can provide both anchor to anchor and agent to anchor range measurements, simulation results show that the SDP solution can serve as a good initialization for the ML estimator. However, for the case when the agents are asynchronous, i.e. synchronization classes PS-Async and FS-Async, the SDP solution is not unique. To alleviate this problem, we propose to take N_t "rough" distance measurements between the agent locations and one of the anchors. It is shown that the calibration result (which is the SDP solution refined with the ML estimator) is less sensitive to the accuracy of these additional distance measurements.

For the measurement system that can only provide agent to anchor range measurements on the other hand, the calibration result for the synchronization class FS-Async is poor. In Chapter 6, it is shown that taking into account the agent location constraints is a key enabler for this case.

6. Performance Evaluation of the Human Posture Capturing System

The proposed localization methods in Chapter 3 and Chapter 4 and the self-calibration method in Chapter 5 are presented in the general framework of wireless sensor network localization. One of the motivations behind this approach is to benefit from the ideas of existing works. Likewise, the methods that are proposed in this thesis can be readily applied to other systems which have similar types of problems. Although such a generic framework is used, as explained in Section 1.5, the considered system setup, the localization and calibration problems and the proposed solutions are motivated by the human posture capturing system. In this chapter[1], we evaluate the performance of the proposed localization and calibration methods for the specific setup of the human posture capturing system. Numerical simulation results that give insight about the tradeoffs that are involved in the design of the system parameters are discussed.

To this end, the remainder of this chapter is organized as follows. In Section 6.1, considering phase synchronous anchors with known locations, the performance of the localization method that accounts the kinematic constraints of the body is discussed. The performance of the proposed self-calibration method for the specific setup of the human posture capturing system is then evaluated in Section 6.2. The impact of anchor location uncertainties (because of the calibration error or anchor movements) on the localization performance is discussed in Section 6.3. The robustness of the localization method which takes into account such anchor location uncertainties is also evaluated.

[1]Parts of this chapter have been published in [105].

6.1. Localization Accounting Body Kinematic Constraints

To understand the impact of the topology of the agents on the estimator performance, we will first consider a 2D setup. More specifically, we consider the two arm topologies that are shown in Figure 6.1. For both arm topologies, the $N_\mathrm{r} = 4$ anchors are located at

$$\boldsymbol{r}_1 = [0, 0]^T, \boldsymbol{r}_2 = [0, 0.5\,\mathrm{m}]^T, \boldsymbol{r}_3 = [0.25\,\mathrm{m}, 0.25\,\mathrm{m}]^T \text{ and } \boldsymbol{r}_4 = [0.25\,\mathrm{m}, -0.25\,\mathrm{m}]^T.$$

The shoulder joint is located at $\boldsymbol{s} = [-0.1\,\mathrm{m}, 0.3\,\mathrm{m}]^T$. For Arm Topology 1 (Figure 6.1a), agent 1 is located at $\boldsymbol{t}_1 = [-0.1\,\mathrm{m}, 0.6\,\mathrm{m}]$ and agent 2 is located at $\boldsymbol{t}_2 = [-0.1\,\mathrm{m}, 0.9\,\mathrm{m}]$. Whereas for Arm Topology 2 (Figure 6.1b), agent 1 is located at the same position $\boldsymbol{t}_1 = [-0.1\,\mathrm{m}, 0.6\,\mathrm{m}]$ but agent 2 is located at $\boldsymbol{t}_2 = [0.2\,\mathrm{m}, 0.6\,\mathrm{m}]$. The length of the upper-arm and the forearm are equal $l_1 = l_2 = 0.3\,\mathrm{m}$. The range measurement errors are assumed to be i.i.d. with a standard deviation $\sigma_{\text{range}} = 1\,\mathrm{cm}$.

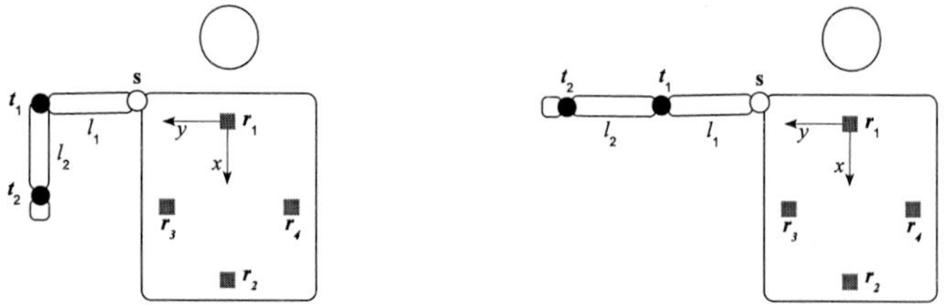

(a) Arm Topology 1

(b) Arm Topology 2

Figure 6.1.: Exemplar arm topologies.

Figure 6.2 shows the estimates of the agents location for both arm topologies. The position estimates for the case when the agents are phase synchronized with the anchors is shown in Figure 6.2a and Figure 6.2b. The asynchronous counter-part is shown in Figure 6.2c and Figure 6.2d. The corresponding RMSE of the agent location estimates are shown in Table 6.1 (for Arm Topology 1) and Table 6.2 (for Arm Topology 1).

We see that for the case of phase synchronous agents, the constrained ML estimates (marked by cyan '×') have a slight improvement compared to the unconstrained ML estimates (marked by blue 'o'). For example, the elbow estimates in Arm Topology 1 has a RMSE of 1.95 cm when the constraints are not taken into account. The RMSE is improved to 0.84 cm when the constraints are taken into account.

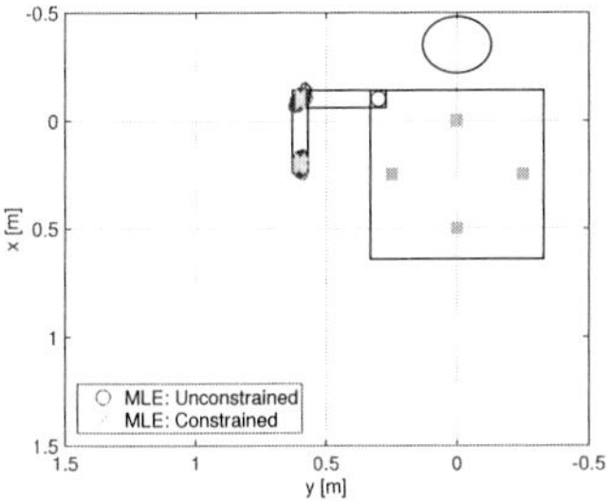

(a) PS agent: Arm Topology 1

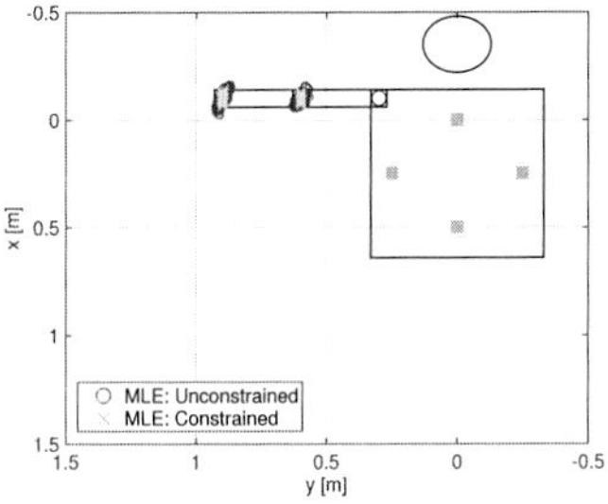

(b) PS agent: Arm Topology 2

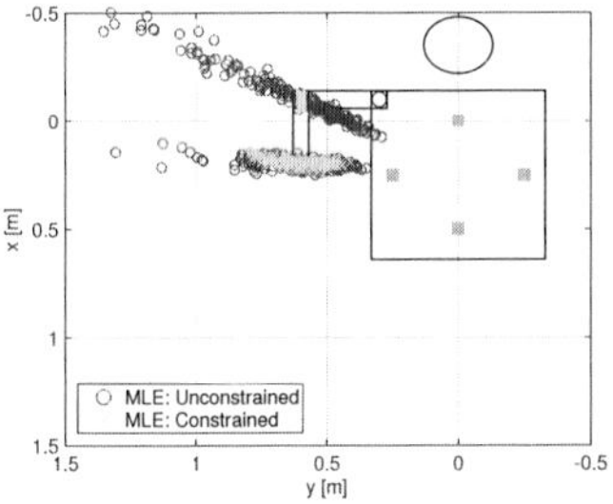

(c) Async. agent: Arm Topology 1

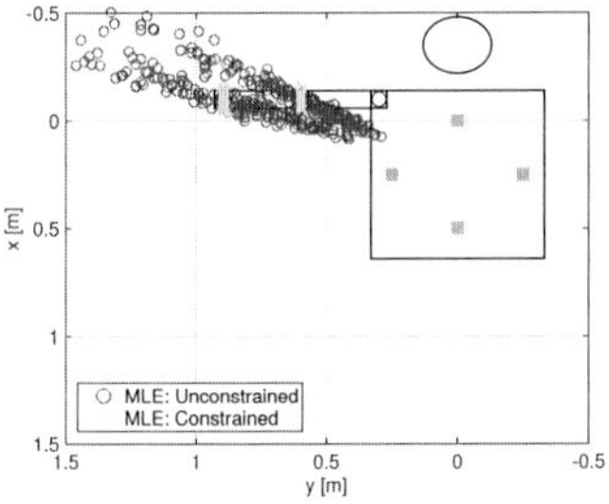

(d) Async. agent: Arm Topology 2

Figure 6.2.: Performance of the ML position estimator for two characteristic agent topologies in synchronous and asynchronous mode.

Table 6.1.: Arm Topology 1: RMSE of agent position estimates.

	Unconstrained ML Estimate (RMSE)	
	phase synchronous	asynchronous
Elbow ($\boldsymbol{t}_1$)	1.95 cm	34.42 cm
Wrist ($\boldsymbol{t}_2$)	1.93 cm	15.41 cm
	Constrained ML Estimate (RMSE)	
	phase synchronous	asynchronous
Elbow ($\boldsymbol{t}_1$)	0.84 cm	1.84 cm
Wrist ($\boldsymbol{t}_2$)	0.98 cm	9.23 cm

The situation completely changes when we look at the asynchronous case. The first thing we notice from the results is that the position estimates for the unconstrained case form an ellipsoidal cloud, which we will call *error cloud*. The center of the cloud

Table 6.2.: Arm Topology 2: RMSE of agent position estimates.

	Unconstrained ML Estimate (RMSE)	
	phase synchronous	asynchronous
Elbow ($\boldsymbol{t}_1$)	1.95 cm	34.69 cm
Wrist ($\boldsymbol{t}_2$)	2.82 cm	40.55 cm
	Constrained ML Estimate (RMSE)	
	phase synchronous	asynchronous
Elbow ($\boldsymbol{t}_1$)	0.94 cm	2.14 cm
Wrist ($\boldsymbol{t}_2$)	1.26 cm	2.96 cm

is located around the true position of the agent and its main axis is approximately oriented in the direction of the line connecting the true position of the agent and the center of the area spanned by the anchors.

In order to get an intuition on this behavior we like to think of the range measurement offset as an error which moves the agent away from or towards the anchor from which the range measurement is taken. This effect is graphically explained in Figure 6.3 for two anchors. As shown in the figure, the measurement offset introduces a position estimation error along the line connecting the anchor and the agent. The joint effect of the error contributions from all the anchors results in a position estimation error whose axis is oriented in the direction of the line connecting the true position of the agent and the midsection of the line between the two anchors.

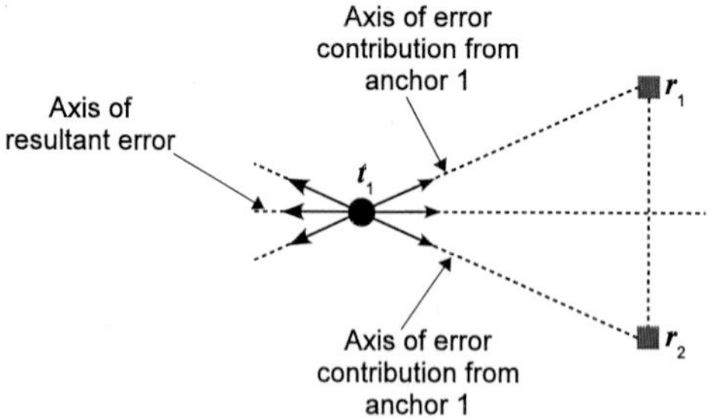

Figure 6.3.: Impact of ranging measurement offset on the position estimates.

From Table 6.1 and Table 6.2, we note the unconstrained estimates of the asynchronous agent located at the elbow has a RMSE above 34 cm (for both topologies).

Keeping in mind that the standard deviation of the ranging error is only 1 cm, unconstrained estimator clearly has unacceptable performance.

A considerable performance improvement is observed when the constraints on the agent locations are taken into account. For example, for Arm Topology 1, the RMSE of the agent located on the elbow is reduced from 34.42 cm (unconstrained) to 1.84 cm (constrained). This is because when the constraints are taken into account the agent on the elbow is constrained to move along a circle, with center at $\boldsymbol{s}$ and radius l_1. Hence, the location uncertainty of the agent is reduced to the intersection of the circle and the ellipsoidal error cloud. A similar performance improvement is observed for the wrist location estimates in Arm Topology 2. For this topology, the RMSE of the agent on the wrist is reduced from 40.55 cm (unconstrained) to 2.96 (constrained).

However, for Arm Topology 1 , the performance improvement due to the constraints is less impressive for the wrist location estimate. We see that the RMSE of the wrist location estimate is reduced from 15.41 cm (unconstrained) to 9.23 cm (constrained). This is because the length constraint between the elbow and the wrist joints allow $\boldsymbol{t}_2$ to be on a circle, with center at $\boldsymbol{t}_1$ and radius l_2. As can be seen from Figure 6.2c, the constraint still allows the wrist to move along the axis of the error cloud and hence the additional location information provided by the constraint is not significant.

From the analysis of the exemplar 2D human posture capturing setup, it is evident that the agents topology has a strong impact on the location estimator's performance. Let us now consider the 3D human posture capturing setup shown in Figure 6.4. The $N_\mathrm{r} = 6$ anchors are located on the torso. Three of the anchors are located in the front torso and the other three are located in the back torso, with locations as given in Table 6.3. Agent 1 is located at the elbow ($\boldsymbol{t}_1$) and agent 2 is located at the wrist ($\boldsymbol{t}_2$). The shoulder joint is positioned at $\boldsymbol{s} = [-0.1\,\mathrm{m}, 0.3\,\mathrm{m}, 0.1\,\mathrm{m}]^T$. The upper-arm and the forearm length are equal and set to $l_1 = l_2 = 0.3\,\mathrm{m}$.

Table 6.3.: Anchor locations. All values are in meters.

Front:	$\boldsymbol{r}_1 = [0, 0, 0]^T$	$\boldsymbol{r}_2 = [0, 0.5, 0]^T$	$\boldsymbol{r}_3 = [0.25, 0.25, 0]^T$
Back:	$\boldsymbol{r}_4 = [0.25, -0.25, 0.25]^T$	$\boldsymbol{r}_5 = [0.5, 0.25, 0.25]^T$	$\boldsymbol{r}_6 = [0, 0.25, 0.25]^T$

We assume the range measurements between all anchors and agents are in a LOS.[2] As before, the range measurement errors are i.i.d. with a standard deviation $\sigma_\mathrm{range} = 1\,\mathrm{cm}$.

[2]NLOS range measurements are considered later.

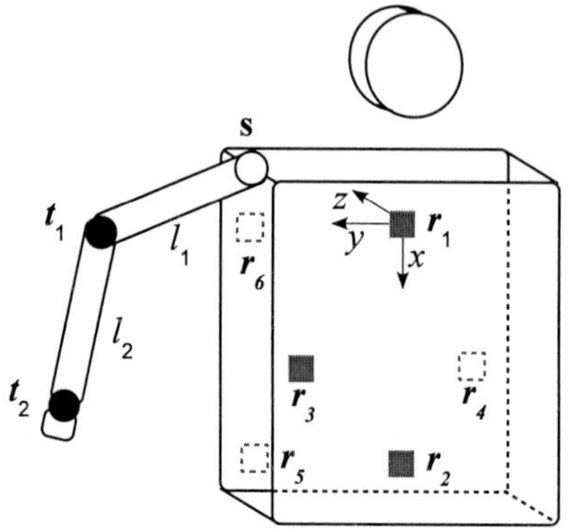

Figure 6.4.: Human posture capturing simulation setup.

The empirical CDF of the RMSE of the agent location estimates is shown in Figure 6.5a (for phase synchronous agents) and Figure 6.5b (for asynchronous agents).

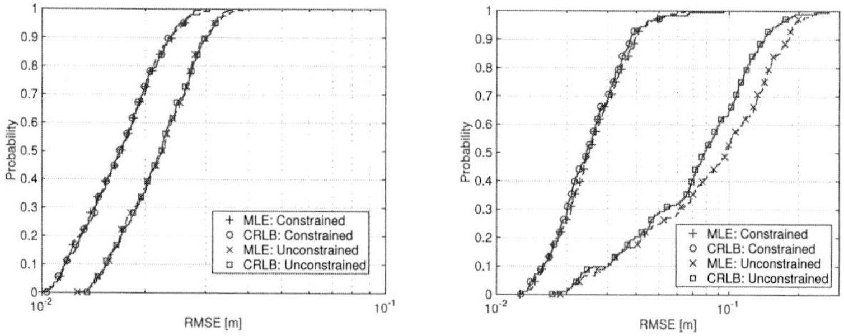

(a) Phase synchronous agent **(b)** Asynchronous agent

Figure 6.5.: Empirical CDF of the RMSE of the agents for random position of the arm.

We see that for the case when the agents are phase synchronous with the anchors, the median (50 %) of the agent location estimates have a RMSE less than 2.2 cm for the unconstrained case. The median RMSE is reduced to 1.7 cm when the constraints are considered.

However, as it is evident in the analysis of the 2D setup, the notable improvement due to the constraints is observed for the case when the agents are asynchronous with the anchors. We note that, for the asynchronous case 90 % of the agent locations have a RMSE less than 4 cm when the constraints are considered. For the unconstrained case on the other hand, only 20 % of the agent locations have a RMSE less than 4 cm. We further see that 50 % of the unconstrained agent estimates has a RMSE above 10 cm. We can hence conclude that the agent location constraints are key performance enablers for a low-cost asynchronous human posture capturing system.

Noting that the agents are low-complexity nodes, one interesting system setup to consider is to place multiple agents per limb. To this end, consider the agent node placement shown in Figure 6.6a. The agents are asynchronous with the anchors. $N_t/2$ agents are placed uniformly on the upper-arm and the other $N_t/2$ agents are placed on the forearm. Hence, the constraints between the agents location are given by

$$\|\boldsymbol{t}_1 - \boldsymbol{s}\|^2 - (2l_1/N_t)^2 = 0, \tag{6.1a}$$

$$\|\boldsymbol{t}_m - \boldsymbol{t}_{m-1}\|^2 - (2l_1/N_t)^2 = 0, \text{ for } m = \{2, \dots, N_t/2\}, \tag{6.1b}$$

$$\|\boldsymbol{t}_m - \boldsymbol{t}_{m-1}\|^2 - (2l_2/N_t)^2 = 0, \text{ for } m = \{N_t/2+1, \dots, N_t\}. \tag{6.1c}$$

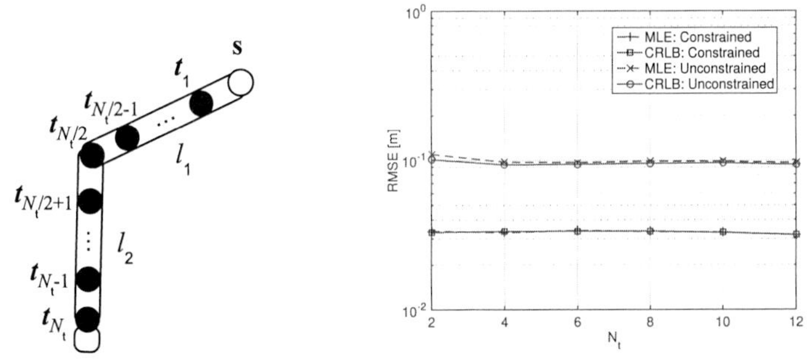

(a) Placement of N_t agents.

(b) Empirical CDF of the RMSE.

Figure 6.6.: Localization performance for varying N_t. The agents are asynchronous with the anchors.

The RMSE of the agent position estimates for varying N_t is shown in Figure 6.6b. It interesting to see that both for the constrained and unconstrained estimators the RMSE performance of the estimator stays almost constant for increasing N_t. As discussed in Section 3.6, such a performance is to be expected for the unconstrained estimator. This is because, when the constraints are not taken into account, the joint estimates of the N_t agent locations can be decoupled to N_t equivalent estimators, where the location of each agent is estimated independently. Hence, on average, RMSE performance should be constant for any N_t.

For the constrained estimator on the other hand, the agent location constraints in (6.1) are similar to the constraints in (3.32). From the result in Figure 3.7, we learn that the RMSE performance of the estimator, which accounts such type of constraints, is improved as N_t increases. This is because the constraints couple the estimation of all the agent locations and hence the joint estimator's performance improves as more and more agents are considered. However, the constrained estimator's performance in Figure 6.6b shows otherwise.

Although this might seem surprising at the first sight, given the agents placement, it is to be expected. For example, consider the agents on the upper-arm. Given one of the agents location (e.g. $\boldsymbol{t}_{N_\mathrm{t}/2}$) and the known parameters (the shoulder location $\boldsymbol{s}$ and the distance between the agents $2l_1/N_\mathrm{t}$), the location of the other $N_\mathrm{t}/2-1$ agents ($\boldsymbol{t}_1, \ldots, \boldsymbol{t}_{N_\mathrm{t}/2-1}$) can be calculated. In other words, if one of the agent location is fixed, the other agents (on the same limb) do not have any degree of freedom (DOF). This implies the range measurements from $N_\mathrm{t}/2-1$ agents do not provide additional location information about $\boldsymbol{t}_{N_\mathrm{t}/2}$. Hence, it is to be expected that estimator performance for $N_\mathrm{t} = 2$ is same as that of, for example, $N_\mathrm{t} = 6$. Note that if the estimator has the *a priori* knowledge of the agents placement, it can add further constraints that calculate $N_\mathrm{t}/2 - 1$ agent locations from one of the agent locations (from $\boldsymbol{t}_{N_\mathrm{t}/2}$ in the above example). For this case, the estimator effectively estimates only one agent location while using the multiple range measurements from all the agents. One can conjecture that such an estimator benefits from the noise reduction due to the multiple range measurements.

Let us now resort back to the setup in Figure 6.4, where $N_\mathrm{t} = 2$. The RMSE performance of the agent location estimates for varying number of anchors N_r is shown in Figure 6.7. The anchors locations are chosen such that they are evenly distributed between the front and the back torso, with the locations given in Table 6.4. For the simulation, the N_r anchors are chosen in the order $\boldsymbol{r}_1, \ldots, \boldsymbol{r}_{N_\mathrm{r}}$.

Table 6.4.: Anchor locations. All values are in meters.

$\boldsymbol{r}_1 = [0, 0, 0]^T$	$\boldsymbol{r}_2 = [0.5, 0.25, 0.25]^T$	$\boldsymbol{r}_3 = [0.25, 0.25, 0]^T$
$\boldsymbol{r}_4 = [0.25, -0.25, 0.25]^T$	$\boldsymbol{r}_5 = [0.5, 0, 0]^T$	$\boldsymbol{r}_6 = [0, 0.25, 0.25]^T$
$\boldsymbol{r}_7 = [0.25, -0.25, 0]^T$	$\boldsymbol{r}_8 = [0, 0, 0.25]^T$	$\boldsymbol{r}_9 = [0.5, 0.25, 0]^T$
$\boldsymbol{r}_{10} = [0.5, 0, 0.25]^T$		

We first note that, both for the constrained and unconstrained estimators, the RMSE of the agent location estimates improves as the number of anchors N_r increases, which is expected. However, it is interesting to see that the performance improvement due to an additional anchor becomes less noticeable as N_r increases, specially for the constrained estimator. For example, the RMSE of the constrained agent location estimates is improved from 3.4 cm (at $N_r = 6$) to 2.8 cm (at $N_r = 10$), less than 20 % improvement.

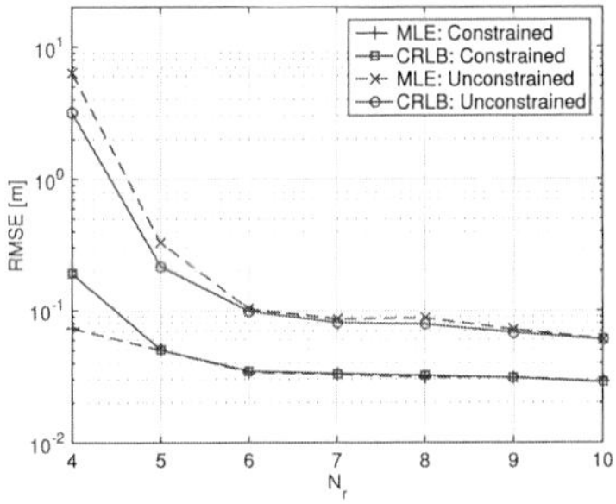

Figure 6.7.: Localization performance for varying number of anchors N_r.

This can be explained by the fact that the RMSE performance of the location estimates depends not only on the number of anchors but also on their location spread. For a given number of anchors N_r, the optimum localization performance is achieved when the anchors are located as symmetric as possible to each other [131]. For example, when $N_r = 4$, the optimum localization performance is achieved when the anchors are located at the vertices of a triangular bi-pyramid centered at the agent's location. For the choice of the anchor locations above, these characteristics have been taken into account. However, as we are restricted to place anchors on the torso, the maximum possible symmetry and location spread between the anchors becomes more and more limited as N_r increases. Hence, the information about the agent's location added by a new anchor becomes smaller as N_r increases.

Another interesting point to note in Figure 6.7 is that, at $N_r = 4$, the RMSE of the constrained ML estimator outperforms the corresponding CRLB. One reason for this might be that the ML estimator is a biased estimator for this setup. Although any unbiased estimator can not be better than the CRLB, the ML estimator (which is not restricted to be an unbiased estimator) may allow a small bias but still achieve a

RMSE performance better than the unbiased estimator.[3]

In summary, from the above results we learn that a median RMSE of around 3 cm is achieved when $N_\mathrm{t} = 2$ and $N_\mathrm{r} = 6$ LOS anchors are available. However, when the available LOS anchors are reduced to $N_\mathrm{r} = 4$, the RMSE of the agent location estimates rises to 7 cm. The estimator performance for this case can be improved by enhancing the accuracy of the range measurements. From the discussion of the range measurement model in Section 2.3, we note that the accuracy of the range measurements can be improved by increasing the signal bandwidth and/or the SNR. Another approach, which is discussed in more detail in the conclusion and outlook chapter, is to propagate location information from one posture capturing stage to the next posture capturing stage. The main motivation for this approach is that for movements such as walking, where the limbs move at a certain speed, the locations of a given agent between two update stages might be close to each other. This behavior can be exploited by the posture capturing procedure system to further improve the localization performance.

6.2. Self-Calibration of the Posture Capturing System

The performance evaluation of the human posture capturing system in Section 6.1 assumes that the positions of the anchors are known and their clocks are phase synchronized. As discussed in Chapter 5 however, in practice, a calibration step is required to estimate the locations and clock offsets of the anchors. Chapter 5 presented a simple and cost effective method that calibrates the location and clock offsets of the anchors based on the measured ranges between the anchors and the agents (which can be realized by a single moving agent). This section discusses the performance of the calibration method when applied to the human posture capturing system setup.

We consider again the human posture capturing system setup shown in Figure 6.4, where $N_\mathrm{r} = 6$ anchors are located on the torso, with locations given in Table 6.5. The $N_\mathrm{t} = 2$ agents are placed on the left arm, agent 1 at elbow joint and agent 2 at the wrist joint. The range measurements are gathered by moving the arm to $N_\mathrm{topo} = 20$ different arm topologies. Hence, in total, $N_{t,\mathrm{total}} = N_\mathrm{topo} N_\mathrm{t}$ agent locations are considered. This implies that $N_{t,\mathrm{total}} N_\mathrm{r}$ range measurements are gathered. The range measurement error standard deviation is set to $\sigma_\mathrm{range} = 1$ cm.

[3]Note that the RMSE of an estimator $\hat{\theta}$ is given by $\mathrm{RMSE}(\hat{\theta}) = \sqrt{\mathrm{Variance}(\hat{\theta}) + (\mathrm{Bias}(\hat{\theta}))^2}$.

Table 6.5.: Anchor locations. All values are in meters.

$\boldsymbol{r}_1 = [0, 0, 0]^T$	$\boldsymbol{r}_2 = [0, 0.5, 0]^T$	$\boldsymbol{r}_3 = [0.25, 0.25, 0]^T$
$\boldsymbol{r}_4 = [0.25, -0.25, 0.25]^T$	$\boldsymbol{r}_5 = [0.5, 0.25, 0.25]^T$	$\boldsymbol{r}_6 = [0, 0.25, 0.25]^T$

Comparing this setup with the calibration setup in Chapter 5, we make the following remarks that need to be considered when applying the calibration algorithm for the human posture capturing system.

- *Available range measurements*: The anchors are a low-complexity nodes that simply relay their received signal to the cluster head. With these types of nodes in mind, it is impractical to assume range measurements between the anchors are available, which would require communication between the anchors. Hence, for the human posture capturing system setup, the only available range measurements are between the agents and the anchors. The ML solution of the calibration problem in (5.4) and the corresponding SDP solution in (5.8) can easily be modified to take this into account by setting the anchor-to-anchor range measurements vector $\boldsymbol{f} = [\,]$, which is equivalent to removing the terms related to $\boldsymbol{f}$ from the estimation process.

- *Agent location constraints*: To keep the exposition short, the distance constraint between the agents is not considered in Chapter 5. We recall that the range measurements are gathered by moving the arm to N_{topo} different topologies, which results in $N_{t,\text{total}} = N_{\text{topo}} N_{\text{t}}$ agent locations in total. Let the locations $\boldsymbol{t}_1, \dots, \boldsymbol{t}_{N_{t,\text{total}}/2}$ be the locations which correspond to agent 1. Likewise, the locations $\boldsymbol{t}_{N_{t,\text{total}}/2+1}, \dots, \boldsymbol{t}_{N_{t,\text{total}}}$ be the locations which correspond to agent 2. With these considerations, the distance constraints between the agent locations can easily be included in the MLE by adding the following constraint in (5.4)

$$\boldsymbol{c}(\boldsymbol{t}) = \begin{bmatrix} \|\boldsymbol{t}_1 - \boldsymbol{s}\|^2 - l_1^2 \\ \vdots \\ \boldsymbol{t}_{N_{t,\text{total}}/2} - \boldsymbol{s}\|^2 - l_1^2 \\ \|\boldsymbol{t}_{N_{t,\text{total}}/2+1} - \boldsymbol{t}_1\|^2 - l_2^2 \\ \vdots \\ \|\boldsymbol{t}_{N_{t,\text{total}}} - \boldsymbol{t}_{N_{t,\text{total}}/2}\|^2 - l_2^2 \end{bmatrix} = 0.$$

Similarly, the agent location constraints can be included in the SDP solution as follows. Recalling the definition $\boldsymbol{X} = [\boldsymbol{r}_1, \dots, \boldsymbol{r}_{N_{\text{r}}}, \boldsymbol{t}_1, \dots, \boldsymbol{t}_{N_{t,\text{total}}}]$ and $\boldsymbol{Y} = \boldsymbol{X}^T \boldsymbol{X}$, the distance constraint between the agents can equivalently be written as

$$\tilde{c}(\boldsymbol{Y},\boldsymbol{X}) = \begin{bmatrix} \boldsymbol{Y}[N_\mathrm{r}{+}1,N_\mathrm{r}{+}1]{+}\boldsymbol{s}^T\boldsymbol{s}{-}2\boldsymbol{s}^T\boldsymbol{X}[:,N_\mathrm{r}{+}1]{-}l_1^2 \\ \vdots \\ \boldsymbol{Y}[N_\mathrm{r}{+}N_{t,\mathrm{total}}/2,N_\mathrm{r}{+}N_{t,\mathrm{total}}/2]{+}\boldsymbol{s}^T\boldsymbol{s}{-}2\boldsymbol{s}^T\boldsymbol{X}[:,N_\mathrm{r}{+}1]{-}l_1^2 \\ \boldsymbol{Y}[N_\mathrm{r}{+}N_{t,\mathrm{total}}/2{+}1,N_\mathrm{r}{+}N_{t,\mathrm{total}}/2{+}1]{+}\boldsymbol{Y}[N_\mathrm{r}{+}1,N_\mathrm{r}{+}1] \\ \qquad {-}2\boldsymbol{Y}[N_\mathrm{r}{+}1,N_\mathrm{r}{+}N_{t,\mathrm{total}}/2{+}1]{-}l_2^2 \\ \vdots \\ \boldsymbol{Y}[N_\mathrm{r}{+}N_{t,\mathrm{total}}/2,N_\mathrm{r}{+}N_{t,\mathrm{total}}]{+}\boldsymbol{Y}[N_\mathrm{r}{+}N_{t,\mathrm{total}}/2,N_\mathrm{r}{+}N_{t,\mathrm{total}}/2] \\ \qquad {-}2\boldsymbol{Y}[N_\mathrm{r}{+}N_{t,\mathrm{total}}/2,N_\mathrm{r}{+}N_{t,\mathrm{total}}]{-}l_2^2 \end{bmatrix} = \boldsymbol{0}. \tag{6.2}$$

Appending the constraint in (6.2) into (5.8) results in the SDP solution of the calibration problem which accounts the agent location constraints.

Figure 6.8 shows the empirical CDF of the RMSE of the anchor location estimates for selected synchronization classes (PS-PS, FS-FS and FS-Async). In Figure 6.8a, the agent location constraints are taken into account. On the other hand in Figure 6.8b, the agent location constraints are not taken into account. The dashed lines represent the ML estimates of the anchor locations and the solid line denote the corresponding CRLB.

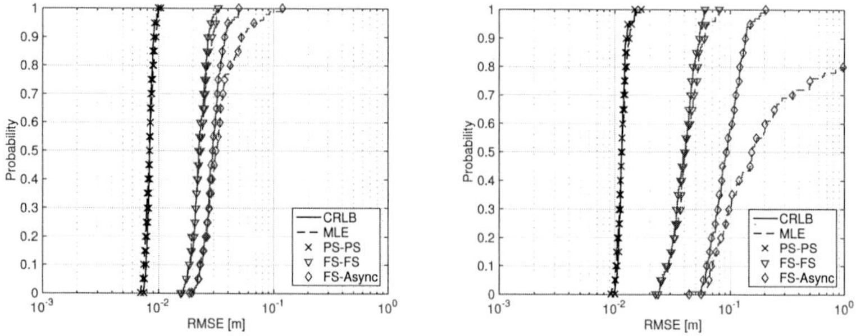

(a) Constrained estimator. **(b)** Unconstrained estimator.

Figure 6.8.: Empirical CDF of RMSE of the anchor position estimates.

We first note that, both for the constrained and the unconstrained estimators, the ML estimator matches the corresponding CRLB for the synchronization classes PS-PS and FS-FS. For the synchronization class FS-Async, on the other hand, the unconstrained ML estimates considerably diverge from the CRLB. However, when the agent location constraints are taken into account, we see that about 80 % of the estimates match the CRLB and only 10 % of the estimates have a RMSE larger than the maximum CRLB value (5 cm). We further see that the median RMSE of the constrained ML estimates are 0.8 cm (PS-PS), 2.3 cm (FS-FS) and 3 cm (FS-Async). For the unconstrained case, on the other hand, the median RMSE values are 1.1 cm (PS-PS), 4 cm (FS-FS) and 15 cm (FS-Async). From these results we can conclude that for the calibration of the human posture capturing setup, where the synchronization class is FS-Async and the available range measurements are only those between the anchors and the agents, the distance constraint between the agents location is the key performance enabler.

The RMSE performance of the calibrated anchors can be improved by increasing the number of the considered arm topologies N_{topo}. Figure 6.9 shows the CRLB of the anchor location estimates for varying number of $N_{t,\text{total}}$. Clearly, when $N_{t,\text{total}}$ is small, the accuracy of the anchor location estimates is very poor. As $N_{t,\text{total}}$ increases however, the number of range measurements increase and hence the accuracy of the anchor location estimates improves.

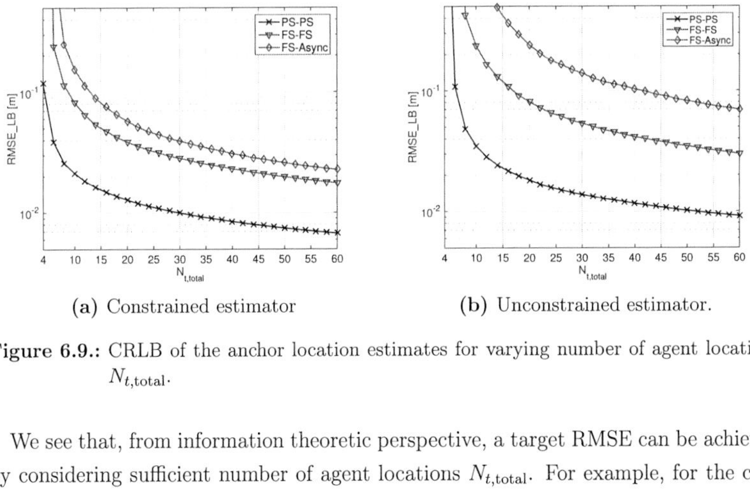

(a) Constrained estimator

(b) Unconstrained estimator.

Figure 6.9.: CRLB of the anchor location estimates for varying number of agent locations $N_{t,\text{total}}$.

We see that, from information theoretic perspective, a target RMSE can be achieved by considering sufficient number of agent locations $N_{t,\text{total}}$. For example, for the constrained estimator and FS-FS synchronization class, a RMSE less than 2 cm can be achieved by considering $N_{t,\text{total}} \geq 50$. Note however that as $N_{t,\text{total}}$ increase the calibration algorithm becomes computationally complex. Hence, in practice, a trade-off between the calibration accuracy and the computational complexity needs to be made. One remark to make here is that the calibration is performed once, before the localization phase. Therefore, although the system needs to be computationally capable to perform calibration within a sensible period of time, the speed requirement in the calibration phase less stringent compared to the localization phase, where the locations of the agents have to be updated fast enough to enable motion capturing.

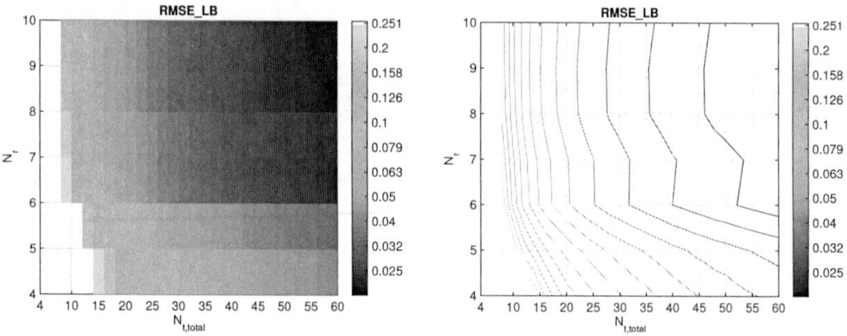

(a) Surface plot. (b) Contour plot.

Figure 6.10.: CRLB of the anchor location estimates for varying N_r and $N_{t,\mathrm{total}}$. FS-Async synchronization class, agent locations constraints accounted .

Next we discuss the impact of the number of anchors on the calibration performance. For this, we consider 10 anchors located as in Table 6.6. Figure 6.10 shows the CRLB of the anchor location estimates for varying N_r and $N_{t,\mathrm{total}}$. The synchronization class FS-Async is considered and the distance constraint of the agent locations is taken into account. In the surface plot, Figure 6.10a, a white point represents RMSE_LB larger than 30 cm. The corresponding contour plot of the CRLB is shown in Figure 6.10b.

Table 6.6.: Anchor locations. All values are in meters.

$\boldsymbol{r}_1 = [0, 0, 0]^T$	$\boldsymbol{r}_2 = [0.5, 0.25, 0.25]^T$	$\boldsymbol{r}_3 = [0.25, 0.25, 0]^T$
$\boldsymbol{r}_4 = [0.25, -0.25, 0.25]^T$	$\boldsymbol{r}_5 = [0.5, 0, 0]^T$	$\boldsymbol{r}_6 = [0, 0.25, 0.25]^T$
$\boldsymbol{r}_7 = [0.25, -0.25, 0]^T$	$\boldsymbol{r}_8 = [0, 0, 0.25]^T$	$\boldsymbol{r}_9 = [0.5, 0.25, 0]^T$
$\boldsymbol{r}_{10} = [0.5, 0, 0.25]^T$		

As expected when N_r increases, the required $N_{t,\mathrm{total}}$ to achieve a target RMSE reduces. What is interesting to note is that $N_\mathrm{r} = 6$ appears to be critical. When $N_\mathrm{r} < 6$, for every reduced anchor, $N_{t,\mathrm{total}}$ needs to be increased considerably to achieve a given target RMSE. From this result, we can conclude that having $N_\mathrm{r} \geq 6$ LOS anchors is recommended to achieve a reasonable calibration accuracy (RMSE of around 3 cm) while keeping the calibration algorithm computationally tractable.

6.3. Localization Under Anchor Position Uncertainties

From the calibration results in Section 6.2, we see that the anchor locations are estimated up to a certain level of accuracy. Furthermore, as the anchors are located on the torso, their location might drift from the calibrated position when the person moves. In this section, we discuss the performance of the localization algorithm under the presence of anchor position uncertainties.

As in the previous sections, we consider the human posture capturing setup shown in Figure 6.4. The location $N_\mathrm{r} = 6$ anchors is given in Table 6.7, same locations as before. The $N_\mathrm{t} = 2$ agents are placed on the left arm, agent 1 at elbow joint and agent 2 at the wrist joint. The range measurement error standard deviation is set to $\sigma_\mathrm{range} = 1\,\mathrm{cm}$. And the anchor location error standard deviation is set to $\sigma_\mathrm{anchor} = 3\,\mathrm{cm}$.

Table 6.7.: Anchor locations. All values are in meters.

$\boldsymbol{r}_1 = [0, 0, 0]^T$	$\boldsymbol{r}_2 = [0, 0.5, 0]^T$	$\boldsymbol{r}_3 = [0.25, 0.25, 0]^T$
$\boldsymbol{r}_4 = [0.25, -0.25, 0.25]^T$	$\boldsymbol{r}_5 = [0.5, 0.25, 0.25]^T$	$\boldsymbol{r}_6 = [0, 0.25, 0.25]^T$

Figure 6.11 shows the empirical CDF of the agent location estimates under the presence of anchor location uncertainties. Here, the localization for each arm topology is performed independently, i.e. $N_\mathrm{topo} = 1$ and $N_{t,\mathrm{total}} = N_\mathrm{t} = 2$. The solid lines denote the ML estimates that account the anchor location uncertainties. The dashed lines represent the ML estimates which does not take into account the anchor location uncertainties.

By comparing this result with the result in Figure 6.5b, where the anchor locations are perfectly known, we see that the anchor location uncertainties lead to a notable performance degradation. Considering the constrained ML estimator, we see that the median RMSE of 2.5 cm (with perfect anchor location) is increased to 15 cm (with anchor location uncertainty, and not accounted). The median RMSE of the later is reduced to 10.5 cm when the anchor location uncertainties are taken into account, which is better but still poor. The reason for this is that, as discussed in Section 4.6, the performance gain of the localization method that accounts the anchor location uncertainties becomes bigger as the number of agents that are estimated jointly increases. Hence, with only $N_{t,\mathrm{total}} = 2$ agents estimated jointly, such a performance is to be expected.

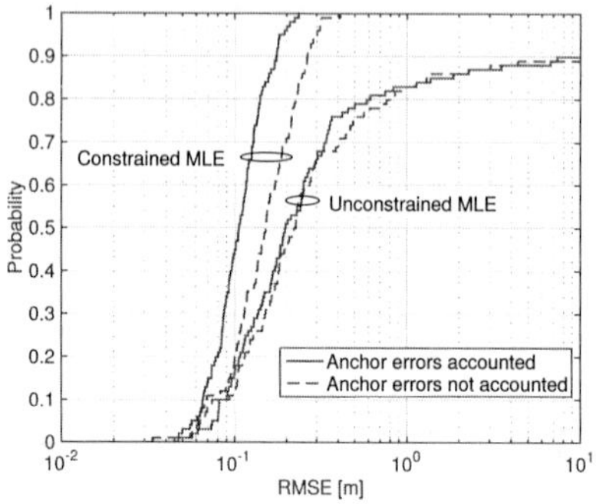

Figure 6.11.: Empirical CDF of RMSE of the agent location estimates in the presence of anchor location uncertainties. A total of $N_{t,\text{total}} = 2$ agents jointly estimated, i.e. $N_{\text{topo}} = 1$.

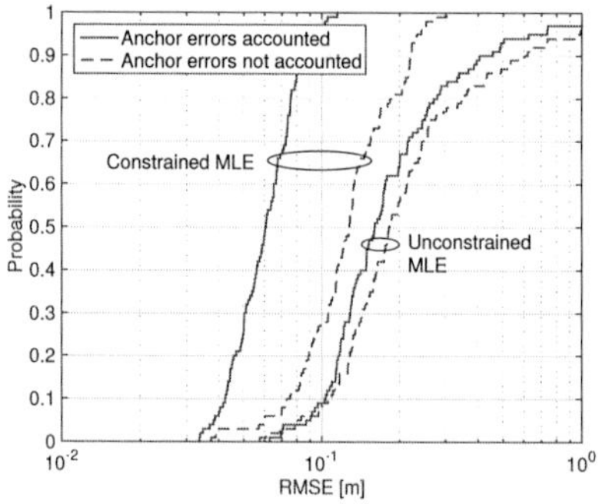

Figure 6.12.: Empirical CDF of RMSE of the agent location estimates in the presence of anchor location uncertainties. A total of $N_{t,\text{total}} = 10$ agents jointly estimated, i.e. $N_{\text{topo}} = 5$.

Figure 6.12 shows the empirical CDF of the RMSE of the agent location estimates for the same setup as above, but now $N_{\text{topo}} = 5$. This means that the location of the agents for 5 arm topologies are estimated jointly, in total $N_{t,\text{total}} = 10$ agent locations are estimated together. Looking at the constrained case, we now see that the median RMSE of 13 cm (anchor errors not accounted) is improved to 6 cm (anchor errors accounted), more than 60 % reduction.

The achievable RMSE of the agent location estimates depends (among others) on σ_{anchor} and $N_{t,\text{total}}$. Figure 6.13a shows the CRLB of the agent location estimate

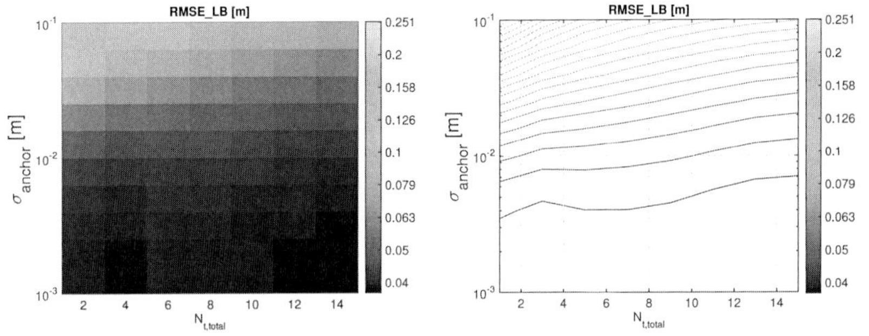

(a) Surface plot. (b) Contour plot.

Figure 6.13.: CRLB of the agent location estimates under the presence of anchor position uncertainties, for varying σ_{anchor} and $N_{t,\text{total}}$. The agent location constraints are taken into account.

under the presence of anchor position error for varying σ_{anchor} and $N_{t,\text{total}}$. The CRLB accounts the distance constraint on the agent locations. The corresponding contour plot is shown in Figure 6.13b. As expected when σ_{anchor} decreases, the required $N_{t,\text{total}}$ to achieve a target RMSE also decreases. For example, RMSE_LB of 5 cm can also be achieved by $N_{t,\text{total}} = 14$ when $\sigma_{\text{anchor}} = 2$ cm. The same RMSE_LB can be achieved by just $N_{t,\text{total}} = 2$ agents when $\sigma_{\text{anchor}} = 1$ cm.

The choice of $N_{t,\text{total}}$ depends on the computational complexity that is affordable by the system, which also relates to the required location update rate. On the other hand, σ_{anchor} depends on the accuracy of the calibration step and the mobility of the torso. Hence, to achieve a given target RMSE, the system parameters need to be chosen carefully such that the appropriate $N_{t,\text{total}}$ is selected and the required σ_{anchor} is achieved at the calibration phase.

6.4. Summary

The performance of the localization and calibration methods presented in the previous chapters are evaluated for the specific setup of the human posture capturing system. For the considered system, where the agents are ultra-low complexity transmit-only asynchronous beacons, accurate human posture capturing is possible when the agent location constraints (imposed by the kinematic constraints of the body) are taken into account. The agent location constraints are specifically important for the considered human posture capturing system setup, where the agents (located on the limbs) are outside the convex-hull of the anchors (located on the torso). The performance evaluation of the self-calibration method further underlines the importance of the agent location constraints. Since the anchors are only frequency synchronous and the agents are asynchronous, the calibration of the clock offsets and locations of the anchors using the simple and cost-effective self-calibration method is possible when the agent location constraints are taken into account.

The anchor position errors, due to the errors in the calibration phase or the movement of the torso, lead to a degradation in the localization performance. Such a performance loss can be minimized by increasing the number of agent locations that are estimated jointly. But this does not necessarily mean increasing the number of agents. In one posture capturing step, the number of agent locations that are estimated jointly can be increased by taking into account agent locations from the previous posture capturing steps.

7. Low-Cost Monobit ADC based Localization Demonstrator System

This chapter presents a low-cost demonstrator system, which practically implements the TOA based localization system discussed in the previous chapters. The agent nodes are realized by integrated UWB radio nodes that generate and transmit DSSS signals. The anchors are realized by finite resolution digital receivers that use monobit analog to digital convertors (ADCs). The chapter starts with the discussion of the motivation behind the use of finite resolution digital receivers in Section 7.1. The details of the monobit ADC based demonstrator system is presented in Section 7.2. The results of the experimental evaluation of the localization and calibration methods is discussed in Section 7.3.

7.1. Finite Resolution Digital UWB Receiver

Finite resolution digital receivers use ADCs that sample a received signal at a certain frequency and represent the samples with finite number of quantization levels. In UWB communication, finite resolution digital receivers are of great interest as they can be realized with several comparators [132]. Moreover, the power consumption of ADCs is proportional to 2^b, where b is the number of bits the ADC uses to represent quantization levels [133]. Hence, ADCs with few number of bits b enable a low-power implementation.

Attracted by their low-complexity and low-power advantages, several previous works have considered finite resolution ADCs for UWB communication and localization systems. In [134], UWB communication system that uses monobit ADCs (i.e. ADCs with a single bit) is considered. The impact of quantization noise and the sampling frequency on the receivers performance is investigated. It is shown that the performance loss due to the monobit ADC operation can be made very small by considering a high sampling frequency. Similarly, in [135, 136], the impact of finite resolution ADCs for UWB based localization is investigated. In these works, it is also shown that receivers with high resolution ADCs can be replaced by ADCs with few bits provided that the signal is sampled at a sampling frequency much higher than Nyquist frequency.

However, the above works that applied finite resolution ADCs for UWB communication and localization systems consider impulse radio signaling, which lead to the requirement for high oversampling. Here, on the other hand, we consider a UWB system that is based on DSSS signaling. Interestingly, for this signaling scheme, a finite resolution digital receiver system with monobit ADCs, which does not require oversampling, is feasible. In the next section, a TOA based localization demonstrator system that is realized by monobit digital receivers is discussed.

7.2. Localization Demonstrator System

The localization demonstrator system, which practically implements the TOA based localization system presented in Section 2.1, is shown in Figure 7.1.

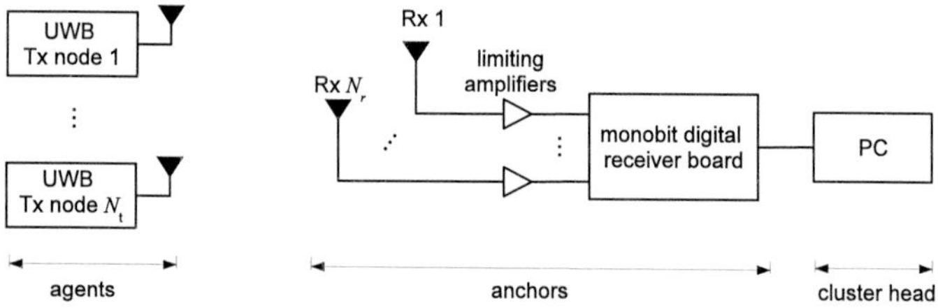

Figure 7.1.: Localization demonstrator system.

The agents are realized by UWB transmitter (Tx for short) nodes that generate and transmit DSSS signals. The signal received at the N_r receiving antennas (Rx for short) is then fed to the limiting amplifiers. The limiting amplifiers have a maximum input amplitude of 2 V (peak to peak) and a bandwidth of approximately 11 GHz. The output of each amplifier, which is a differential signal with a maximum amplitude of 700 mV (peak to peak), is then fed to the monobit digital receiver board. The monobit digital receiver board then digitizes the differential input signals and correlates the signal from each receiving antenna with the stored templates of all the agent nodes, which results in the estimate of the channel impulse response between all agents and all anchors. The channel impulse response estimates are then transferred to a PC via Ethernet for further processing.

7.2.1. Integrated UWB transmitter node

The integrated UWB transmitter nodes, shown in Figure 7.2a, were developed by the author of [137]. The main building blocks of the transmitter node are depicted in Figure 7.2b. The transmitter has of two main components: the digital baseband transmitter and the analog front-end. The digital baseband part consists of a field programmable gate array (FPGA) chip which is operated by a 125 MHz clock. The FPGA chip implements a linear feedback shift register that generates periodic M-sequences. The user input/output interface with pushbuttons and control LEDs enables the user to select different sequences. For our demonstrator setup, M-sequences with length of $2^{13} - 1$ are chosen.

(a) UWB transmitter node.

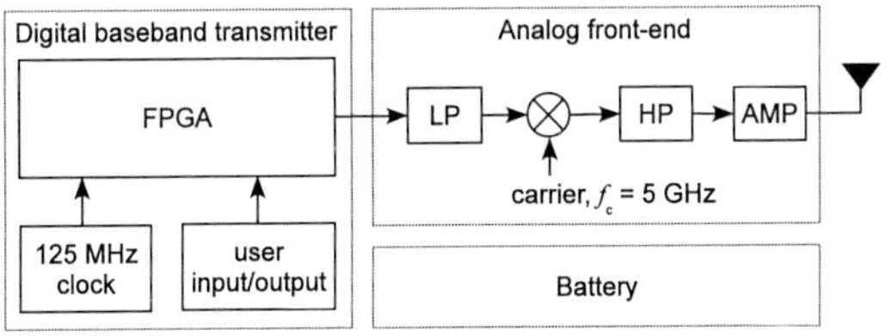

(b) Block diagram of the transmitter node.

Figure 7.2.: UWB transmitter node that generates and transmits DSSS signal [39]. LP: lowpass, HP: highpass and AMP: amplifier.

The digital baseband transmitter generates an M-sequence with a chip rate of 2.4375 Gbps and a frequency range spanning between DC and 2.5 GHz. The analog front-end part then mixes this signal with a carrier of 5 GHz, amplifies and transmits it. The spectrum of the signal transmitted by the integrated UWB transmitter node is shown in Figure 7.3. The transmitter node is operated by a battery, which allows autonomous operation of up to 10 hours. Each of the UWB transmitter nodes use their own local clocks, which are asynchronous with respect to each other and with respect to the clock that is used by the receiver board.

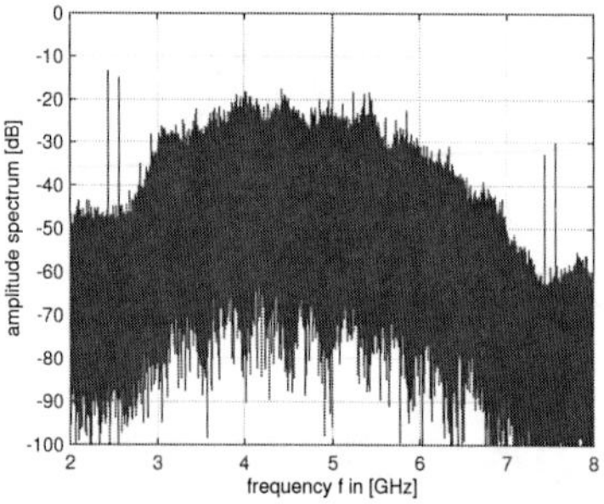

Figure 7.3.: Spectrum of the transmit signal.

7.2.2. Integrated monobit digital UWB receiver

The integrated monobit digital receiver board is shown in Figure 7.4. In its current implementation, the receiver board has $N_r = 6$ channels. The functional block diagram of the receiver board, for one of the receive channels, is depicted in Figure 7.5. The implementation details of the receiver board can be found in [138], which was supervised as a part of this PhD project. The main building blocks and the functional flow of the system can be summarized as follows.

The first block in the receiver board is the receiver input buffer. This block detects the input signal and applies appropriate equalization and DC gain. After measurement evaluation however, for the considered application, it is opted not to apply equalization and DC gain. Hence, the receiver input buffer only detects the input signal and forwards it to the clock and data recovery (CDR) unit.

The CDR unit, as the name implies, recovers the data from the incoming signal. It digitizes the input signal with 1-bit quantization and forwards it to the de-serializer. The unit has two operating modes: lock-to-data (LTD) mode and lock-to-reference (LTR) mode. In the LTD mode, the CDR unit recovers the clock from the incoming

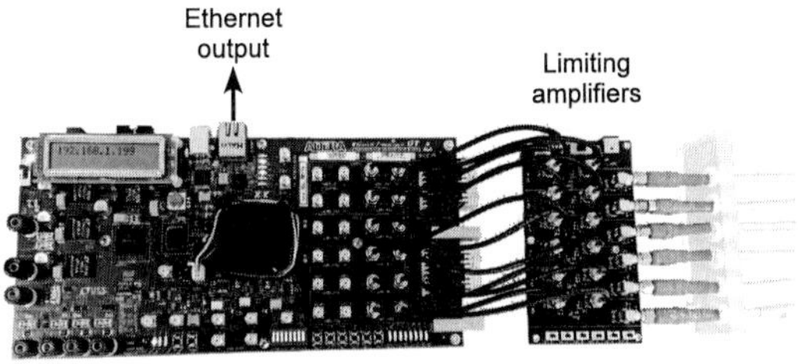

Figure 7.4.: Integrated monobit digital receiver board (with limiting amplifiers attached to the right).

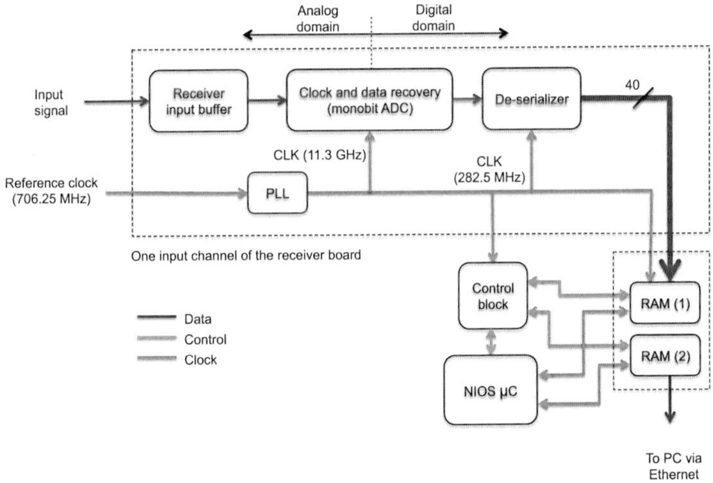

Figure 7.5.: Block diagram of the monobit digital receiver board.

signal, which can then be used to sample the signal and recover the data contained in it. On the other hand, in the LTR mode, the CDR unit uses an external reference clock with a frequency of 11.3 GHz. For the considered application, the LTR mode is used. The 11.3 GHz clock (which is used by the CDR unit) and the 285.2 MHz clock (which is used by the de-serializer) are generated by phase locked loop (PLL) from a reference clock of 706.25 MHz.

The output of the CDR unit has a rate of 11.3 Gbps. This high speed serial data is read by the de-serializer which then gives out low-speed 40 parallel data streams, each with a speed of 285.2 Mbps. The output of the de-serializer is written on the memory unit RAM (1), which can be accessed by the control unit and NIOS micro-controller (μC). The sampled received signal (in RAM (1)) is then correlated with the stored template of the transmitted signal to result in the channel impulse response estimate. The correlation result is serialized to a high speed data stream of 11.3 Gbps and saved to RAM (2). The content of this memory block is then transferred to a PC via Ethernet. In its current implementation, the receiver board can handle $N_\mathrm{r} = 6$ receive channels. And it can perform the correlation of the signals transmitted by $N_\mathrm{t} = 2$ transmit nodes.

From Figure 7.5, we see that the clocks that are used by the CDR unit and the de-serializer are generated by a PLL from the reference clock. All of the 6 receive channels have their own PLLs that generate their corresponding clocks from the same reference clock. Since all PLLs operate independently, the phase of the 11.3 GHz clocks (for the CDR unit) and 285.2 MHz clocks (for the de-serializer) they generate might not be the same for different channels. However, as all channels use the same reference clock, the clocks of the different channels are synchronized in frequency. Recalling that the clocks of the UWB transmitters are asynchronous, the localization demonstrator system shown in Figure 7.1 falls in the synchronization class of asycnronous agents and frequency synchronous anchors.

Before we proceed to the discussion of the measurement results using the demonstrator system in Figure 7.1, it is worth to understand the effect of the 1-bit quantization on the channel impulse response estimate, which is the subject of the next sub-section.

7.2.3. Effect of 1-bit quantization

To ease the discussion, consider the bandpass signal transmitted by one of the agents within one full period of the M-sequence, which can be written in the following form

$$s(t) = c(t)\cos(2\pi f_\mathrm{c} t), \quad 0 \leq t \leq T_s$$

where $c(t)$ denotes the chip sequence, f_c is the carrier frequency and T_s is one full period of the M-sequence. The chip sequence $c(t)$ is given by

$$c(t) = \sum_{i=0}^{N_\mathrm{ch}-1} c_i p(t - iT_\mathrm{ch}), \quad \text{with} \quad p(t) = \begin{cases} 1/\sqrt{T_\mathrm{ch}}, & 0 \leq t \leq T_\mathrm{ch}, \\ 0, & \text{otherwise.} \end{cases}$$

As defined in Section 2.2, $\{c_i\}$ denotes the code sequence, T_{ch} is the chip period and N_{ch} is the number of chips of the M-sequence. A portion of such a transmit signal is visualized in Figure 7.6 with parameters $f_{\mathrm{c}} = 10\,\mathrm{GHz}$ and $T_{\mathrm{ch}} = 0.5\,ns$.

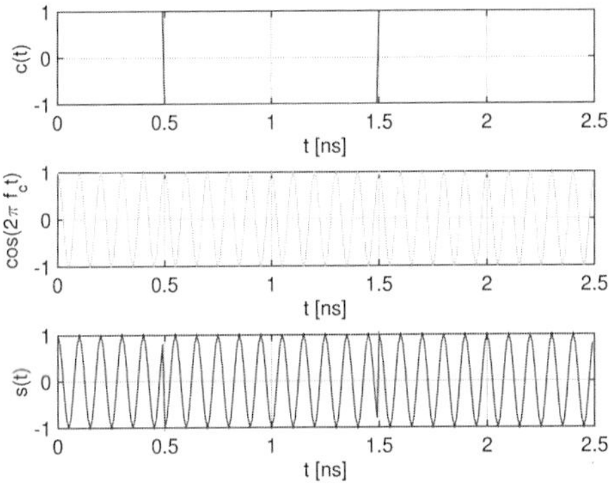

Figure 7.6.: Visualization of the transmit signal $s(t)$, $f_{\mathrm{c}} = 10\,\mathrm{GHz}, T_{\mathrm{ch}} = 0.5\,ns$.

Considering the simplified scenario where only a single agent is transmitting, the signal received at one of the anchors can be written as

$$\begin{aligned} r(t) &= \sum_{l=1}^{L} a^{(l)} s(t - \tau^{(l)}) + w(t) \\ &= \sum_{l=1}^{L} a^{(l)} c(t - \tau^{(l)}) \cos(2\pi f_{\mathrm{c}}(t - \tau^{(l)})) + w(t), \end{aligned}$$

where L is number of multipath components of the channel, $a^{(l)}$ and $\tau^{(l)}$ are the amplitude and the delay of the lth path, respectively, and $w(t)$ is an additive noise. After receiving the signal $r(t)$, the mono-bit digital receiver samples it with the sampling frequency $f_s = 11.3\,\mathrm{GHz}$, quantizes it with 1-bit (i.e. takes the signs of each sample). The 1-bit quantized signal is then correlated with the local stored copy of the transmitted signal to result in the channel impulse response estimate.

To understand the effect of the 1-bit quantization on the channel impulse response estimate, let us consider the noiseless received signal ($w(t) = 0$) and a two path channel ($L = 2$). Also assume that the first path is the strongest path, i.e. $a^{(1)} > a^{(2)}$. With this consideration, the received signal for the time duration where the chip sequence is constant can be depicted as shown in Figure 7.7a. Figure 7.7b shows the sampling instances of the received signal and also differentiates the time period within which the quantizer output is dominated by a certain path. The blue background means that the quantizer output is dominated by the first path. The pink background means the quantizer output is dominated by the second path.

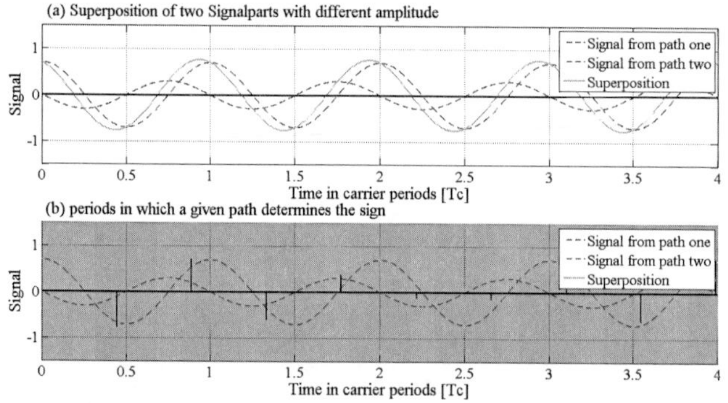

Figure 7.7.: Visualization of the received signal for the time duration where the chip sequence is constant. (a) Superposition of the signals from the two paths. (b) Sampling instances and the time periods dominated by the paths.

From the very simple and constructed example of the received signal in Figure 7.7, the following interesting insight about the choice of the sampling frequency f_s in relation to the carrier frequency f_c can be deduced. If f_s is chosen to be an integer multiple of f_c, the sampling instances, with respect to the start and the end of a carrier period, will be constant throughout the whole M-sequence. Hence, if by chance these sampling instances are on the blue region, the second path (the week path) will not be visible. A similar effect can be observed if, for example $f_s = 12.5\,\text{GHz}$ and $f_c = 5\,\text{GHz}$. For this case, the sampling instances repeat after 4 carrier periods.

The optimal solution to cope with this effect is to chose the sampling frequency such that the sampling instances through out the whole M-sequence period are not repeated. For the considered localization demonstrator system, $f_s = 11.3\,\text{GHz}$ and $f_c = 5\,\text{GHz}$. This implies that on average 2.26 samples are taken per each carrier period and the sampling instances repeat after 50 carrier periods. This corresponds to 113 equally spaced different sampling instances, which is a reasonably good choice. However, it should be mentioned that slightly changing the sampling frequency to $f_s = 11.35\,\text{GHz}$ leads to 226 different sampling instances.

To further assess the effect of 1-bit quantization, let us now consider the case where the noise is present and the transmit signal $s(t)$ is the actual signal which is transmitted by the integrated UWB transmitter node. The measured transmitted signal is passed through a two-tap channel with path amplitudes $a^{(1)} = 0.7$ and $a^{(2)} = 0.3$. The delay of the first path $\tau^{(1)}$ is fixed while the delay of the second path $\tau^{(2)}$ is varied from $\tau^{(1)}$ up to $10/f_c$. The received signal is then sampled, quantized with 1-bit and correlated with the copy of the transmit signal.

Figure 7.8 shows the maximum, minimum and mean value of the peak amplitudes of the correlator output for both paths for varying SNR. For comparison, the results of the correlator when the samples are not quantized (full resolution) is also shown. Let us first consider the full resolution case. We note that the peak amplitude of the strong path is almost unaffected by varying delay of the second path. On the other hand, for the weak path, there is a discrepancy of around 0.04 between the maximum and minimum peak. This is because the autocorrelation of the transmit signal has side-lobes and since the first path is strong it affects the second path.

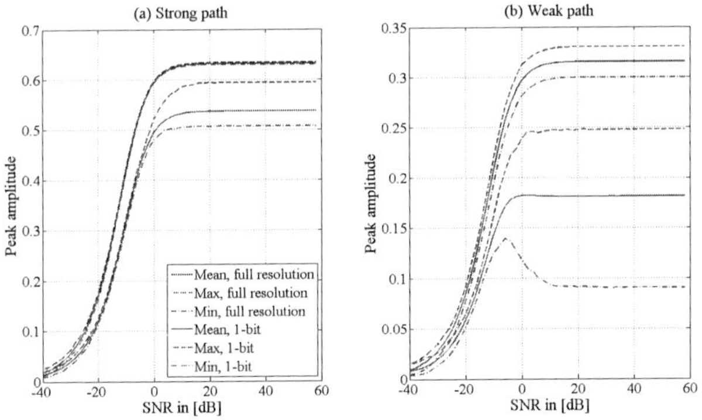

Figure 7.8.: Maximum, minimum and mean value of the peak amplitude for varying SNR. (a) Strong path. (b) Weak path.

Also for the 1-bit quantized case, at high SNR, there is a difference of around 0.1 between the maximum and minimum peak amplitudes of the strong path. What is more interesting however is the result for the weak path. We note that, at high SNR, the discrepancy between the maximum and minimum peak amplitude is more than 0.15. However, as the SNR decreases (in the range between 10 dB and −5 dB), the minimum peak amplitude improves. Then below the SNR value of −5 dB, decreasing the SNR leads to a reduction in the minimum peak amplitude. This has an interesting implication that a "right level" of noise actually helps in detecting the weaker path.

The reason behind this interesting effect of noise on the weaker path can be explained with the probability tree shown in Figure 7.9. At a give sampling instance of the received signal, the probability that the signal contributions from both paths to have the same sign is 0.5 (and opposite sign 0.5). Let the probability the noise flips the sign of the constructively added sample of the received signal be p_1. Hence, with a probability of $0.5p_1$, the 1-bit quantized signal will have the wrong sign because of the noise. This leads to reduction in the amplitude of the correlator output for both paths. The probabilities of the other cases can be calculated similarly.

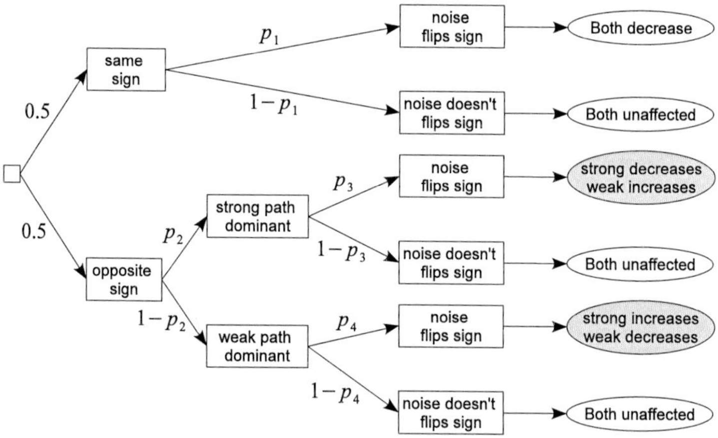

Figure 7.9.: Probability tree: effect of noise on the correlator output.

The two cases in which the noise discriminates between the two paths are highlighted with blue background in Figure 7.9. We see that, with the probability of $0.5p_2p_3$, the noise helps to improves the weak path while decreasing the strong path. And with the probability of $0.5(1-p_2)p_4$, the noise improves the strong path while decreasing the weak path. Hence, the noise helps to improve the weak path when $p_2p_3 > (1-p_2)p_4$. Clearly, when the two paths are of opposite sign, the probability that the strong path dominates is larger than the probability the weak path dominates, i.e. $p_2 > (1-p_2)$. But it should also be noted that, depending on the amplitude difference of the two paths and the noise level, it might be easier to flip the sign when the weak path is dominant than when the strong path is dominant, i.e $p_3 < p_4$. Hence, if the noise level is such that p_3 is close to p_4 (the "right level" of noise), then noise can indeed improve the correlator output for the weak path.

In summary, from the above analysis, it is understandable that the relation between the sampling frequency and the carrier frequency plays an important role in the estimation of the channel impulse response from a 1-bit quantized version of the received signal. We further understood that the noise also has an interesting effect on the channel impulse response estimate. It should however be noted that these effects are observed in the amplitude estimates of the channel impulse response. Although the path amplitudes might be estimated higher or lower, a strong effect is not observed on the time delay of the paths. Hence, for the considered application (where the time delay estimates of the paths are important), the demonstrator system which is based on a low-complexity monobit digital receiver is well suited. For other type of applications, where the exact value of the path amplitudes is relevant however, a careful consideration is required when using such type of systems.

7.3. Measurement Results

In this section, the performance of the localization and human posture capturing methods presented in the previous chapters are evaluated using the demonstrators system shown in Figure 7.1. First the TOA estimation (and hence the range estimation) accuracy is evaluated. Then the performance of the TOA based localization method presented in Chapter 3 is assessed. The discussion is then extended to the problem of human posture capturing.

7.3.1. TOA estimation accuracy

As discussed in Section 1.4, the problem of TOA estimation for UWB communication is a well investigated topic. Several previous works have proposed different methods with their own merits of accuracy and computational complexity. For this measurement evaluation, we use the method called search back window and thresholding (SBWT), as it provides a reasonable tradeoff between accuracy and computational complexity for the considered application. The SBWT TOA estimation method is presented in [73], which can be briefly revised as follows.

Let $\hat{h}(t)$ be the correlator output of the monobit ADC receiver board for a given agent and anchor link, which corresponds to the channel impulse response estimate of the link. In Figure 7.10, the blue plot shows such a typical output of the correlator for a LOS channel. Given $\hat{h}(t)$, the TOA estimation based on the SBWT method follows Algorithm 4. The algorithm requires two parameters: the threshold factor $\eta \in [0,1]$ and the search back window size $W^{(\text{SBWT})}$. These parameters need to be chosen carefully according to the characteristics of the channel. For example, when the channel has a clear LOS path that is distinct from the other multipath components, then the TOA estimate is almost the delay which corresponds to the maximum value of $\hat{h}(t)$. Hence for this case η needs to be chosen high and $W^{(\text{SBWT})}$ needs to be short. On the other hand, if the LOS is smeared with the other multipath components, then η needs to be lowered and $W^{(\text{SBWT})}$ needs to be widened such that the LOS path can be detected.

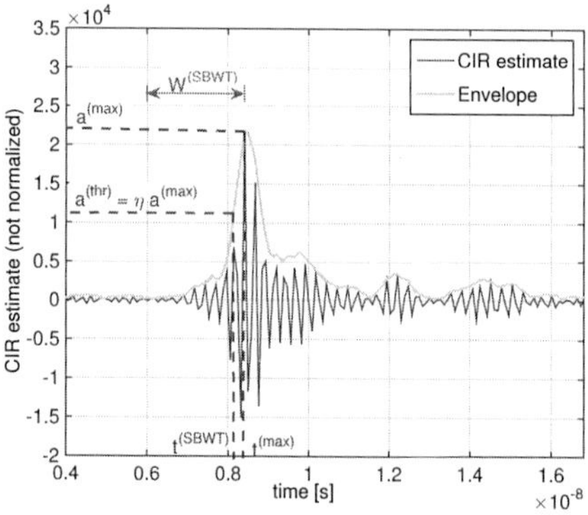

Figure 7.10.: TOA estimation based on search back window and thresholding (SBWT) method.

Algorithm 4 TOA estimation based on search back window and thresholding (SBWT) method.

1: *Input*: $\hat{h}(t)$, η, $W^{(\text{SBWT})}$.
2: Calculate envelope: $\bar{h}(t) = |\hat{h}(t) + j\mathcal{H}\{\hat{h}(t)\}|$, $\mathcal{H}\{\cdot\}$ denotes Hilbert transform.
3: Search max.: $t_{\text{max}} = \arg\max_t \bar{h}(t)$, $a_{\text{max}} = \bar{h}(t_{\text{max}})$.
4: Calculate threshold: $a^{(\text{thr})} = \eta a_{\text{max}}$.
5: Search back for the first threshold crossing: $t^{(\text{SBWT})} = \min t$, s.t. $\bar{h}(t) \geq a^{(\text{thr})}$, $t_{\text{max}} - W^{(\text{SBWT})} \leq t \leq t_{\text{max}}$.
6: *Output*: TOA estimate $t^{(\text{SBWT})}$.

To evaluate the TOA estimation accuracy that can be achieved when using the correlator output of the monobit digital receiver, we use the setup shown in Figure 7.11.

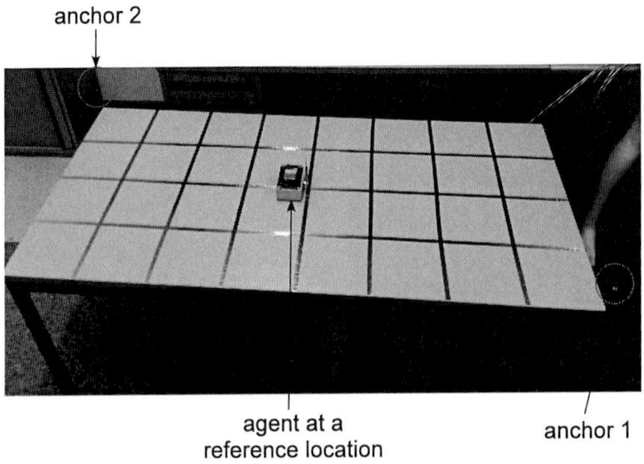

(a) Locations of the agent and the anchors on a table.

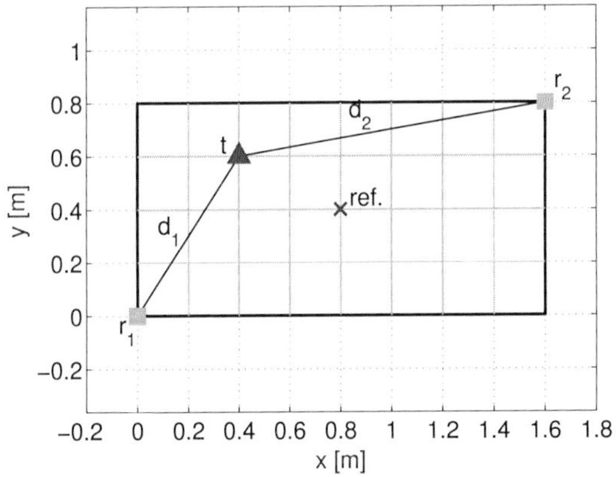

(b) Measurement grid.

Figure 7.11.: Measurement setup for TOA estimator evaluation.

Two anchors are located on the corners of a $1.6\,\mathrm{m} \times 0.8\,\mathrm{m}$ table. The table is partitioned as shown in the Figure and the agent is moved to all points in the grid except where the anchors are located (43 points in total). The channel impulse response estimates from both anchors are recored from all the agent locations. The TOA estimation accuracy is then evaluated using these recorded channel impulse responses.

Before we move to the discussion of the TOA estimation performance however, we need to make two important remarks:

- TOA estimates with bias: Since the clock of the agent is not synchronized with the anchors, as discussed in Section 2.3, the TOA estimates contain a bias due to clock asynchronicity of the agent with that of the anchors clock. For this reason we evaluate difference of the TOA estimates from the two anchors. Assuming the anchors clocks are phase synchronized, the ranges calculated from the TOA estimates of the two anchors can be written as

$$\hat{d}_1 = d_1 + b_t + e_1 \quad \text{and} \quad \hat{d}_2 = d_2 + b_t + e_2,$$

  where d_1 and d_2 are the true distances, b_t is the ranging offset due to the clock asynchronicity of the agent, e_1 and e_2 are the errors. The metric that is used to quantify the TOA estimation accuracy is the RMSE of the difference of the two range estimates given by

$$\mathrm{RMSE}_{\mathrm{range}} = \sqrt{\mathbb{E}\left\{\left((\hat{d}_1 - \hat{d}_2) - (d_1 - d_2)\right)^2\right\}}. \tag{7.1}$$

  It is worth to mention that the metric in (7.1) might be a pessimistic performance measure. Due to the subtraction of the two ranges, if the two measurement errors are statistically independent, the variance of the error is in fact doubled. Nevertheless, the metric can help us to understand the accuracy of the TOA estimation that can be achieved using the demonstrator system.

- Calibration of the anchor ranging offsets: As discussed in Section 7.2.2, the clocks of the anchors are only frequency synchronous, which leads to range measurement offsets. Furthermore, the constant propagation delays through the cables connecting the receive antennas to the input channels of the receiver board are unknown, which also results in ranging offsets. To calibrate out these offsets, range measurements are gathered from a reference agent location (see Figure 7.11b). The excess range measurements of the anchors are then used to calibrate out the unknown ranging offsets of the anchors.

The TOA estimation accuracy is evaluated using the measurement setup and the above procedure. The SBWT algorithm parameters are chosen as $\eta = 0.85$ and $W^{(\mathrm{SBWT})} = 1\,\mathrm{ns}$. Figure 7.12 shows the empirical CDF of the RMSE of the difference of the range estimates using the metric in (7.1). We see that the estimates have a median RMSE of around 1.1 cm. And more than 90 % of the estimates have an RMSE less than 1.3 cm. Noting the fact that we are using the metric in (7.1), where the error is almost doubled, one may conjecture that the actual range estimates have an RMSE in the range of sub-centimeters. Hence, the standard deviation of the range measurements $\sigma_{\text{range}} = 1\,\text{cm}$ that is considered in the previous chapters is indeed practically achievable.

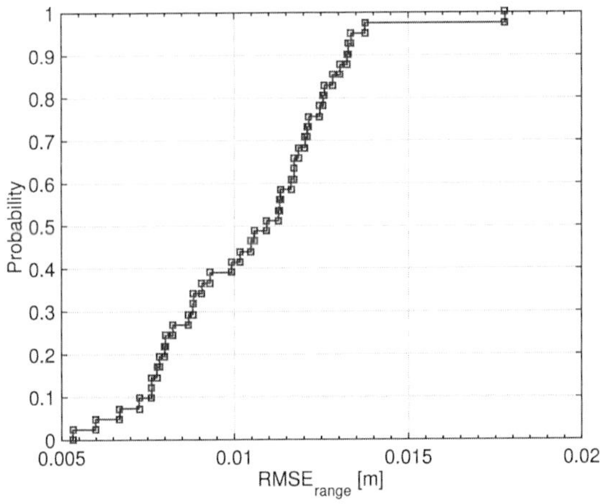

Figure 7.12.: Empirical CDF: RMSE of the difference of the range estimates.

7.3.2. TOA based localization accuracy

To evaluate the performance of TOA based localization, four anchors are placed at the corners of the table as shown in Figure 7.13. Before the localization phase, a calibration is performed to determine the locations and ranging offsets of the anchors. We applied two calibration methods: manual and self-calibration. In the manual calibration method, the anchor locations are measured using a digital laser distance measurement tape. To determine the ranging offsets, the agent is placed at a known location (marked as ref. in the figure) and the excess range of the anchors is estimated. For the self-calibration method on the other hand, the agent is moved to 25 different locations on the table and the range measurement between the agent and all anchors is recored. The locations and ranging offsets of the anchors is then estimated using the self-calibration method presented in Chapter 5. The anchor locations from both calibration methods are given in Table 7.1.

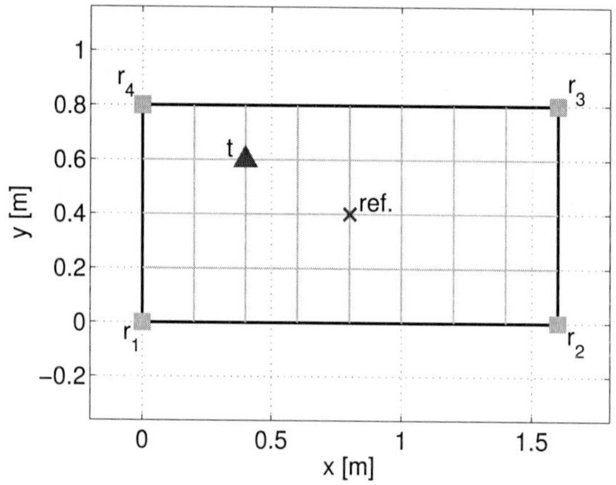

Figure 7.13.: Measurement setup: 2D localization.

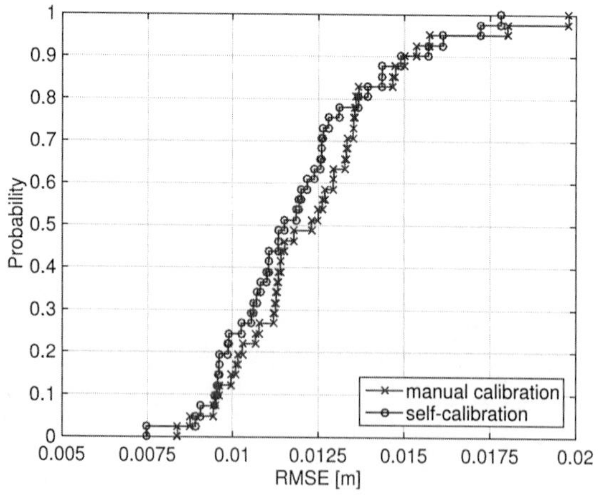

Figure 7.14.: TOA based localization: Empirical CDF RMSE of the agent location estimates.

Table 7.1.: Anchor locations: manual calibration and self-calibration. All values in meters.

anchor location	manual calibration	self-calibration
r_1	$[0, 0]^T$	$[0, 0]^T$
r_2	$[1.603, 0]^T$	$[1.5942, 0]^T$
r_3	$[1.598, 0.796]^T$	$[1.6094, 0.785]^T$
r_4	$[0, 0.804]^T$	$[-0.0125, 0.8029]^T$

The empirical CDF of the RMSE of the agent location estimates is shown in Figure 7.14. We see that, both for manual calibration and self-calibration, the median of the RMSE of the location estimates is around 1.2 cm. We further note that 90 % of the estimates have an RMSE less than 1.5 cm. Comparing the results with manual calibration and self-calibration, we see that their performance difference is small. Note however that manual calibration involves measurement of the anchors locations and also the measurement of the distance between all anchors and the reference point, which all have to be done by hand. This might be manageable for the considered simple localization setup. However, for more realistic sensor network localization problem, it might be a cumbersome and error prone task to perform such a manual calibration.

7.3.3. Human posture capturing accuracy

The localization setup discussed above is extended and applied for the human posture capturing problem. Here, it is worth to mention that the 1-bit ADC receiver board (with its current implementation) can realize up to 6 anchors, which can enable a 3D demonstration. Our initial evaluation however shows that the results for the 3D case were not satisfactory. As discussed in the outlook, one possible reason for this might be the antennas that are used for the evaluation which are not tailored for the human posture capturing setup.

Because of the aforementioned reason, we demonstrate a 2D human posture capturing setup. The agents and the anchors are located on a mannequin as shown in Figure 7.15. Two agents are located on the elbow and wrist joints of the left arm. Four anchors are located on the torso. With the reference coordinate system defined by anchors 1 and 2, the locations of the anchors is given by

$$r_1 = [0, 0]^T, \quad r_2 = [0.38\,\mathrm{m}, 0]^T,$$
$$r_3 = [0.235\,\mathrm{m}, 0.11\,\mathrm{m}]^T, \quad \text{and} \quad r_4 = [0.22\,\mathrm{m}, -0.115\,\mathrm{m}].$$

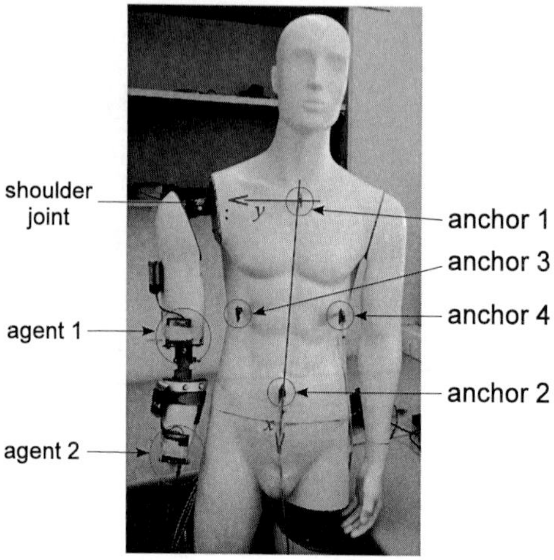

Figure 7.15.: Agent and anchor placement for 2D human posture capturing.

An example of the posture estimate, for a given arm posture, is shown in Figure 7.16. At the arm position shown in the figure, 20 estimates of the agents locations are recoded. To estimate the locations of the agents, the method discussed in Section 6.1 is applied. The 20 location estimates of agent 1 are marked with blue crosses and the mean value of the estimates is marked by a cyan cross. Similarly, for agent 2 the raw location estimates are marked with red crosses and their mean value is marked with a green cross. The corresponding standard deviations of the agent location estimates are also given in the figure (in cm). We see that raw agent location estimates form a cloud around their mean value, similar to the error-cloud observed in the simulation results discussed in Section 6.1.

To further assess the performance of the posture estimates, the arm is moved to different positions. Figure 7.17 shows the different postures of the arm and their corresponding estimates. From these results, we see that the cloudy nature of the agent location estimates is observed for all arm postures. It is interesting to also note that the cloud is relatively bigger (and hence the standard deviation of the estimates) for postures 1 and 5. As explained in Section 6.1, this is because for the agent locations in postures 1 and 5, the constraints allow the agents to move in the axis of the error cloud. On the other hand, for posture 3, where the constraints cut the error cloud perpendicularly, the variance of the agent location estimates is small.

7.4. Summary

A real-time demonstrator system for TOA based localization and human posture capturing is presented. The agents are realized by integrated UWB transmit nodes that generate and transmit DSSS signals. The anchors, on the other hand, are realized by a low-complexity finite resolution digital receiver board that uses monobit ADCs. It is shown that when the channel impulse responses are estimated from 1-bit quantized version of the received signals, system parameters (such as sampling frequency and carrier frequency) and noise can have an effect in the amplitude estimates but not on the time delay estimates. Although the presented demonstrator system is suitable for the considered application (where the time delay estimates are important), care must be taken when using the same system for other type of applications where the exact value of the amplitude estimates might be important.

From the experimental evaluation of the TOA estimates using the demonstrator system, it is shown that a range estimation accuracy is the range of centimeters can be achieved. The performance of the localization and calibration methods presented in Chapters 3 and 5, respectively, have been experimentally evaluated. It is shown that a localization accuracy with a median RMSE value of 1.2 cm is achieved. The evaluation is extended to the 2D human posture capturing problem. The agent location estimate error cloud, due to the clock asynchronousity of the agent, that is observed in the numerical evaluation in Section 6.1 is confirmed by the measurement results.

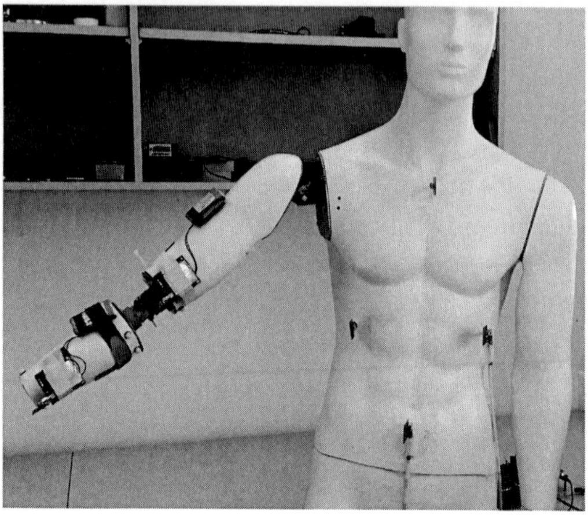

(a) Posture.

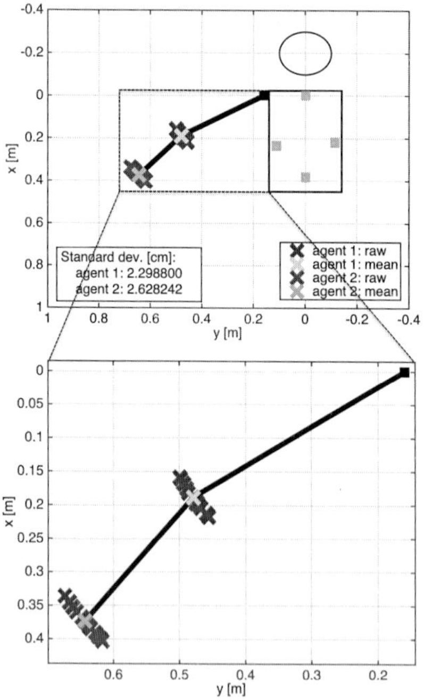

(b) Posture estimates: location estimates of agent 1 and agent 2.

Figure 7.16.: Human posture estimate.

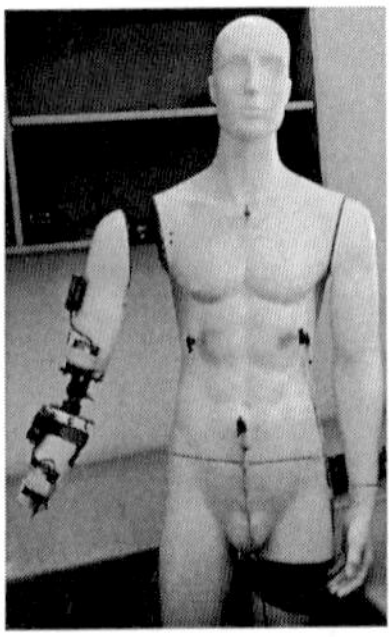

(a) Posture 1.

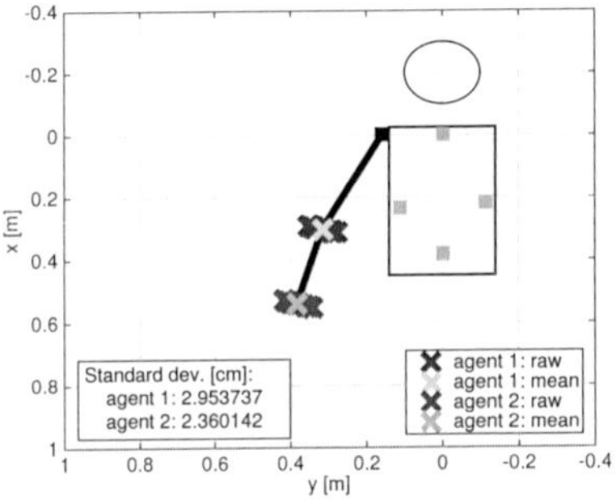

(b) Posture 1 estimate.

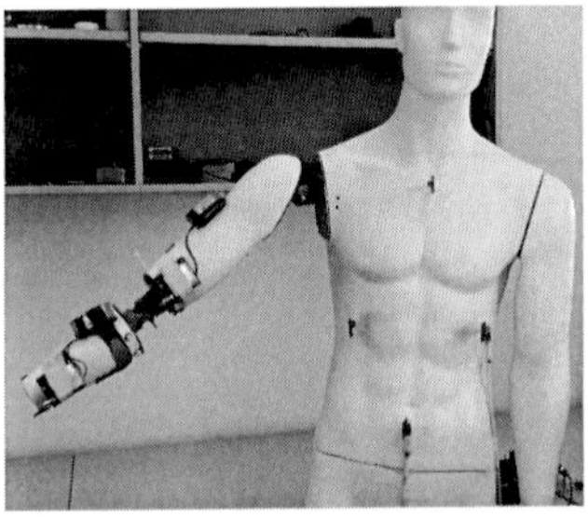

(c) Posture 2.

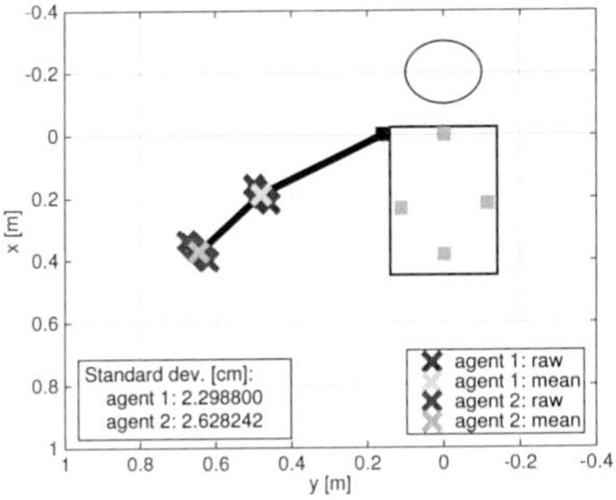

(d) Posture 2 estimate.

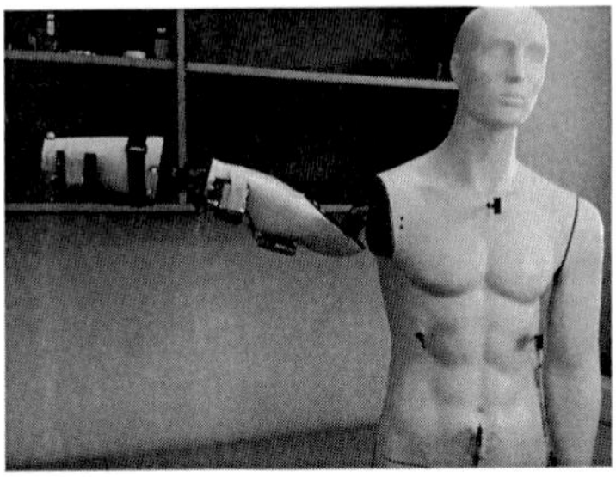

(e) Posture 3.

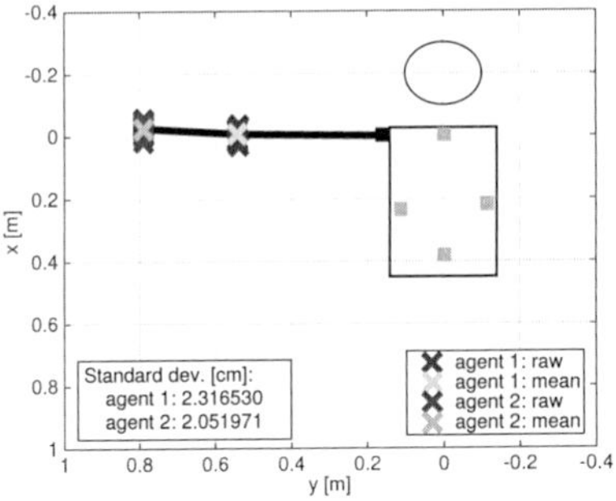

(f) Posture 3 estimate.

Figure 7.17.: Human posture estimate.

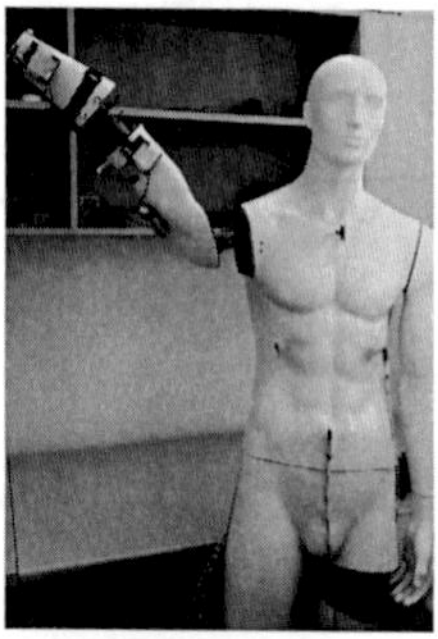

(g) Posture 4.

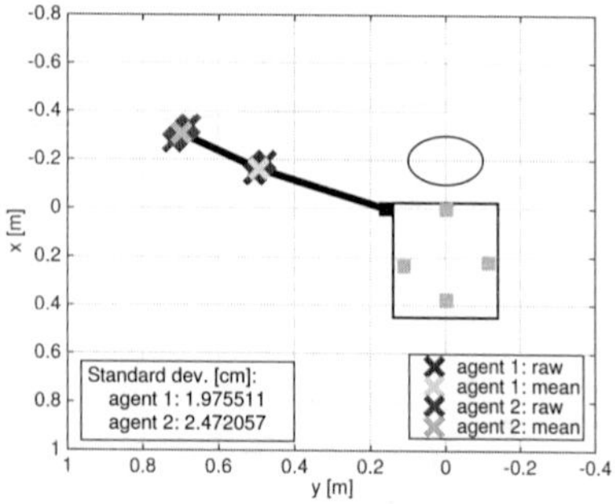

(h) Posture 4 estimate.

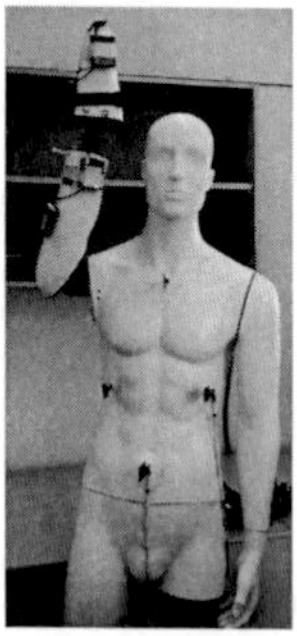

(i) Posture 5.

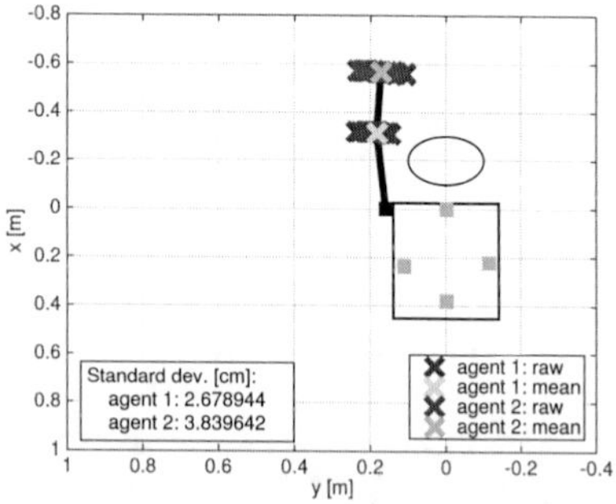

(j) Posture 5 estimate.

Figure 7.17.: Human posture estimate.

8. Conclusion and Outlook

8.1. Conclusion

TOA based human posture capturing system has potential distinct advantages compared to currently commercially available approaches. To unleash the full potential of such a system and enable ubiquitous use, a highly asymmetric system which is based on UWB communications technology is proposed and studied.

The clocks of the ultra-low complexity and ultra-low power transmit-only agents are asynchourous with each other. The TOA measurement biases due to the clock asynchronoucity of the agents have a considerable impact on the localization performance, most notably for the human posture capturing setup where the agents are located outside the convex-hull of the anchors. Accounting the location information of the agents offered by the kinematic constraints of the body is a key performance enabler for the localization of asynchronous agents. The ML solution of the localization problem of asynchronous agents with position constraints is a non-convex optimization problem. The relaxation of the ML estimator to SOCP problem results in a solution that is not unique and hence, the approach is not suitable for the considered system setup. On the other hand, the relaxation to SDP problem results in a solution that is close to the global optimum, which can further be refined with the ML estimator.

A NLOS situation between the agents and the anchors, which leads to an unknown TOA measurement bias, can be detected by performing a likelihood ration test on the features of the received signals. A simple likelihood ration test based on the SNR of the received signal provides a NLOS detection rate of more than 99 % while keeping the false alarm rate below 9 %.

Unaccounted location uncertainties of the anchors, e.g. due to the movement of the torso or errors from the calibration phase, can lead to a considerable degradation in the localization performance. Pervious related works assume the anchor location errors are small and simplify the localization problem by approximating the ranges with their first order Taylor-series expansion around the measured anchor positions. In this thesis however, we we propose a localization method which jointly estimates the locations of the anchors along with the locations of the agents without performing prior approximation. The proposed method outperforms the existing method, most notably when the anchor location errors are the dominant source of error and the number of jointly estimated agent locations are large. On the other hand, large number of jointly estimated agent locations means increased computationally complexity and hence, slow location update rate. Hence, in practice a reasonable tradeoff needs to be made between localization accuracy and the update rate.

A self-calibration method that enables the human posture capturing system to calibrate the location and clock offsets of the anchors without relying on external infrastructure is proposed and analyzed. The calibration method reuses the localization method to gather range measurements between the anchors and moving agent(s), which makes the calibration procedure simple and cost effective. The calibration problem is generalized such that different practically relevant clock synchronization scenarios between the anchors and the agents are taken into account. The ML solution of the calibration problem, which is a non-convex optimization problem, is relaxed to SDP problem. The SDP solution is then refined with the ML estimator. Numerical and experimental evaluations confirm that the proposed method is capable of accurately calibrating TOA based localization systems.

A low-cost measurement system that practically demonstrates the proposed human posturing system is presented. The agents are realized by integrated UWB transmitter nodes that generate and transmit DSSS signals. The anchors are realized by a finite resolution digital receiver board that uses monobit ADCs. Receiver systems with monobit ADCs are attractive as they enable a low-power and low-complexity implementation. Although the monobit quantization may have undesired effect on the amplitude response of the channel impulse response, the time delay estimates are not affected. Hence, the demonstrator system is suitable for the considered application. Experimental evaluation results show that a TOA based localization accuracy in the order of centimeters is achievable.

8.2. Outlook

Wireless channel between the anchors and the cluster head: In the scope of this thesis, the second hop channel between the anchors and the cluster head is assumed to be a wired channel, which only introduces a constant propagation delay and amplitude attenuation. To make the system fully wireless, a communication protocol that considers a wireless second hop channel needs be studied. One approach is to realize the anchors as a variant of AF relays, which amplify the received signals, add their specific signatures and forward them to the cluster head. From the received superposition signal, the cluster head should be able to estimate the channels between all anchors and agents as well as the channels between the anchors and the cluster head. For this case, the proposed localization and calibration methods may need to be extended to account the propagation delay through the second hop channel, which might not be constant. Another approach is to perform TOA estimation at the anchors and forward them to the cluster head for further processing, which can be seen as a decode and forward (DF) relaying strategy. The advantage of this approach is that the propagation delay of the second hop channel will not have an effect on posture capturing. The downside however is that it may increase the complexity of the anchors.

Hybrid system: From the discussion of the different commercially available human posture capturing systems, we note that inertial systems offer a high update rate and moderate system complexity. Their main drawback however is that it is prone to drift errors due to the integration operation of the gyroscope and accelerometer measurements. A hybrid system that combines inertial system and the proposed TOA based human posture capturing system can benefit from the advantages of both systems. It is interesting to also note that, for the inertial systems, the gyroscope and accelerometer readings have to be anyway communicated to a central processing unit using radio technology. Hence, in the hybrid system the TOA based system can serve both for communicating the sensor data and for posture capturing.

Antenna design: The antennas that are used in Chapter 7 are general purpose triangular monopole antennas, which were manufactured as presented in [139] and the design is based on [140]. The employed antennas have an undesired effect that the channel impulse response is affected by the relative orientation of the transmit and receive antennas. That is the reason why, in Chapter 7, the experimental evaluation of the localization and posture capturing methods is restricted to a 2D setup. To enable an accurate channel impulse response that is dependent only on the propagation channel between the agents and the anchors, antennas with radiation patters that are specifically optimized for on-body communications can be designed.

System for targeted applications: Compared to vision based and magnetic systems (which provide an accuracy in the sub-millimeter range), the accuracy of the proposed TOA based system is moderate (in the range of centimeters). However, the key advantages of the proposed system are independence from external infrastructure, non-intrusiveness and the low-cost. Some of the potential applications that can greatly benefit from these advantages (while accepting the moderate accuracy) are rehabilitation of patients with gait disorder, early detection of person's malpositions that may lead to chronic back pain and fall detection. With this in mind, the proposed posture capturing system can be optimized such that it meets the needs of the specific applications.

A. Definition of Common Distributions

For the likelihood ratio test in Section 2.4, the empirical distributions of the channel parameters are fitted to commonly used distributions. In the following, the PDFs of these commonly used distributions is defined.

Normal Distribution

The normal (also referred to as Gaussian) distribution is parametrized by the mean $\mu \in \mathbb{R}$ and the standard deviation $\sigma \in \mathbb{R}^+$. The PDF of a normal distributed random variable x is given by

$$p(x) = \frac{1}{\sqrt{2\pi\sigma^2}} \exp\left(-\frac{(x-\mu)^2}{2\sigma^2}\right).$$

Gaussian Extreme Value (GEV) Distribution

The GEV distribution is parametrized by a shape parameter $k \in \mathbb{R}$, a scale parameter $\sigma \in \mathbb{R}^+$ and a location parameter $\mu \in \mathbb{R}$. The PDF of a GEV distributed random variable x is defined as

$$p(x) = \frac{1}{\sigma}\left(1 + k\frac{(x-\mu)}{\sigma}\right)^{-(1+1/k)} \exp\left(-\left(1 + k\frac{(x-\mu)}{\sigma}\right)^{-1/k}\right).$$

T-Location-Scale Distribution

The t-location-scale distribution is parameterized by a shape parameter $k \in \mathbb{R}^+$, a scale parameter $\sigma \in \mathbb{R}^+$ and a location parameter $\mu \in \mathbb{R}$. The PDF of a t-location-scale distributed random variable x takes the form

$$p(x) = \frac{\Gamma((k+1)/2)}{\sqrt{k\pi\sigma^2}\Gamma(k/2)} \left(1 + \frac{(x-\mu)^2}{k\sigma^2}\right)^{-(k+1)/2},$$

where the Gamma function is defined as $\Gamma(a) = \int_0^\infty t^{a-1} \exp(-t)\,\mathrm{d}t$, for $a > 0$.

Nakagami Distribution

The Nakagami distribution is parametrized by a shape parameter $\mu \in \mathbb{R}^+$ and a scale parameter $\sigma \in \mathbb{R}^+$. The PDF of a normal distributed random variable $x > 0$ is given by

$$p(x) = \frac{2\mu^\mu}{\sigma\Gamma(\mu)} x^{2\mu-1} \exp\left(-\frac{\mu}{\sigma}x^2\right).$$

Gamma Distribution

The Gamma distribution is parametrized by a shape parameter $\mu \in \mathbb{R}^+$ and a scale parameter $\sigma \in \mathbb{R}^+$. The PDF of a Gamma distributed random variable $x > 0$ is defined as

$$p(x) = \frac{x^{\mu-1}}{\sigma^\mu\Gamma(\mu)} \exp\left(-\frac{x}{\sigma}\right).$$

B. SOCP Problem

Let $\boldsymbol{x} \in \mathbb{R}^{N\times 1}$ be the optimization variable . A second order cone programming (SOCP) problem is a convex optimization problem of the form [119]

$$\hat{\boldsymbol{x}} = \arg\min_{\boldsymbol{x}} \boldsymbol{f}^T\boldsymbol{x} \tag{B.1a}$$

$$\text{s.t. } \|\boldsymbol{A}_i\boldsymbol{x} + \boldsymbol{b}_i\| \leq \boldsymbol{c}_i^T\boldsymbol{x} + d_i, \quad \text{for } i \in \{1, \dots, M\}, \tag{B.1b}$$

$$\boldsymbol{F}\boldsymbol{x} = \boldsymbol{g}, \tag{B.1c}$$

where $\boldsymbol{f} \in \mathbb{R}^{N\times 1}$, $\boldsymbol{A}_i \in \mathbb{R}^{N_i\times N}$, $\{\boldsymbol{b}_i, \boldsymbol{c}_i\} \in \mathbb{R}^{N_i\times 1}$, $d_i \in \mathbb{R}$, $\boldsymbol{F} \in \mathbb{R}^{P\times N}$ and $\boldsymbol{g} \in \mathbb{R}^{P\times 1}$ are known. We see that the SOCP problem has a linear objective function as in (B.1a), a second order cone constraint (B.1b) and a linear equality constraint (B.1c).

Note that if $\boldsymbol{c}_i = \boldsymbol{0}$ for $i \in \{1, \dots, M\}$, then both side of the constraint in (B.1b) to result in a quadratic constraint. In this case, the problem in (B.1) is equivalent to a quadratically constrained quadratic problem (QCQP).

C. SDP Problem

Given an optimization variable $\boldsymbol{x} \in \mathbb{R}^{N\times 1}$. A semi-definite programing problem is a convex optimization problem of the following form [141]

$$\hat{\boldsymbol{x}} = \arg\min_{\boldsymbol{x}} \boldsymbol{f}^T\boldsymbol{x} \tag{C.1a}$$

$$\text{s.t. } \boldsymbol{c}_k^T\boldsymbol{x} = b_k, \quad \text{for } k \in \{1,\ldots,K\}, \tag{C.1b}$$

$$\boldsymbol{F}(\boldsymbol{x}) \succeq \boldsymbol{0}, \tag{C.1c}$$

where $\boldsymbol{F}(\boldsymbol{x}) = \boldsymbol{F}_0 + \sum_{n=1}^{N} x_n\boldsymbol{F}_n$, with known matrices and vectors $\boldsymbol{f} \in \mathbb{R}^{N\times 1}$, $\boldsymbol{c}_k \in \mathbb{R}^{N\times 1}$, $\{\boldsymbol{F}_0,\ldots,\boldsymbol{F}_N\} \in \mathbb{R}^{M\times M}$ and $b_k \in \mathbb{R}$.

The objective function of the SDP problem in (C.1a) is linear and the constraint in (C.1b) is also linear with respect to the variable $\boldsymbol{x}$. The constraint in (C.1c) is a linear matrix inequality constraint, which subjects $\boldsymbol{F}(\boldsymbol{x})$ to be a semi-definite matrix.

D. Calculation of the Fisher Information Matrix $\boldsymbol{J}$

D.1. Localization with Perfectly Known Anchor Locations

The FIM of the unknown agent locations $\boldsymbol{t}$ and ranging offsets $\boldsymbol{b}_\mathrm{t}$ is given by

$$\begin{aligned}\boldsymbol{J} &= \begin{bmatrix} \mathbb{E}\left\{\left(\frac{\partial \mathcal{L}}{\partial \boldsymbol{t}}\right)^T\left(\frac{\partial \mathcal{L}}{\partial \boldsymbol{t}}\right)\right\} & \mathbb{E}\left\{\left(\frac{\partial \mathcal{L}}{\partial \boldsymbol{t}}\right)^T\left(\frac{\partial \mathcal{L}}{\partial \boldsymbol{b}_\mathrm{t}}\right)\right\} \\ \mathbb{E}\left\{\left(\frac{\partial \mathcal{L}}{\partial \boldsymbol{b}_\mathrm{t}}\right)^T\left(\frac{\partial \mathcal{L}}{\partial \boldsymbol{t}}\right)\right\} & \mathbb{E}\left\{\left(\frac{\partial \mathcal{L}}{\partial \boldsymbol{b}_\mathrm{t}}\right)^T\left(\frac{\partial \mathcal{L}}{\partial \boldsymbol{b}_\mathrm{t}}\right)\right\} \end{bmatrix} \\ &\triangleq \begin{bmatrix} \boldsymbol{J}_1 & \boldsymbol{J}_2 \\ \boldsymbol{J}_2^T & \boldsymbol{J}_3 \end{bmatrix},\end{aligned}$$

with the log-likelihood function

$$\mathcal{L}\left(\boldsymbol{d}\middle|\, \boldsymbol{t}, \boldsymbol{b}_\mathrm{t}\right) = \ln\left(\frac{|\boldsymbol{\Sigma}|^{-\frac{1}{2}}}{(2\pi)^{\frac{N_\mathrm{r}N_\mathrm{t}}{2}}}\right) - \frac{1}{2}\left(\boldsymbol{d} - \boldsymbol{g} - \boldsymbol{\Gamma}_\mathrm{t}\boldsymbol{b}_\mathrm{t}\right)^T \boldsymbol{\Sigma}^{-1}\left(\boldsymbol{d} - \boldsymbol{g} - \boldsymbol{\Gamma}_\mathrm{t}\boldsymbol{b}_\mathrm{t}\right).$$

Taking the partial derivative of $\mathcal{L}\left(\boldsymbol{d}\middle|\, \boldsymbol{t}, \boldsymbol{b}_\mathrm{t}\right)$ with respect to $\boldsymbol{t}$ gives us

$$\begin{aligned}\frac{\partial \mathcal{L}}{\partial \boldsymbol{t}} &= -\left(\boldsymbol{d} - \boldsymbol{g} - \boldsymbol{\Gamma}_\mathrm{t}\boldsymbol{b}_\mathrm{t}\right)^T \boldsymbol{\Sigma}^{-1}\frac{\partial(\boldsymbol{d} - \boldsymbol{g} - \boldsymbol{\Gamma}_\mathrm{t}\boldsymbol{b}_\mathrm{t})}{\partial \boldsymbol{t}} \\ &= \left(\boldsymbol{d} - \boldsymbol{g} - \boldsymbol{\Gamma}_\mathrm{t}\boldsymbol{b}_\mathrm{t}\right)^T \boldsymbol{\Sigma}^{-1}\frac{\partial \boldsymbol{g}}{\partial \boldsymbol{t}}. \end{aligned} \tag{D.1}$$

Hence, the first sub-matrix of the FIM $\boldsymbol{J}_1$ takes the form

$$\begin{aligned}\boldsymbol{J}_1 &= \mathbb{E}\left\{\left(\frac{\partial \mathcal{L}}{\partial \boldsymbol{t}}\right)^T\left(\frac{\partial \mathcal{L}}{\partial \boldsymbol{t}}\right)\right\} \\ &= \left(\frac{\partial \boldsymbol{g}}{\partial \boldsymbol{t}}\right)^T \boldsymbol{\Sigma}^{-1}\mathbb{E}\left\{\left(\boldsymbol{d} - \boldsymbol{g} - \boldsymbol{\Gamma}_\mathrm{t}\boldsymbol{b}_\mathrm{t}\right)\left(\boldsymbol{d} - \boldsymbol{g} - \boldsymbol{\Gamma}_\mathrm{t}\boldsymbol{b}_\mathrm{t}\right)^T\right\}\boldsymbol{\Sigma}^{-1}\frac{\partial \boldsymbol{g}}{\partial \boldsymbol{t}} \\ &= \left(\frac{\partial \boldsymbol{g}}{\partial \boldsymbol{t}}\right)^T \boldsymbol{\Sigma}^{-1}\boldsymbol{\Sigma}\boldsymbol{\Sigma}^{-1}\frac{\partial \boldsymbol{g}}{\partial \boldsymbol{t}}\end{aligned}$$

$$= \left(\frac{\partial \boldsymbol{g}}{\partial \boldsymbol{t}}\right)^T \boldsymbol{\Sigma}^{-1} \frac{\partial \boldsymbol{g}}{\partial \boldsymbol{t}}.$$

Similarly, taking the partial derivative of $\mathcal{L}(\boldsymbol{d}|\,\boldsymbol{t}, \boldsymbol{b}_{\mathrm{t}})$ with respect to $\boldsymbol{b}_{\mathrm{t}}$ results in

$$\frac{\partial \mathcal{L}}{\partial \boldsymbol{b}_{\mathrm{t}}} = (\boldsymbol{d} - \boldsymbol{g} - \boldsymbol{\Gamma}_{\mathrm{t}}\boldsymbol{b}_{\mathrm{t}})^T \boldsymbol{\Sigma}^{-1}\boldsymbol{\Gamma}_{\mathrm{t}}.$$

This leads to the second sub-matrix of the FIM $\boldsymbol{J}_2$

$$\begin{aligned}\boldsymbol{J}_2 &= \mathbb{E}\left\{\left(\tfrac{\partial \mathcal{L}}{\partial \boldsymbol{t}}\right)^T \left(\tfrac{\partial \mathcal{L}}{\partial \boldsymbol{b}_{\mathrm{t}}}\right)\right\} \\ &= \left(\frac{\partial \boldsymbol{g}}{\partial \boldsymbol{t}}\right)^T \boldsymbol{\Sigma}^{-1}\mathbb{E}\left\{(\boldsymbol{d} - \boldsymbol{g} - \boldsymbol{\Gamma}_{\mathrm{t}}\boldsymbol{b}_{\mathrm{t}})(\boldsymbol{d} - \boldsymbol{g} - \boldsymbol{\Gamma}_{\mathrm{t}}\boldsymbol{b}_{\mathrm{t}})^T\right\}\boldsymbol{\Sigma}^{-1}\boldsymbol{\Gamma}_{\mathrm{t}} \\ &= \left(\frac{\partial \boldsymbol{g}}{\partial \boldsymbol{t}}\right)^T \boldsymbol{\Sigma}^{-1}\boldsymbol{\Gamma}_{\mathrm{t}}.\end{aligned}$$

We further see that the third sub-matrix of the FIM $\boldsymbol{J}_3$ is give by

$$\begin{aligned}\boldsymbol{J}_3 &= \mathbb{E}\left\{\left(\tfrac{\partial \mathcal{L}}{\partial \boldsymbol{b}_{\mathrm{t}}}\right)^T \left(\tfrac{\partial \mathcal{L}}{\partial \boldsymbol{b}_{\mathrm{t}}}\right)\right\} \\ &= \boldsymbol{\Gamma}_{\mathrm{t}}^T\boldsymbol{\Sigma}^{-1}\mathbb{E}\left\{(\boldsymbol{d} - \boldsymbol{g} - \boldsymbol{\Gamma}_{\mathrm{t}}\boldsymbol{b}_{\mathrm{t}})(\boldsymbol{d} - \boldsymbol{g} - \boldsymbol{\Gamma}_{\mathrm{t}}\boldsymbol{b}_{\mathrm{t}})^T\right\}\boldsymbol{\Sigma}^{-1}\boldsymbol{\Gamma}_{\mathrm{t}} \\ &= \boldsymbol{\Gamma}_{\mathrm{t}}^T\boldsymbol{\Sigma}^{-1}\boldsymbol{\Gamma}_{\mathrm{t}}.\end{aligned}$$

D.2. Localization with Anchor Position Uncertainties

Given the range measurements $\boldsymbol{d}$ and the imperfect anchor positions $\tilde{\boldsymbol{r}}$, the log-likelihood function of the unknown parameters $\{\boldsymbol{t}, \boldsymbol{b}_{\mathrm{t}}, \boldsymbol{r}\}$ takes the form in (4.7)

$$\begin{aligned}\mathcal{L}(\boldsymbol{d}, \tilde{\boldsymbol{r}}|\boldsymbol{t}, \boldsymbol{b}_{\mathrm{t}}, \boldsymbol{r}) = &-\tfrac{1}{2}(\boldsymbol{d} - \boldsymbol{g} - \boldsymbol{\Gamma}_{\mathrm{t}}\boldsymbol{b}_{\mathrm{t}})^T\boldsymbol{\Sigma}^{-1}(\boldsymbol{d} - \boldsymbol{g} - \boldsymbol{\Gamma}_{\mathrm{t}}\boldsymbol{b}_{\mathrm{t}}) - \tfrac{1}{2}(\tilde{\boldsymbol{r}} - \boldsymbol{r})^T\boldsymbol{\Delta}^{-1}(\tilde{\boldsymbol{r}} - \boldsymbol{r}) \\ &+ \ln\left(\frac{|\boldsymbol{\Sigma}|^{-\frac{1}{2}}}{(2\pi)^{\frac{N_{\mathrm{r}}N_{\mathrm{t}}}{2}}} \times \frac{|\boldsymbol{\Delta}|^{-\frac{1}{2}}}{(2\pi)^{\frac{3N_{\mathrm{r}}}{2}}}\right)\end{aligned}$$

The FIM of the unknown parameters is hence given by

$$\boldsymbol{J} = \left[\begin{array}{c|cc} \mathbb{E}\left\{\left(\frac{\partial \mathcal{L}}{\partial \boldsymbol{t}}\right)^T\left(\frac{\partial \mathcal{L}}{\partial \boldsymbol{t}}\right)\right\} & \mathbb{E}\left\{\left(\frac{\partial \mathcal{L}}{\partial \boldsymbol{t}}\right)^T\left(\frac{\partial \mathcal{L}}{\partial \boldsymbol{b}_{\mathrm{t}}}\right)\right\} & \mathbb{E}\left\{\left(\frac{\partial \mathcal{L}}{\partial \boldsymbol{t}}\right)^T\left(\frac{\partial \mathcal{L}}{\partial \boldsymbol{r}}\right)\right\} \\ \hline \mathbb{E}\left\{\left(\frac{\partial \mathcal{L}}{\partial \boldsymbol{b}_{\mathrm{t}}}\right)^T\left(\frac{\partial \mathcal{L}}{\partial \boldsymbol{t}}\right)\right\} & \mathbb{E}\left\{\left(\frac{\partial \mathcal{L}}{\partial \boldsymbol{b}_{\mathrm{t}}}\right)^T\left(\frac{\partial \mathcal{L}}{\partial \boldsymbol{b}_{\mathrm{t}}}\right)\right\} & \mathbb{E}\left\{\left(\frac{\partial \mathcal{L}}{\partial \boldsymbol{b}_{\mathrm{t}}}\right)^T\left(\frac{\partial \mathcal{L}}{\boldsymbol{r}}\right)\right\} \\ \mathbb{E}\left\{\left(\frac{\partial \mathcal{L}}{\partial \boldsymbol{r}}\right)^T\left(\frac{\partial \mathcal{L}}{\partial \boldsymbol{t}}\right)\right\} & \mathbb{E}\left\{\left(\frac{\partial \mathcal{L}}{\partial \boldsymbol{r}}\right)^T\left(\frac{\partial \mathcal{L}}{\partial \boldsymbol{b}_{\mathrm{t}}}\right)\right\} & \mathbb{E}\left\{\left(\frac{\partial \mathcal{L}}{\partial \boldsymbol{r}}\right)^T\left(\frac{\partial \mathcal{L}}{\partial \boldsymbol{r}}\right)\right\} \end{array}\right] \triangleq \begin{bmatrix} \boldsymbol{J}_1 & \boldsymbol{J}_2 \\ \boldsymbol{J}_2^T & \boldsymbol{J}_3 \end{bmatrix}.$$

Taking the partial derivative of $\mathcal{L}\left(\boldsymbol{d}, \tilde{\boldsymbol{r}}|\boldsymbol{t}, \boldsymbol{b}_{\mathrm{t}}, \boldsymbol{r}\right)$ with respect to $\boldsymbol{t}$ results in

$$\frac{\partial \mathcal{L}}{\partial \boldsymbol{t}} = \left(\boldsymbol{d} - \boldsymbol{g} - \boldsymbol{\Gamma}_{\mathrm{t}}\boldsymbol{b}_{\mathrm{t}}\right)^T \boldsymbol{\Sigma}^{-1} \frac{\partial \boldsymbol{g}}{\partial \boldsymbol{t}}.$$

Noting that this is the same as in (D.1), the first sub-matrix of the FIM $\boldsymbol{J}_1$ takes the form

$$\boldsymbol{J}_1 = \left(\frac{\partial \boldsymbol{g}}{\partial \boldsymbol{t}}\right)^T \boldsymbol{\Sigma}^{-1} \frac{\partial \boldsymbol{g}}{\partial \boldsymbol{t}}.$$

Taking the partial derivative of the log-likelihood function with respect to $\boldsymbol{b}_{\mathrm{t}}$ gives us

$$\frac{\partial \mathcal{L}}{\partial \boldsymbol{b}_{\mathrm{t}}} = \left(\boldsymbol{d} - \boldsymbol{g} - \boldsymbol{\Gamma}_{\mathrm{t}}\boldsymbol{b}_{\mathrm{t}}\right)^T \boldsymbol{\Sigma}^{-1} \boldsymbol{\Gamma}_{\mathrm{t}}.$$

Hence, the first building block of the sub-matrix of the FIM $\boldsymbol{J}_2$ takes the form

$$\mathbb{E}\left\{\left(\tfrac{\partial \mathcal{L}}{\partial \boldsymbol{t}}\right)^T \left(\tfrac{\partial \mathcal{L}}{\partial \boldsymbol{b}_{\mathrm{t}}}\right)\right\} = \left(\frac{\partial \boldsymbol{g}}{\partial \boldsymbol{t}}\right)^T \boldsymbol{\Sigma}^{-1} \boldsymbol{\Gamma}_{\mathrm{t}}.$$

The partial derivative of the log-likelihood with respect to $\boldsymbol{r}$ results in

$$\begin{aligned}\frac{\partial \mathcal{L}}{\partial \boldsymbol{r}} &= -\left(\boldsymbol{d} - \boldsymbol{g} - \boldsymbol{\Gamma}_{\mathrm{t}}\boldsymbol{b}_{\mathrm{t}}\right)^T \boldsymbol{\Sigma}^{-1} \frac{\partial(\boldsymbol{d} - \boldsymbol{g} - \boldsymbol{\Gamma}_{\mathrm{t}}\boldsymbol{b}_{\mathrm{t}})}{\partial \boldsymbol{t}} - (\tilde{\boldsymbol{r}} - \boldsymbol{r})^T \boldsymbol{\Delta}^{-1}(-\boldsymbol{I}) \\ &= \left(\boldsymbol{d} - \boldsymbol{g} - \boldsymbol{\Gamma}_{\mathrm{t}}\boldsymbol{b}_{\mathrm{t}}\right)^T \boldsymbol{\Sigma}^{-1} \frac{\partial \boldsymbol{g}}{\partial \boldsymbol{r}} + (\tilde{\boldsymbol{r}} - \boldsymbol{r})^T \boldsymbol{\Delta}^{-1}.\end{aligned}$$

The second building block of the sub-matrix of the FIM $\boldsymbol{J}_2$ is hence given by

$$\begin{aligned}\mathbb{E}\left\{\left(\tfrac{\partial \mathcal{L}}{\partial \boldsymbol{t}}\right)^T \left(\tfrac{\partial \mathcal{L}}{\partial \boldsymbol{r}}\right)\right\} &= \left(\frac{\partial \boldsymbol{g}}{\partial \boldsymbol{t}}\right)^T \boldsymbol{\Sigma}^{-1} \frac{\partial \boldsymbol{g}}{\partial \boldsymbol{r}} + \left(\frac{\partial \boldsymbol{g}}{\partial \boldsymbol{t}}\right)^T \boldsymbol{\Sigma}^{-1} \mathbb{E}\left\{\left(\boldsymbol{d} - \boldsymbol{g} - \boldsymbol{\Gamma}_{\mathrm{t}}\boldsymbol{b}_{\mathrm{t}}\right)(\tilde{\boldsymbol{r}} - \boldsymbol{r})^T\right\} \boldsymbol{\Delta}^{-1} \\ &= \left(\frac{\partial \boldsymbol{g}}{\partial \boldsymbol{t}}\right)^T \boldsymbol{\Sigma}^{-1} \frac{\partial \boldsymbol{g}}{\partial \boldsymbol{r}}.\end{aligned}$$

Here, we have used the assumption that the range measurement error $(\boldsymbol{d} - \boldsymbol{g} - \boldsymbol{\Gamma}_{\mathrm{t}}\boldsymbol{b}_{\mathrm{t}})$ and $(\tilde{\boldsymbol{r}} - \boldsymbol{r})$ are statistically independent zero-mean random vectors.

Similarly, the building blocks of the third sub-matrix of the FIM $\boldsymbol{J}_3$ can be calculated as follows.

$$\mathbb{E}\left\{\left(\tfrac{\partial \mathcal{L}}{\partial \boldsymbol{b}_{\mathrm{t}}}\right)^T \left(\tfrac{\partial \mathcal{L}}{\partial \boldsymbol{b}_{\mathrm{t}}}\right)\right\} = \boldsymbol{\Gamma}_{\mathrm{t}}^T \boldsymbol{\Sigma}^{-1} \boldsymbol{\Gamma}_{\mathrm{t}}.$$

$$\mathbb{E}\left\{\left(\frac{\partial\mathcal{L}}{\partial \boldsymbol{b}_{\mathrm{t}}}\right)^{T}\left(\frac{\partial\mathcal{L}}{\partial \boldsymbol{r}}\right)\right\} = \boldsymbol{\Gamma}_{\mathrm{t}}^{T}\boldsymbol{\Sigma}^{-1}\frac{\partial \boldsymbol{g}}{\partial \boldsymbol{r}}.$$

$$\begin{aligned}\mathbb{E}\left\{\left(\frac{\partial\mathcal{L}}{\partial \boldsymbol{r}}\right)^{T}\left(\frac{\partial\mathcal{L}}{\partial \boldsymbol{r}}\right)\right\} &= \left(\frac{\partial \boldsymbol{g}}{\partial \boldsymbol{r}}\right)^{T}\boldsymbol{\Sigma}^{-1}\frac{\partial \boldsymbol{g}}{\partial \boldsymbol{r}} + \boldsymbol{\Delta}^{-1}\mathbb{E}\left\{(\tilde{\boldsymbol{r}}-\boldsymbol{r})(\tilde{\boldsymbol{r}}-\boldsymbol{r})^{T}\right\}\boldsymbol{\Delta}^{-1}\\ &= \left(\frac{\partial \boldsymbol{g}}{\partial \boldsymbol{r}}\right)^{T}\boldsymbol{\Sigma}^{-1}\frac{\partial \boldsymbol{g}}{\partial \boldsymbol{r}} + \boldsymbol{\Delta}^{-1}.\end{aligned}$$

D.3. Self-Calibration Method

For the calibration problem, the FIM of all the unknown parameters $\boldsymbol{\theta} = \left[\boldsymbol{\theta}_1^T, \boldsymbol{\theta}_2^T\right]^T$ is given by

$$\boldsymbol{J} = \mathbb{E}\left\{\left(\frac{\partial\mathcal{L}}{\partial\boldsymbol{\theta}}\right)^{T}\frac{\partial\mathcal{L}}{\partial\boldsymbol{\theta}}\right\} \triangleq \begin{bmatrix}\boldsymbol{J}_1 & \boldsymbol{J}_2\\ \boldsymbol{J}_2^T & \boldsymbol{J}_3\end{bmatrix},$$

where the sub-matrices of the FIM are constructed as

$$\boldsymbol{J}_1 = \mathbb{E}\left\{\left(\frac{\partial\mathcal{L}}{\partial\boldsymbol{\theta}_1}\right)^{T}\frac{\partial\mathcal{L}}{\partial\boldsymbol{\theta}_1}\right\} = \begin{bmatrix}\mathbb{E}\left\{\left(\frac{\partial\mathcal{L}}{\partial\boldsymbol{r}}\right)^{T}\left(\frac{\partial\mathcal{L}}{\partial\boldsymbol{r}}\right)\right\} & \mathbb{E}\left\{\left(\frac{\partial\mathcal{L}}{\partial\boldsymbol{r}}\right)^{T}\left(\frac{\partial\mathcal{L}}{\partial\boldsymbol{b}_{\mathrm{r}}}\right)\right\}\\ \mathbb{E}\left\{\left(\frac{\partial\mathcal{L}}{\partial\boldsymbol{b}_{\mathrm{r}}}\right)^{T}\left(\frac{\partial\mathcal{L}}{\partial\boldsymbol{r}}\right)\right\} & \mathbb{E}\left\{\left(\frac{\partial\mathcal{L}}{\partial\boldsymbol{b}_{\mathrm{r}}}\right)^{T}\left(\frac{\partial\mathcal{L}}{\partial\boldsymbol{b}_{\mathrm{r}}}\right)\right\}\end{bmatrix},$$

$$\boldsymbol{J}_2 = \mathbb{E}\left\{\left(\frac{\partial\mathcal{L}}{\partial\boldsymbol{\theta}_1}\right)^{T}\frac{\partial\mathcal{L}}{\partial\boldsymbol{\theta}_2}\right\} = \begin{bmatrix}\mathbb{E}\left\{\left(\frac{\partial\mathcal{L}}{\partial\boldsymbol{r}}\right)^{T}\left(\frac{\partial\mathcal{L}}{\partial\boldsymbol{t}}\right)\right\} & \mathbb{E}\left\{\left(\frac{\partial\mathcal{L}}{\partial\boldsymbol{r}}\right)^{T}\left(\frac{\partial\mathcal{L}}{\partial\boldsymbol{b}_{\mathrm{t}}}\right)\right\}\\ \mathbb{E}\left\{\left(\frac{\partial\mathcal{L}}{\partial\boldsymbol{b}_{\mathrm{r}}}\right)^{T}\left(\frac{\partial\mathcal{L}}{\partial\boldsymbol{t}}\right)\right\} & \mathbb{E}\left\{\left(\frac{\partial\mathcal{L}}{\partial\boldsymbol{b}_{\mathrm{r}}}\right)^{T}\left(\frac{\partial\mathcal{L}}{\partial\boldsymbol{b}_{\mathrm{t}}}\right)\right\}\end{bmatrix},$$

$$\boldsymbol{J}_3 = \mathbb{E}\left\{\left(\frac{\partial\mathcal{L}}{\partial\boldsymbol{\theta}_2}\right)^{T}\frac{\partial\mathcal{L}}{\partial\boldsymbol{\theta}_2}\right\} = \begin{bmatrix}\mathbb{E}\left\{\left(\frac{\partial\mathcal{L}}{\partial\boldsymbol{t}}\right)^{T}\left(\frac{\partial\mathcal{L}}{\partial\boldsymbol{t}}\right)\right\} & \mathbb{E}\left\{\left(\frac{\partial\mathcal{L}}{\partial\boldsymbol{t}}\right)^{T}\left(\frac{\partial\mathcal{L}}{\partial\boldsymbol{b}_{\mathrm{t}}}\right)\right\}\\ \mathbb{E}\left\{\left(\frac{\partial\mathcal{L}}{\partial\boldsymbol{b}_{\mathrm{t}}}\right)^{T}\left(\frac{\partial\mathcal{L}}{\partial\boldsymbol{t}}\right)\right\} & \mathbb{E}\left\{\left(\frac{\partial\mathcal{L}}{\partial\boldsymbol{b}_{\mathrm{t}}}\right)^{T}\left(\frac{\partial\mathcal{L}}{\partial\boldsymbol{b}_{\mathrm{t}}}\right)\right\}\end{bmatrix}.$$

The log-likelihood of unknown parameters $\boldsymbol{\theta} = [\boldsymbol{\theta}_1^T, \boldsymbol{\theta}_2^T]^T$ is given by

$$\begin{aligned}\mathcal{L}(\boldsymbol{d}, \boldsymbol{f}\,|\,\boldsymbol{r}, \boldsymbol{t}, \boldsymbol{b}_{\mathrm{r}}, \boldsymbol{b}_{\mathrm{t}}) = &-\frac{1}{2}\left(\boldsymbol{d}-\boldsymbol{g}-\boldsymbol{\Gamma}_{\mathrm{t}}\boldsymbol{b}_{\mathrm{t}}-\boldsymbol{\Gamma}_{\mathrm{r}}\boldsymbol{b}_{\mathrm{r}}\right)^{T}\boldsymbol{\Sigma}_{\mathrm{d}}^{-1}\left(\boldsymbol{d}-\boldsymbol{g}-\boldsymbol{\Gamma}_{\mathrm{t}}\boldsymbol{b}_{\mathrm{t}}-\boldsymbol{\Gamma}_{\mathrm{r}}\boldsymbol{b}_{\mathrm{r}}\right)\\ &-\frac{1}{2}\left(\boldsymbol{f}-\boldsymbol{h}-\boldsymbol{\Lambda}\boldsymbol{b}_{\mathrm{r}}\right)^{T}\boldsymbol{\Sigma}_{\mathrm{f}}^{-1}\left(\boldsymbol{f}-\boldsymbol{h}-\boldsymbol{\Lambda}\boldsymbol{b}_{\mathrm{r}}\right)\\ &+\ln\left(\frac{|\boldsymbol{\Sigma}_{\mathrm{d}}|^{-\frac{1}{2}}}{(2\pi)^{\frac{N_{\mathrm{t}}N_{\mathrm{r}}}{2}}}\times\frac{|\boldsymbol{\Sigma}_{\mathrm{f}}|^{-\frac{1}{2}}}{(2\pi)^{\frac{N_{\mathrm{r}}N_{\mathrm{r}}}{2}}}\right).\end{aligned}$$

Following the derivation in Appendix D.1 and Appendix D.2 and noting the additional term in the log-likelihood function, the building blocks of the FIM can be calculated as follows.

Taking the partial derivative of the log-likelihood with respect to $\boldsymbol{r}$ results in

$$\frac{\partial \mathcal{L}}{\partial \boldsymbol{r}} = \left(\boldsymbol{d} - \boldsymbol{g} - \boldsymbol{\Gamma}_{\mathrm{t}}\boldsymbol{b}_{\mathrm{t}} - \boldsymbol{\Gamma}_{\mathrm{r}}\boldsymbol{b}_{\mathrm{r}}\right)^T \boldsymbol{\Sigma}_{\mathrm{d}}^{-1}\frac{\partial \boldsymbol{g}}{\partial \boldsymbol{r}} + \left(\boldsymbol{f} - \boldsymbol{h} - \boldsymbol{\Lambda}\boldsymbol{b}_{\mathrm{r}}\right)^T \boldsymbol{\Sigma}_{\mathrm{f}}^{-1}\frac{\partial \boldsymbol{h}}{\partial \boldsymbol{r}}.$$

Noting that the range measurement errors $(\boldsymbol{d} - \boldsymbol{g} - \boldsymbol{\Gamma}_{\mathrm{t}}\boldsymbol{b}_{\mathrm{t}} - \boldsymbol{\Gamma}_{\mathrm{r}}\boldsymbol{b}_{\mathrm{r}})$ and $(\boldsymbol{f} - \boldsymbol{h} - \boldsymbol{\Lambda}\boldsymbol{b}_{\mathrm{r}})$ are zero mean and independent random vectors, the first block of the matrix $\boldsymbol{J}_{\boldsymbol{\theta}_1}$ takes the form

$$\mathbb{E}\left\{\left(\tfrac{\partial \mathcal{L}}{\partial \boldsymbol{r}}\right)^T\left(\tfrac{\partial \mathcal{L}}{\partial \boldsymbol{r}}\right)\right\} = \left(\frac{\partial \boldsymbol{g}}{\partial \boldsymbol{r}}\right)^T \boldsymbol{\Sigma}_{\mathrm{d}}^{-1}\frac{\partial \boldsymbol{g}}{\partial \boldsymbol{r}} + \left(\frac{\partial \boldsymbol{h}}{\partial \boldsymbol{r}}\right)^T \boldsymbol{\Sigma}_{\mathrm{f}}^{-1}\frac{\partial \boldsymbol{h}}{\partial \boldsymbol{r}}.$$

Similarly, taking the partial derivative of the log-likelihood with respect to $\boldsymbol{b}_{\mathrm{r}}$ results in

$$\frac{\partial \mathcal{L}}{\partial \boldsymbol{b}_{\mathrm{r}}} = \left(\boldsymbol{d} - \boldsymbol{g} - \boldsymbol{\Gamma}_{\mathrm{t}}\boldsymbol{b}_{\mathrm{t}} - \boldsymbol{\Gamma}_{\mathrm{r}}\boldsymbol{b}_{\mathrm{r}}\right)^T \boldsymbol{\Sigma}_{\mathrm{d}}^{-1}\boldsymbol{\Gamma}_{\mathrm{r}} + \left(\boldsymbol{f} - \boldsymbol{h} - \boldsymbol{\Lambda}\boldsymbol{b}_{\mathrm{r}}\right)^T \boldsymbol{\Sigma}_{\mathrm{f}}^{-1}\boldsymbol{\Lambda}.$$

Hence, the other blocks of the matrix $\boldsymbol{J}_1$ are given by

$$\mathbb{E}\left\{\left(\tfrac{\partial \mathcal{L}}{\partial \boldsymbol{r}}\right)^T\left(\tfrac{\partial \mathcal{L}}{\partial \boldsymbol{b}_{\mathrm{r}}}\right)\right\} = \left(\frac{\partial \boldsymbol{g}}{\partial \boldsymbol{r}}\right)^T \boldsymbol{\Sigma}_{\mathrm{d}}^{-1}\boldsymbol{\Gamma}_{\mathrm{r}} + \left(\frac{\partial \boldsymbol{h}}{\partial \boldsymbol{r}}\right)^T \boldsymbol{\Sigma}_{\mathrm{f}}^{-1}\boldsymbol{\Lambda}.$$

$$\mathbb{E}\left\{\left(\tfrac{\partial \mathcal{L}}{\partial \boldsymbol{b}_{\mathrm{r}}}\right)^T\left(\tfrac{\partial \mathcal{L}}{\partial \boldsymbol{b}_{\mathrm{r}}}\right)\right\} = \boldsymbol{\Gamma}_{\mathrm{r}}^T\boldsymbol{\Sigma}_{\mathrm{d}}^{-1}\boldsymbol{\Gamma}_{\mathrm{r}} + \boldsymbol{\Lambda}^T\boldsymbol{\Sigma}_{\mathrm{f}}^{-1}\boldsymbol{\Lambda}.$$

Following similar steps and calculating the building blocks of sub-matrix $\boldsymbol{J}_2$ leads to

$$\mathbb{E}\left\{\left(\tfrac{\partial \mathcal{L}}{\partial \boldsymbol{r}}\right)^T\left(\tfrac{\partial \mathcal{L}}{\partial \boldsymbol{t}}\right)\right\} = \left(\frac{\partial \boldsymbol{g}}{\partial \boldsymbol{r}}\right)^T \boldsymbol{\Sigma}_{\mathrm{d}}^{-1}\frac{\partial \boldsymbol{g}}{\partial \boldsymbol{t}}.$$

$$\mathbb{E}\left\{\left(\tfrac{\partial \mathcal{L}}{\partial \boldsymbol{r}}\right)^T\left(\tfrac{\partial \mathcal{L}}{\partial \boldsymbol{b}_{\mathrm{t}}}\right)\right\} = \left(\frac{\partial \boldsymbol{g}}{\partial \boldsymbol{r}}\right)^T \boldsymbol{\Sigma}_{\mathrm{d}}^{-1}\boldsymbol{\Gamma}_{\mathrm{t}}.$$

$$\mathbb{E}\left\{\left(\tfrac{\partial \mathcal{L}}{\partial \boldsymbol{b}_{\mathrm{r}}}\right)^T\left(\tfrac{\partial \mathcal{L}}{\partial \boldsymbol{t}}\right)\right\} = \boldsymbol{\Gamma}_{\mathrm{r}}^T\boldsymbol{\Sigma}_{\mathrm{d}}^{-1}\frac{\partial \boldsymbol{g}}{\partial \boldsymbol{t}}.$$

$$\mathbb{E}\left\{\left(\tfrac{\partial \mathcal{L}}{\partial \boldsymbol{b}_{\mathrm{r}}}\right)^T\left(\tfrac{\partial \mathcal{L}}{\partial \boldsymbol{b}_{\mathrm{t}}}\right)\right\} = \boldsymbol{\Gamma}_{\mathrm{r}}^T\boldsymbol{\Sigma}_{\mathrm{d}}^{-1}\boldsymbol{\Gamma}_{\mathrm{t}}.$$

The building blocks of sub-matrix $\boldsymbol{J}_3$ are given by

$$\mathbb{E}\left\{\left(\tfrac{\partial \mathcal{L}}{\partial \boldsymbol{t}}\right)^T\left(\tfrac{\partial \mathcal{L}}{\partial \boldsymbol{t}}\right)\right\} = \left(\frac{\partial \boldsymbol{g}}{\partial \boldsymbol{t}}\right)^T \boldsymbol{\Sigma}_{\mathrm{d}}^{-1}\frac{\partial \boldsymbol{g}}{\partial \boldsymbol{t}}.$$

$$\mathbb{E}\left\{\left(\tfrac{\partial \mathcal{L}}{\partial \boldsymbol{t}}\right)^T\left(\tfrac{\partial \mathcal{L}}{\partial \boldsymbol{b}_{\mathrm{t}}}\right)\right\} = \left(\frac{\partial \boldsymbol{g}}{\partial \boldsymbol{t}}\right)^T \boldsymbol{\Sigma}_{\mathrm{d}}^{-1}\boldsymbol{\Gamma}_{\mathrm{t}}.$$

$$\mathbb{E}\left\{\left(\frac{\partial \mathcal{L}}{\partial \boldsymbol{b}_{\mathrm{t}}}\right)^T\left(\frac{\partial \mathcal{L}}{\partial \boldsymbol{b}_{\mathrm{t}}}\right)\right\} = \boldsymbol{\Gamma}_{\mathrm{t}}^T \boldsymbol{\Sigma}_{\mathrm{d}}^{-1} \boldsymbol{\Gamma}_{\mathrm{t}}.$$

Acronyms

2D	2-dimensional.
3D	3-dimensional.
ADC	analog to digital convertor.
AF	amplify and forward.
AOA	angle of arrival.
Async	asynchronous.
AWGN	additive white Gaussian noise.
CDF	cumulative distribution function.
CDR	clock and data recovery.
CIR	channel impulse response.
CRLB	Cramér-Rao lower bound.
DF	decode and forward.
DS	direct sequence.
DS-IR	direct sequence impulse radio.
DS-SS	direct sequence spread spectrum.
FCC	federal communications commission.
FPGA	field programmable gate array.
FS	frequency synchronous.
GEV	generalized extrem value.

LOS	line of sight.
LOS	non-line of sight.
LTD	lock-to-data.
LTR	lock-to-reference.
MED	mean excess delay.
ML	maximum likelihood.
PDF	probability density function.
PLL	phase locked loop.
PN	pseudo-random noise.
PS	phase synchronous.
PSD	power spectral density.
RMS	root mean squared.
RMS-DS	root mean squared delay spread.
RMSE	root mean squared error.
RSS	received signal strength.
s.t.	such that.
SBWT	search back window and thresholding.
SDP	semi-definite programming.
SNR	signal to noise ratio.
SOCP	second order cone programming.
TDOA	time difference of arrival.
TDOA	time of flight.
TH	time hopping.
TOA	time of arrival.
ULA	uniform linear array.
UWB	ultra-wideband.

Notation

N_t	number of agents.
N_r	number of anchors.
$\boldsymbol{a}$	a column vector $\boldsymbol{a}$.
$\boldsymbol{A}$	matrix $\boldsymbol{A}$.
$\boldsymbol{A}[i,j]$	The entry of matrix $\boldsymbol{A}$ in the ith row and jth column.
$\boldsymbol{A}[i,:]$	the ith row of matrix $\boldsymbol{A}$.
$\boldsymbol{A}[:,j]$	the jth column of matrix $\boldsymbol{A}$.
$\boldsymbol{A}=[\,]$	empty matrix $\boldsymbol{A}$.
$\boldsymbol{a}^T$	transpose of vector $\boldsymbol{a}$.
$\boldsymbol{A}^T$	transpose of matrix $\boldsymbol{A}$.
$\mathrm{Tr}\{\boldsymbol{A}\}$	trace of matrix $\boldsymbol{A}$.
$\mathrm{diag}\{\boldsymbol{A}_1,\ldots,\boldsymbol{A}_N\}$	a block diagonal matrix with matrices $\boldsymbol{A}_1,\ldots,\boldsymbol{A}_N$ on its block diagonal.
$\boldsymbol{A}\succeq\boldsymbol{B}$	$\boldsymbol{A}-\boldsymbol{B}$ is a postive semi-definite matrix.
$\odot$	element-wise (Hadamard) product operator.
$\boldsymbol{E}^{(i)}_{M\times N}$	$M\times N$ matrix with all zero elements except the ith column which contains all ones.
$\lceil x\rceil$	the smallest integer larger than or equal to x.
$\mathcal{N}(m,\sigma)$	Gaussian distributed random variable with mean m and variance σ.
$\delta(t)$	Dirac delta function.

c_0	speed of light.
arg max	maximizing argument of a function or a set.
arg min	minimizing argument of a function or a set.
$\mathbb{E}\{\cdot\}$	expectation operator.

Bibliography

[1] J. Kim, S. Yang, and M. Gerla, "Stroketrack: wireless inertial motion tracking of human arms for stroke telerehabilitation," in *Proceedings of the First ACM Workshop on Mobile Systems, Applications, and Services for Healthcare*. ACM, 2011, p. 4.

[2] S. Das, L. Trutoiu, A. Murai, D. Alcindor, M. Oh, F. De la Torre, and J. Hodgins, "Quantitative measurement of motor symptoms in parkinson's disease: a study with full-body motion capture data," in *Engineering in Medicine and Biology Society, EMBC, 2011 Annual International Conference of the IEEE*. IEEE, 2011, pp. 6789–6792.

[3] K. F. Sim and K. Sundaraj, "Human motion tracking of athlete using optical flow & artificial markers," in *Intelligent and Advanced Systems (ICIAS), 2010 International Conference on*. IEEE, 2010, pp. 1–4.

[4] X. Liu, J. Sun, Y. He, Y. Liu, and L. Cao, "Overview of virtual reality apply to sports," *Journal of Convergence Information Technology*, vol. 6, no. 12, 2011.

[5] C. Bregler, "Motion capture technology for entertainment," *Signal Processing Magazine, IEEE*, vol. 24, no. 6, pp. 160–158, 2007.

[6] G. Welch and E. Foxlin, "Motion tracking: no silver bullet, but a respectable arsenal," *Computer Graphics and Applications, IEEE*, vol. 22, no. 6, pp. 24–38, Nov 2002.

[7] H. Zhou and H. Hu, "Human motion tracking for rehabilitation – a survey," *Biomedical Signal Processing and Control*, vol. 3, no. 1, pp. 1–18, 2008.

[8] J. G. Richards, "The measurement of human motion: a comparison of commercially available systems," *Human Movement Science*, vol. 18, no. 5, pp. 589–602, 1999.

[9] "Vicon motion capture," www.vicon.com, accessed: 28-08-2015.

[10] "Motion analysis: Raptor digital real time system," www.motionanalysis.com, accessed: 28-08-2015.

[11] "Motus Digital: motion capture," www.motusdigital.com, accessed: 28-08-2015.

[12] "Qualisys: motion capture systems," www.optitrack.com, accessed: 28-08-2015.

[13] "OptiTrack: motion capture systems," www.qualisys.com, accessed: 23-10-2015.

[14] D. Thewlis, C. Bishop, N. Daniell, and G. Paul, "Next generation low-cost motion capture systems can provide comparable spatial accuracy to high-end systems," *Journal of applied biomechanics*, vol. 29, no. 1, pp. 112–117, 2013.

[15] B. Carse, B. Meadows, R. Bowers, and P. Rowe, "Affordable clinical gait analysis: An assessment of the marker tracking accuracy of a new low-cost optical 3D motion analysis system," *Physiotherapy*, vol. 99, no. 4, pp. 347–351, 2013.

[16] H. Shaban, M. A. El-Nasr, R. M. Buehrer *et al.*, "Toward a highly accurate ambulatory system for clinical gait analysis via UWB radios," *Information Technology in Biomedicine, IEEE Transactions on*, vol. 14, no. 2, pp. 284–291, 2010.

[17] R. Poppe, "Vision-based human motion analysis: An overview," *Computer vision and image understanding*, vol. 108, no. 1, pp. 4–18, 2007.

[18] "Xsens MTV: Motion Capture," www.xsens.com, accessed: 01-09-2015.

[19] "InertiaCube3," www.intersense.com, accessed: 01-09-2015.

[20] "Inertia-Link: Microstrain inertial motion capture," www.microstrain.com, accessed: 01-09-2015.

[21] A. D. Young, "Wireless realtime motion tracking system using localised orientation estimation," 2010.

[22] C. Hu, S. Song, X. Wang, M. Q.-H. Meng, and B. Li, "A novel positioning and orientation system based on three-axis magnetic coils," *Magnetics, IEEE Transactions on*, vol. 48, no. 7, pp. 2211–2219, 2012.

[23] C. Hu, M. Li, S. Song, W. Yang, R. Zhang, and M. Q. Meng, "A cubic 3-axis magnetic sensor array for wirelessly tracking magnet position and orientation," *Sensors Journal, IEEE*, vol. 10, no. 5, pp. 903–913, 2010.

[24] C. Hu, M. Q. Meng, and M. Mandal, "A linear algorithm for tracing magnet position and orientation by using three-axis magnetic sensors," *Magnetics, IEEE Transactions on*, vol. 43, no. 12, pp. 4096–4101, 2007.

[25] F. H. Raab, E. B. Blood, T. O. Steiner, and H. R. Jones, "Magnetic position and orientation tracking system," *Aerospace and Electronic Systems, IEEE Transactions on*, no. 5, pp. 709–718, 1979.

[26] E. Slottke and A. Wittneben, "Accurate localization of passive sensors using multiple impedance measurements," in *IEEE Vehicular Technology Conference*, May 2014.

[27] "Polhemus: Wireless motion trackers," www.polhemus.com, accessed: 05-09-2015.

[28] K. Mitobe, T. Kaiga, T. Yukawa, T. Miura, H. Tamamoto, A. Rodgers, and N. Yoshimura, "Development of a motion capture system for a hand using a magnetic three dimensional position sensor."

[29] U. Blanke and B. Schiele, "Towards human motion capturing using gyroscopeless orientation estimation." in *ISWC*, 2010, pp. 1–2.

[30] R. Zhu and Z. Zhou, "A real-time articulated human motion tracking using tri-axis inertial/magnetic sensors package," *Neural Systems and Rehabilitation Engineering, IEEE Transactions on*, vol. 12, no. 2, pp. 295–302, 2004.

[31] D. Roetenberg, H. Luinge, and P. Slycke, "Xsens MVN: full 6DOF human motion tracking using miniature inertial sensors."

[32] E. R. Bachmann, "Inertial and magnetic tracking of limb segment orientation for inserting humans into synthetic environments," DTIC Document, Tech. Rep., 2000.

[33] M.-G. Di Benedetto, *UWB communication systems: a comprehensive overview.* Hindawi Publishing Corporation, 2006, vol. 5.

[34] L. Yang and G. Giannakis, "Ultra-wideband communications: an idea whose time has come," *Signal Processing Magazine, IEEE*, vol. 21, no. 6, pp. 26–54, Nov 2004.

[35] F. Trösch, "Novel low duty cycle schemes: From ultra wide band to ultra low power," Ph.D. dissertation, PhD Thesis, 2009.

[36] S. Gezici, Z. Tian, G. B. Giannakis, H. Kobayashi, A. F. Molisch, H. V. Poor, and Z. Sahinoglu, "Localization via ultra-wideband radios: a look at positioning aspects for future sensor networks," *Signal Processing Magazine, IEEE*, vol. 22, no. 4, pp. 70–84, 2005.

[37] S. Gezici and H. V. Poor, "Position estimation via ultra-wide-band signals," *Proceedings of the IEEE*, vol. 97, no. 2, pp. 386–403, 2009.

[38] S. Gezici, "A survey on wireless position estimation," *Wireless personal communications*, vol. 44, no. 3, pp. 263–282, 2008.

[39] H. Luecken, "Communication and localization in UWB sensor networks: A synergetic approach," Ph.D. dissertation, PhD Thesis, 2013.

[40] F. C. Commission *et al.*, "Revision of part 15 of the commission's rules regarding ultra-wideband transmission systems," *V48, April*, 2002.

[41] C. Steiner, "Location fingerprinting for ultra-wideband systems - the key to efficient and robust localization," Ph.D. dissertation, PhD Thesis, 2010.

[42] H. Arslan, Z. N. Chen, and M.-G. Di Benedetto, *Ultra-wideband wireless communication.* John Wiley & Sons, 2006.

[43] Y. Qi and H. Kobayashi, "On relation among time delay and signal strength based geolocation methods," in *Global Telecommunications Conference, 2003. GLOBECOM '03. IEEE*, vol. 7, Dec 2003, pp. 4079–4083.

[44] Y. Qi, "Wireless geolocation in a non-line-of-sight environment," *Ph.D. dissertation, Princeton University*, December 2003.

[45] C. Nerguizian, C. Despins, and S. Affès, "Geolocation in mines with an impulse response fingerprinting technique and neural networks," *Wireless Communications, IEEE Transactions on*, vol. 5, no. 3, pp. 603–611, 2006.

[46] C. Nerguizian and V. Nerguizian, "Indoor fingerprinting geolocation using wavelet-based features extracted from the channel impulse response in conjunction with an artificial neural network," in *Industrial Electronics, 2007. ISIE 2007. IEEE International Symposium on.* IEEE, 2007, pp. 2028–2032.

[47] C. Steiner, F. Althaus, F. Troesch, and A. Wittneben, "Ultra-wideband georegioning: A novel clustering and localization technique," *EURASIP Journal on Advances in Signal Processing*, vol. 2008, p. 84, 2008.

[48] C. Steiner and A. Wittneben, "Low complexity location fingerprinting with generalized uwb energy detection receivers," *Signal Processing, IEEE Transactions on*, vol. 58, no. 3, pp. 1756–1767, 2010.

[49] ——, "Clustering of wireless sensors based on ultra-wideband geo-regioning," in *Asilomar Conference on Signals, Systems, and Computers*, Nov. 2007.

[50] J. Li and R. Wu, "An efficient algorithm for time delay estimation," *Signal Processing, IEEE Transactions on*, vol. 46, no. 8, pp. 2231–2235, 1998.

[51] H. Saarnisaari, "ML time delay estimation in a multipath channel," in *Spread Spectrum Techniques and Applications Proceedings, 1996., IEEE 4th International Symposium on*, vol. 3. IEEE, 1996, pp. 1007–1011.

[52] T. G. Manickam, R. J. Vaccaro, and D. W. Tufts, "A least-squares algorithm for multipath time-delay estimation," *Signal Processing, IEEE Transactions on*, vol. 42, no. 11, pp. 3229–3233, 1994.

[53] C. Falsi, D. Dardari, L. Mucchi, and M. Z. Win, "Time of arrival estimation for UWB localizers in realistic environments," *EURASIP Journal on Applied Signal Processing*, vol. 2006, pp. 152–152, 2006.

[54] D. Dardari, C.-C. Chong, and M. Z. Win, "Threshold-based time-of-arrival estimators in UWB dense multipath channels," *Communications, IEEE Transactions on*, vol. 56, no. 8, pp. 1366–1378, 2008.

[55] K. Haneda, K.-i. Takizawa, J.-i. Takada, M. Dashti, and P. Vainikainen, "Performance evaluation of threshold-based UWB ranging methods-leading edge vs. search back," in *Antennas and Propagation, 2009. EuCAP 2009. 3rd European Conference on*. IEEE, 2009, pp. 3673–3677.

[56] A. Rabbachin, I. Oppermann, and B. Denis, "GML ToA estimation based on low complexity UWB energy detection," in *Personal, Indoor and Mobile Radio Communications, 2006 IEEE 17th International Symposium on*. IEEE, 2006, pp. 1–5.

[57] ——, "ML time-of-arrival estimation based on low complexity UWB energy detection," in *Ultra-Wideband, The 2006 IEEE 2006 International Conference on*. IEEE, 2006, pp. 599–604.

[58] H. Luecken, C. Steiner, and A. Wittneben, "ML timing estimation for generalized UWB-IR energy detection receivers," in *Ultra-Wideband, 2009. ICUWB 2009. IEEE International Conference on*. IEEE, 2009, pp. 829–833.

[59] I. Guvenc and Z. Sahinoglu, "Threshold-based TOA estimation for impulse radio UWB systems," in *Ultra-Wideband, 2005. ICU 2005. 2005 IEEE International Conference on*. IEEE, 2005, pp. 420–425.

[60] D. Dardari, A. Conti, U. Ferner, A. Giorgetti, and M. Win, "Ranging with ultrawide bandwidth signals in multipath environments," *Proceedings of the IEEE*, vol. 97, no. 2, pp. 404–426, Feb 2009.

[61] M. Dashti, J.-i. Takada, K. Haneda, and M. Ghoraishi, *High-precision time-of-arrival estimation for UWB localizers in indoor multipath channels.* INTECH Open Access Publisher, 2011.

[62] J. C. Chen, R. E. Hudson, and K. Yao, "Maximum-likelihood source localization and unknown sensor location estimation for wideband signals in the near-field," *Signal Processing, IEEE Transactions on*, vol. 50, no. 8, pp. 1843–1854, 2002.

[63] A. Kannan, G. Mao, B. Vucetic *et al.*, "Simulated annealing based localization in wireless sensor network," in *Local Computer Networks, 2005. 30th Anniversary. The IEEE Conference on.* IEEE, 2005, pp. 2–pp.

[64] P. Biswas and Y. Ye, "Semidefinite programming for ad hoc wireless sensor network localization," in *Information Processing in Sensor Networks, 2004. IPSN 2004. Third International Symposium on*, April 2004, pp. 46–54.

[65] P. Biswas, T.-C. Liang, K.-C. Toh, Y. Ye, and T.-C. Wang, "Semidefinite programming approaches for sensor network localization with noisy distance measurements," *Automation Science and Engineering, IEEE Transactions on*, vol. 3, no. 4, pp. 360–371, October 2006.

[66] K. W. Cheung, W.-K. Ma, and H.-C. So, "Accurate approximation algorithm for TOA-based maximum likelihood mobile location using semidefinite programming," in *Acoustics, Speech, and Signal Processing, 2004. Proceedings.(ICASSP'04). IEEE International Conference on*, vol. 2. IEEE, 2004, pp. ii–145.

[67] P. Tseng and I. M. O. J. Sturm, "Second-order cone programming relaxation of sensor network localization," *SIAM J. Optimization*, pp. 156–185, 2007.

[68] S. Srirangarajan, A. Tewfik, and Z.-Q. Luo, "Distributed sensor network localization using socp relaxation," *Wireless Communications, IEEE Transactions on*, vol. 7, no. 12, pp. 4886–4895, December 2008.

[69] W. H. Foy, "Position-location solutions by Taylor-series estimation," *IEEE Transactions on Aerospace and Electronic Systems*, pp. 187–194, 1976.

[70] K. W. Cheung, H.-C. So, W.-K. Ma, and Y.-T. Chan, "Least squares algorithms for time-of-arrival-based mobile location," *Signal Processing, IEEE Transactions on*, vol. 52, no. 4, pp. 1121–1130, 2004.

[71] W. Kim, J. G. Lee, and G.-I. Jee, "The interior-point method for an optimal treatment of bias in trilateration location," *Vehicular Technology, IEEE Transactions on*, vol. 55, no. 4, pp. 1291–1301, 2006.

[72] S. Valaee, B. Champagne, and P. Kabal, "Localization of wideband signals using least-squares and total least-squares approaches," *Signal Processing, IEEE Transactions on*, vol. 47, no. 5, pp. 1213–1222, 1999.

[73] M. Di Renzo, R. Buehrer, and J. Torres, "Pulse shape distortion and ranging accuracy in UWB-based body area networks for full-body motion capture and gait analysis," *IEEE Global Telecommunications Conference, 2007. GLOBECOM '07.*, pp. 3775–3780, Nov. 2007.

[74] Y. Qi, C. B. Soh, E. Gunawan, K.-S. Low, and A. Maskooki, "Using wearable UWB radios to measure foot clearance during walking," in *Engineering in Medicine and Biology Society (EMBC), 2013 35th Annual International Conference of the IEEE.* IEEE, 2013, pp. 5199–5202.

[75] R. Bharadwaj, S. Swaisaenyakorn, C. G. Parini, J. Batchelor, and A. Alomainy, "Localization of wearable ultrawideband antennas for motion capture applications," *Antennas and Wireless Propagation Letters, IEEE*, vol. 13, pp. 507–510, 2014.

[76] E. Xu, Z. Ding, and S. Dasgupta, "Source localization in wireless sensor networks from signal time-of-arrival measurements," *Signal Processing, IEEE Transactions on*, vol. 59, no. 6, pp. 2887–2897, June 2011.

[77] J. N. Laneman, D. N. Tse, and G. W. Wornell, "Cooperative diversity in wireless networks: Efficient protocols and outage behavior," *Information Theory, IEEE Transactions on*, vol. 50, no. 12, pp. 3062–3080, 2004.

[78] L. Michael and R. Kohno, *Ultra-Wideband Signals and Systems in Communication Engineering.* Wiley, 2004.

[79] J. Proakis, *Digital Communications*, ser. McGraw-Hill Series in Electrical and Computer Engineering. Computer Engineering. McGraw-Hill, 2001.

[80] Y.-C. Wu, Q. Chaudhari, and E. Serpedin, "Clock synchronization of wireless sensor networks," *Signal Processing Magazine, IEEE*, vol. 28, no. 1, pp. 124–138, Jan. 2011.

[81] J. R. Vig, "Introduction to quartz frequency standards. revision," DTIC Document, Tech. Rep., 1992.

[82] Y. Qi, H. Kobayashi, and H. Suda, "Analysis of wireless geolocation in a non-line-of-sight environment," *Wireless Communications, IEEE Transactions on*, vol. 5, no. 3, pp. 672–681, Mar. 2006.

[83] H. Koorapaty, H. Grubeck, and M. Cedervall, "Effect of biased measurement errors on accuracy of position location methods," in *Global Telecommunications Conference, 1998. IEEE*, vol. 3, 1998, pp. 1497–1502 vol.3.

[84] D. Jourdan, D. Dardari, and M. Win, "Position error bound for UWB localization in dense cluttered environments," in *Communications, 2006. IEEE International Conference on*, vol. 8, Jun. 2006, pp. 3705–3710.

[85] Y. Shen and M. Z. Win, "Fundamental limits of wideband localization: part I - a general framework," *IEEE Trans. Inf. Theor.*, vol. 56, no. 10, pp. 4956–4980, Oct. 2010.

[86] L. Mailaender, "On the geolocation bounds for round-trip time-of-arrival and all non-line-of-sight channels," *EURASIP Jour. on Adv. in Signal Process*, Jan. 2008.

[87] S. Al-Jazzar and J. Caffery, "ML and bayesian TOA location estimators for NLOS environments," in *Vehicular Technology Conference, IEEE 56th*, vol. 2, 2002, pp. 1178–1181.

[88] S. Al-Jazzar, J. Caffery, and H.-R. You, "A scattering model based approach to nlos mitigation in toa location systems," in *Vehicular Technology Conference, IEEE 55th*, vol. 2, 2002, pp. 861–865 vol.2.

[89] W. Wang, "A new location algorithm for mitigating NLOS propagation errors in microcell environment," in *Communication Technology Proceedings. International Conference on*, vol. 2, Apr. 2003, pp. 850–853.

[90] P.-C. Chen, "A non-line-of-sight error mitigation algorithm in location estimation," in *Wireless Communications and Networking Conference, IEEE*, vol. 1, 1999, pp. 316–320.

[91] L. Xiong, "A selective model to suppress NLOS signals in angle-of-arrival (AOA) location estimation," in *Personal, Indoor and Mobile Radio Communications. The Ninth IEEE International Symposium on*, vol. 1, Sep. 1998, pp. 461–465.

[92] S. Gezici, Z. Tian, G. Giannakis, H. Kobayashi, A. Molisch, H. Poor, and Z. Sahinoglu, "Localization via ultra-wideband radios: a look at positioning aspects for future sensor networks," *Signal Processing Magazine, IEEE*, vol. 22, no. 4, pp. 70–84, Jul. 2005.

[93] J. Khodjaev, Y. Park, and A. S. Malik, "Survey of NLOS identification and error mitigation problem in UWB-based positioning algorithms for dense environments," in *Annals of Telecommunications*, vol. 65, Aug. 2009, pp. 301–311.

[94] J. Schroeder, S. Galler, K. Kyamakya, and K. Jobmann, "NLOS detection algorithms for ultra-wideband localization," in *Positioning, Navigation and Communication, 2007. WPNC '07. 4th Workshop on*, Mar. 2007, pp. 159–166.

[95] J. Borras, P. Hatrack, and N. Mandayam, "Decision theoretic framework for NLOS identification," in *Vehicular Technology Conference. IEEE*, vol. 2, May 1998, pp. 1583–1587.

[96] S. Gezici, H. Kobayashi, and H. Poor, "Nonparametric nonline-of-sight identification," in *Vehicular Technology Conference. IEEE*, vol. 4, Oct. 2003, pp. 2544–2548.

[97] Y.-H. Jo, J.-Y. Lee, D.-H. Ha, and S.-H. Kang, "Accuracy enhancement for UWB indoor positioning using ray tracing," in *Position, Location, And Navigation Symposium, 2006 IEEE/ION*, Apr. 2006, pp. 565–568.

[98] D. Gustafson, J. Elwell, and J. Soltz, "Innovative indoor geolocation using RF multipath diversity," in *Position, Location, And Navigation Symposium, 2006 IEEE/ION*, Apr. 2006, pp. 904–912.

[99] I. Guvenc, C.-C. Chong, and F. Watanabe, "NLOS identification and mitigation for UWB localization systems," in *Wireless Communications and Networking Conference. IEEE*, Mar. 2007, pp. 1571–1576.

[100] M. Heidari, F. Akgul, and K. Pahlavan, "Identification of the absence of direct path in indoor localization systems," in *Personal, Indoor and Mobile Radio Communications, 2007. PIMRC 2007. IEEE 18th International Symposium on*, Sep. 2007, pp. 1–6.

[101] S. Venkatesh and R. Buehrer, "Non-line-of-sight identification in ultra-wideband systems based on received signal statistics," *Microwaves, Antennas Propagation, IET*, vol. 1, no. 6, pp. 1120–1130, Dec. 2007.

[102] I. Guvenc, C.-C. Chong, F. Watanabe, and H. Inamura, "NLOS identification and weighted least-squares localization for UWB systems using multipath channel statistics," *EURASIP Journal on Advances in Signal Processing*, no. 1, p. 271984, 2008.

[103] F. Heer, "Localization of asynchronous agents under NLOS conditions: application to UWB-based human motion tracking," Master's thesis, Communication Technology Laboratory, ETH Zurich, 2013, Supervisor: Z. W. Mekonnen.

[104] H. Van Trees, *Detection, Estimation, and Modulation Theory: Part I-III.* John Wiley & Sons, Inc., 2001.

[105] Z. Mekonnen, E. Slottke, H. Luecken, C. Steiner, and A. Wittneben, "Constrained maximum likelihood positioning for UWB based human motion tracking," in *Indoor Positioning and Indoor Navigation (IPIN), 2010 International Conference on*, September 2010, pp. 1–10.

[106] Z. W. Mekonnen and A. Wittneben, "Robust TOA based localization for wireless sensor networks with anchor position uncertainties," in *PIMRC'14*, Sep. 2014.

[107] Y. Chan and K. Ho, "A simple and efficient estimator for hyperbolic location," *Signal Processing, IEEE Transactions on*, vol. 42, no. 8, pp. 1905–1915, Aug 1994.

[108] K. Yang, G. Wang, and Z.-Q. Luo, "Efficient convex relaxation methods for robust target localization by a sensor network using time differences of arrivals," *Signal Processing, IEEE Transactions on*, vol. 57, no. 7, pp. 2775–2784, July 2009.

[109] K. Yang and Z.-Q. Luo, "Robust target localization with multiple sensors using time difference of arrivals," in *Radar Conference, 2008. RADAR '08. IEEE*, May 2008, pp. 1–6.

[110] G. Shirazi, M. Shenouda, and L. Lampe, "Second order cone programming for sensor network localization with anchor position uncertainty," in *Positioning Navigation and Communication (WPNC), 2011 8th Workshop on*, April 2011, pp. 51–55.

[111] P. Biswas and Y. Ye, "A distributed method for solving semidefinite programs arising from ad hoc wireless sensor network localization," in *Multiscale optimization methods and applications.* Springer, 2006, pp. 69–84.

[112] G. Wang, Y. Li, and N. Ansari, "A semidefinite relaxation method for source localization using tdoa and fdoa measurements," *Vehicular Technology, IEEE Transactions on*, vol. 62, no. 2, pp. 853–862, Feb 2013.

[113] M. Gholami, S. Gezici, and E. Strom, "TDOA based positioning in the presence of unknown clock skew," *Communications, IEEE Transactions on*, vol. 61, no. 6, pp. 2522–2534, June 2013.

[114] K. B. Petersen and M. S. Pedersen, "The matrix cookbook," Nov. 2012. [Online]. Available: http://www2.imm.dtu.dk/pubdb/p.php?3274

[115] A. Kannan, G. Mao, and B. Vucetic, "Simulated annealing based localization in wireless sensor network," in *Local Computer Networks, 2005. 30th Anniversary. The IEEE Conference on*, Nov 2005.

[116] P. Namin and M. Tinati, "Node localization using particle swarm optimization," in *Intelligent Sensors, Sensor Networks and Information Processing (ISSNIP), 2011 Seventh International Conference on*, Dec 2011.

[117] Q. Zhang, J. Wang, C. Jin, J. Ye, C. Ma, and W. Zhang, "Genetic algorithm based wireless sensor network localization," in *Natural Computation, 2008. ICNC '08. Fourth International Conference on*, vol. 1, Oct 2008, pp. 608–613.

[118] K. W. K. Lui, W.-K. Ma, H. So, and F. K. W. Chan, "Semi-definite programming algorithms for sensor network node localization with uncertainties in anchor positions and/or propagation speed," *Signal Processing, IEEE Transactions on*, vol. 57, no. 2, pp. 752–763, February 2009.

[119] S. Boyd and L. Vandenberghe, *Convex Optimization.* Cambridge University Press, 2004.

[120] S. Boyd, L. El Ghaoui, E. Feron, and V. Balakrishnan, *Linear Matrix Inequalities in System and Control Theory*, ser. Studies in Applied Mathematics. SIAM, 1994, vol. 15.

[121] M. Grant and S. Boyd, "MATLAB software for disciplined convex programming." [Online]. Available: http://cvxr.com

[122] F. Zhang, *The Schur Complement and Its Applications.* Springer Science & Business Media, Inc., 2005.

[123] P. Stoica and B. C. Ng, "On the Cramer-Rao bound under parametric constraints," *IEEE Sig. Proc. Lett.*, vol. 5, no. 7, pp. 177–179, Jul. 1998.

[124] Z. W. Mekonnen and A. Wittneben, "Self-calibration method for TOA based localization systems with generic synchronization requirement," in *IEEE International Conference on Communications, ICC 2015, London, UK*, 2015.

[125] M. Crocco, A. Del Bue, and V. Murino, "A bilinear approach to the position self-calibration of multiple sensors," *Signal Processing, IEEE Transactions on*, vol. 60, no. 2, pp. 660–673, Feb. 2012.

[126] R. L. Moses, D. Krishnamurthy, and R. Patterson, "A self-localization method for wireless sensor networks," *EURASIP Journal on Applied Signal Processing*, vol. 4, pp. 348–358, 2002.

[127] J. D. Hol, T. B. Schön, and F. Gustafsson, "Ultra-wideband calibration for indoor positioning," in *Ultra-Wideband (ICUWB), 2010 IEEE International Conference on*, vol. 2, Sep. 2010.

[128] Galarza, Ana Irene Ramirez and J. Seade, *Introduction to classical geometries.* Birkhäuser Basel, 2007.

[129] G. Wahba, "A least squares estimates of spacecraft attitude," *SIAM Review*, vol. 7, no. 3, p. 409, Jul. 1965.

[130] F. L. Markley, "Attitude determination using vector observations and the singular value decomposition," *The Journal of the Astronautical Sciences*, vol. 36, no. 3, pp. 245–258, Jul. 1988.

[131] G. Han, D. Choi, and W. Lim, "Reference node placement and selection algorithm based on trilateration for indoor sensor networks," *Wireless Communications and Mobile Computing*, vol. 9, no. 8, pp. 1017–1027, 2009.

[132] H. Khani, H. Nie, W. Xiang, and Z. Chen, "Finite-resolution digital receiver for high rate ultra-wideband weighted-transmitted reference system," in *Ultra-Wideband (ICUWB), 2011 IEEE International Conference on*, 2011, pp. 200–204.

[133] Y. Chiu, B. Nikoli, and P. Gray, "Scaling of analog-to-digital converters into ultra-deep-submicron cmos," in *Custom Integrated Circuits Conference, 2005. Proceedings of the IEEE 2005*, 2005, pp. 375–382.

[134] S. Hoyos, B. M. Sadler, and G. R. Arce, "Monobit digital receivers for ultra-wideband communications," *Wireless Communications, IEEE Transactions on*, vol. 4, no. 4, pp. 1337–1344, 2005.

[135] F. Sun, Y. Zhang, H. Yin, and W. Wang, "A low complexity UWB localization algorithm using finite-resolution quantization," in *Vehicular Technology Conference (VTC Spring), 2013 IEEE 77th*, 2013, pp. 1–5.

[136] F. Sun, H. Yin, and W. Wang, "Finite-resolution digital receiver for uwb toa estimation," *Communications Letters, IEEE*, vol. 16, no. 1, pp. 76–79, 2012.

[137] C. Sulser, "UWB transmitter nodes," ETH Zurich, Wireless Communications Group, Hardware Presentation, 2011.

[138] M. Eppenberger, "Implementation of an FPGA based multi-channel UWB receiver with smart correlation," ETH Zurich, Wireless Communications Group, Semester Thesis, Supervisor: Z. W. Mekonnen and C. Sulser, 2014.

[139] C. Sulser, "UWB antenna design," ETH Zurich, Wireless Communications Group, Antenna Design Presentation, 2011.

[140] C.-C. Lin and H.-R. Chuang, "A 3-12 ghz uwb planar triangular monopole antenna with ridged ground-plane," *Progress In Electromagnetics Research*, vol. 83, pp. 307–321, 2008.

[141] L. Vandenberghe and S. Boyd, "Semidefinite programming," *SIAM Review*, vol. 38, pp. 49–95, 1994.

Curriculum Vitae

Name:	Zemene Walle Mekonnen
Birthday:	January 19, 1986
Birthplace:	Gonder, Ethiopia

Work Experience

12/2009-present **Research assistant at ETH Zurich, Switzerland**
In the Communication Technology Laboratory, headed by Prof. Dr.-Ing. Armin Wittneben.

- Performed research on signal processing for wireless sensor networks and TOA based human posture capturing.
- Participated on a research project work with Wärtsilä Switzerland AG.
- Supervised several master thesis and semester thesis projects.
- Thought and assisted lectures.
- Gave presentations at international conferences. Reviewed international conference and journal submissions.

11/2008-03/2009 **Student assistant at University of Kassel, Germany**
In the Communications Laboratory headed by Prof. Dr. sc. Dirk Dahlhaus.

09/2007-03/2008 **Junior Electrical Engineer at ZTE (H.K.) Limited, Ethiopia**

Education

02/2010 - present **PhD in Electrical Engineering**
ETH Zurich, Switzerland.

04/2008 - 11/2009 **MSc in Electrical Communication Engineering**
University of Kassel, Germany.

10/2003 - 08/2007 **BSc in Electrical and Computer Engineering**
Addis Ababa University, Ethiopia.

09/2001-07/2003 **Higher Education Preparatory Studies**
Fasiledes Preparatory School, Gonder, Ethiopia.

Peer-Reviewed Publications

- **Self-Calibration Method for TOA Based Localization Systems Under Generic Synchronization Requirements**
  Z. W. Mekonnen and A. Wittneben, IEEE International Conference on Communications (ICC), London, UK, June 2015.

- **Robust TOA Based Localization for Wireless Sensor Networks with Anchor Position Uncertainties**
  Z. W. Mekonnen and A. Wittneben, IEEE International Symposium on Personal, Indoor and Mobile Radio Communications (PIMRC), Washington, DC, USA, September 2014.

- **Localization via Taylor-Series Approximation for UWB Based Human Motion Tracking**
  Z. W. Mekonnen and A. Wittneben, 8th Workshop on Positioning, Navigation and Communication (WPNC), Dresden, Germany, April 2011.

- **Constrained Maximum Likelihood Positioning for UWB Based Human Motion Tracking**
  Z. W. Mekonnen, E. Slottke, H. Luecken, C. Steiner and A. Wittneben, International Conference on Indoor Positioning and Indoor Navigation (IPIN), Zurich, Switzerland, September 2010.

Patent

- **CTI Project Patent on UWB Telemetry Sensor Networks**
  A. Wittneben, Z. W. Mekonnen, E. Slottke, M. Kuhn, and C. Cartalemi, patent application, title and filing information to be disclosed.

Bisher erschienene Bände der Reihe

Series in Wireless Communications

ISSN 1611-2970

1	Dirk Benyoucef	Codierte Multiträgerverfahren für Powerline- und Mobilfunkanwendungen ISBN 978-3-8325-0137-2 40.50 EUR
2	Marc Kuhn	Space-Time Codes und ihre Anwendungen in zukünftigen Kommunikationssystemen ISBN 978-3-8325-0159-4 40.50 EUR
3	Frank Althaus	A New Low-Cost Approach to Wireless Communication over Severe Multipath Fading Channels ISBN 978-3-8325-0158-7 40.50 EUR
4	Ingmar Hammerström	Cooperative Relaying and Adaptive Scheduling for Low Mobility Wireless Access Networks ISBN 978-3-8325-1466-2 40.50 EUR
5	Thomas Zasowski	A System Concept for Ultra Wideband (UWB) Body Area Networks ISBN 978-3-8325-1715-1 40.50 EUR
6	Boris Rankov	Spectral Efficient Cooperative Relaying Strategies for Wireless Networks ISBN 978-3-8325-1744-1 40.50 EUR
7	Stephan Sand	Joint Iterative Channel and Data Estimation in High Mobility MIMO-OFDM Systems ISBN 978-3-8325-2385-5 39.00 EUR
8	Florian Troesch	Design and Optimization of Distributed Multiuser Cooperative Wireless Networks ISBN 978-3-8325-2400-5 42.50 EUR
9	Celal Esli	Novel Low Duty Cycle Schemes: From Ultra Wide Band to Ultra Low Power ISBN 978-3-8325-2484-5 42.00 EUR

10	Stefan Berger	Coherent Cooperative Relaying in Low Mobility Wireless Multiuser Networks ISBN 978-3-8325-2536-1 42.00 EUR
11	Christoph Steiner	Location Fingerprinting for Ultra-Wideband Systems. The Key to Efficient and Robust Localization ISBN 978-3-8325-2567-5 36.00 EUR
12	Jian Zhao	Analysis and Design of Communication Techniques in Spectrally Efficient Wireless Relaying Systems ISBN 978-3-8325-2585-9 39.50 EUR
13	Azadeh Ettefagh	Cooperative WLAN Protocols for Multimedia Communication ISBN 978-3-8325-2774-7 37.50 EUR
14	Georgios Psaltopoulos	Affordable Nonlinear MIMO Systems ISBN 978-3-8325-2824-9 36.50 EUR
15	Jörg Wagner	Distributed Forwarding in Multiuser Multihop Wireless Networks ISBN 978-3-8325-3193-5 36.00 EUR
16	Etienne Auger	Wideband Multi-user Cooperative Networks: Theory and Measurements ISBN 978-3-8325-3209-3 38.50 EUR
17	Heinrich Lücken	Communication and Localization in UWB Sensor Networks. A Synergetic Approach ISBN 978-3-8325-3332-8 36.50 EUR
18	Raphael T. L. Rolny	Future Mobile Communication: From Cooperative Cells to the Post-Cellular Relay Carpet ISBN 978-3-8325-4229-0 42.00 EUR
19	Zemene Walle Mekonnen	Time of Arrival Based Infrastructureless Human Posture Capturing System ISBN 978-3-8325-4429-4 36.00 EUR
20	Eric Slottke	Inductively Coupled Microsensor Networks: Relay Enabled Cooperative Communication and Localization ISBN 978-3-8325-4438-6 38.00 EUR